Politics
and Verbal Play

Politics and Verbal Play

The Ludic Poetry of Angel González

Martha LaFollette Miller

Madison • Teaneck
Fairleigh Dickinson University Press
London: Associated University Presses

© 1995 by Associated University Presses, Inc.

All rights reserved. Authorization to photocopy items for internal or personal use, or the internal or personal use of specific clients, is granted by the copyright owner, provided that a base fee of $10.00, plus eight cents per page, per copy is paid directly to the Copyright Clearance Center, 222 Rosewood Drive, Danvers, Massachusetts 01923. [0-8386-3552-0/95 $10.00 + 8¢ pp, pc.]

Associated University Presses
440 Forsgate Drive
Cranbury, NJ 08512

Associated University Presses
25 Sicilian Avenue
London WC1A 2QH, England

Associated University Presses
P.O. Box 338, Port Credit
Mississauga, Ontario
Canada L5G 4L8

The paper used in this publication meets the requirements of the American National Standard for Permanence of Paper for Printed Library Materials Z39.48–1984.

Library of Congress Cataloging-in-Publication Data

Miller, Martha LaFollette, 1944–
    Politics and verbal play : The ludic poetry of Angel González / Martha LaFollette Miller.
    p. cm.
    Includes bibliographical references (p.) and index.
    ISBN 0-8386-3552-0 (alk. paper)
    1. González, Angel, 1925– —Criticism and interpretation.
2. Politics and literature. 3. Play in literature.
4. Postmodernism (Literature) I. Title
PQ6613.0489Z78 1995
861'.64—dc20   94-24276
                                                              CIP

PRINTED IN THE UNITED STATES OF AMERICA

For Matthew

Contents

Acknowledgments / 9
Chronology of Life and Works / 11

1. Introduction / 15
2. Roots and Connections: The Genesis of *Palabra sobre palabra* / 24
3. The Poetry of *Engagement:* From Inner Exile to Expressive Freedom / 47
4. The Textures of Politics and Verbal Play in González's Second Period / 68
5. Play with the Logic of Time and Place / 94
6. Play with Spheres of Discourse in González's Second Period / 115
7. Literary Tradition versus Speaker Experience in the Poetry of Angel González / 137
8. Iconoclastic Images of Self and Other in *Palabra sobre palabra* / 162
9. Conclusion / 186

Notes / 191
Works Cited / 211
Index / 221

Acknowledgments

Without the generous help and encouragement of teachers, friends, and colleagues over a period of many years, this book would never have been written. For inspired instruction in the close readings of contemporary Spanish poets, I am indebted to Antonio Sánchez Barbudo. For introducing me to Angel González and to his works, I am grateful to Alfred Rodríguez. For not only making the academic community a more hospitable place but for contributing specifically to my development as a scholar, I thank John Kronik, Julian Palley, John Wilcox, and Salvador Jiménez-Fajardo. For his characteristically generous assistance and advice I am especially indebted to Andrew P. Debicki. Many other colleagues have provided stimulation, example, camaraderie, and suggestions. I am grateful to Doug Benson, Rafael Espejo-Saavedra, Maria Nowakowska Stycos, Katherine Stephenson, and Anita Hart for their friendship, encouragement, and help. The graciousness shown me by Angel González and Susana Rivera as this project developed made my work considerably easier and more pleasant.

I would also like to acknowledge the institutional support that helped make my study possible. The University of North Carolina Charlotte and its Foundation have made faculty research grants and time off from teaching duties available. A fellowship to the School of Criticism and Theory allowed me to acquire part of the theoretical background for my study. Two National Endowment for the Humanities fellowships—one for a Summer Seminar taught by Andrew Debicki in 1978, the other, a Summer Stipend in 1992—have also contributed to my project.

Additionally, I would like to thank those who have helped make this book possible by granting me permission to incorporate previously published material. First of all, I extend my gratitude to Angel González for allowing me to quote from his poetry, essays, and interviews. I wish also to acknowledge Princeton University Press for permitting me to use Donald D. Walsh's excellent translations of a number of González's poems. I am grateful as well to Francisco Hernández-Pinzón, who on behalf of the heirs of Juan Ramón Jiménez has consented to my quoting from Jiménez's poetry.

I am indebted also to those who have allowed me to incorporate into my study some of my own previously published work on González. I thank the editors of *Simposio-Homenaje a Angel González* for permission to reproduce parts of my article "The Uses of Play and Humor in Angel González' Second Period"; the University Press of Kentucky for allowing use of my article "Political Intent Versus Verbal Play in 'La paloma' by Angel González," published in *Perspectives on Contemporary Literature;* Luis González-del-Valle, editor of *Anales de la Literatura Española Contemporánea* and director of Publictions of the Society of Spanish and Spanish-American Studies for permission to use parts of my essays "Literary Tradition Versus Speaker Experience in the Poetry of Angel González," "The Ludic Poetry of Angel González," and "Inestabilidad temporal y textual en Angel González." Please see the list of works cited for complete bibliographical reference for these items.

Three friends deserve special words of thanks. I am deeply indebted to Judith Suther for her example and encouragement, to Sharon Kellum for her staunch friendship and generous editorial advice, and to Margaret Persin for her loyalty and critical acumen. Finally, I am fortunate to have had the support over the years of my mother, Martha LaFollette, my brother, Jere LaFollette, and my son, Matthew Miller.

Chronology of Life and Works

6 Sept. 1925	Born in Oviedo, Spain, to María Muñiz and Pedro González Cano
1927	Death of father (after elective surgery on knee)
Oct. 1934	Miners' uprising in Asturias, followed by brutal reprisals
1936	Civil War. Brother Manolo detained and executed by Nationalists in Asturian town of Salas
1937–44	Completes secondary education at the Instituto de Oviedo (4 years) and the Colegio Fruela (3 years)
1944	Diagnosed with tuberculosis and sent to Páramo de Sil (León) to recuperate for three years; begins law studies on his own
1949	Receives law degree from the University of Oviedo
1951	Certified as a journalist through an intensive course in Madrid
1954	Brief stint as government bureaucrat in Seville
1955	Year in Barcelona as an editorial assistant; *Accésit* [finalist], Adonais Prize for manuscript of *Aspero mundo*
1956	*Aspero mundo* [Harsh world][1] Returns to government bureaucracy (Ministry of Public Works)
1961	*Sin esperanza, con convencimiento* [Without hope, but with conviction]
1962	*Grado elemental* [Elementary grade]
1965	*Palabra sobre palabra* [Word upon word]
1967	*Tratado de urbanismo* [Treatise on urban development]
1968	*Palabra sobre palabra* (collected works)
1969	Death of mother in Oviedo
1970	First trip to United States, Venezuela, and Mexico—lectures and poetry readings
1971	*Breves acotaciones para una biografía* [Brief marginal notes for a biography]
1972	Visiting Professor, University of New Mexico; 2d ed., *Palabra sobre palabra*; *Procedimientos narrativos*

1975	Becomes permanent member of University of New Mexico faculty
1976	*Muestra de algunos procedimientos narrativos y de las actitudes sentimentales que habitualmente comportan* [Sample of some narrative procedures and the sentimental attitudes they habitually entail]; 2d ed., *Tratado de urbanismo*
1977	*Muestra, corregida y aumentada, de algunos procedimientos narrativos y de las actitudes sentimentales que habitualmente comportan* [Sample, revised and enlarged, of some narrative procedures and the sentimental attitudes they habitually entail]; 3d ed., *Palabra sobre palabra*; *"Harsh World" and Other Poems*
1980	*Poemas: Edición del autor* [Poems: Author's edition]
1982	*Antología poética* [Anthology of poetry]
1984	*Prosemas o menos*[2] [Prosemores or less]
1985	Príncipe de Asturias [Prince of Asturias] Prize for Letters; Visiting Professor, University of Oviedo; 2d ed., *Prosemas o menos*
1986	Acebo de Plata [Silver holly] Prize (sponsored by Editorial "Azucel" de Corvera); 4th ed., *Palabra sobre Palabra*
1992	*Deixis en fantasma*[3] [Deictics phantasmafied]
1993	Retires from University of New Mexico faculty

Politics
and Verbal Play

1
Introduction

By some standards, Angel González began to publish poetry late in life. His first book, *Aspero mundo* (1956), appeared when he was thirty-one. Since that time his writing career has developed steadily. Eight additional volumes of poetry and four editions of his complete works have appeared in the last three decades. Through these books, as well as through other milestones—a bilingual anthology published by Princeton University Press in 1977, conferences and homage volumes on both sides of the Atlantic, and the Príncipe de Asturias Prize in 1985—he has won recognition as an important member of his poetic generation. Although his work has been termed difficult to characterize,[1] from early on its double thrust has been obvious; it has expressed, on the one hand, an attitude of social criticism, at times bitter, and on the other, an intense lyricism, mostly elegiac in tone. His recent books show that he has never completely abandoned these two modalities. Poems of open political *engagement* have been replaced in the eighties with occasional social satire, but his elegiac bent has if anything grown stronger.[2]

González's comments on his poems reveal his awareness of the different directions his poetry has taken as well as offering his view of the artistic evolution he has undergone. Although like many of his contemporaries he was convinced early in his career of the importance of political commitment, solidarity, and a testimonial stance, he nevertheless describes his early work as more existential than "social," pointing out that in all his books except *Grado elemental* elegiac and amorous poems occupy more space than those of a political nature.[3] Other constants of his work permeate both his political and his personal poems. His nearly ubiquitous irony has served, he says, to confuse censors and to help him avoid expressing his emotions in too personal or revealing a way.[4] Furthermore, the poems that address collective issues as well as those based on individual experiences are infused with a pessimism that he attributes on the one hand to negative attitudes he acquired in early childhood and on the other to a feeling he shared with various writers in his generation: the sense of having wasted his life at the margin of a society based on premises with which he disagreed.[5] Critics have noted still other constants within his works. Andrew P. Debicki and Douglas K. Benson, for example, have described with acumen how he undercuts conventional attitudes and parodies various poetic and nonpoetic types of discourse.[6]

Despite the persistence in González's work of certain characteristic elements, his poetry in the late sixties began to undergo a significant transformation. He himself attributes this change to disillusionment about the effectiveness of the poetic word:

> Creo que *Tratado de urbanismo* marca el final de una etapa—o de una actitud—y también el comienzo de otra. El poema «Preámbulo a un silencio» viene a ser la negación de mi intermitente, pero hasta entonces sostenida, ilusión en la capacidad activa de la palabra poética.
>
> [I believe that *Tratado de urbanismo* marks the end of one stage—or attitude—as well as the beginning of another one. The poem "Preámbulo a un silencio" ("Prelude to Silence" [DDW]) becomes the negation of my intermittent, but until that time sustained, illusion regarding the active power of the poetic word.]

González links his abandonment of faith in the word to his loss of hope for political change. In the books that followed *Tratado de urbanismo* (*Breves acotaciones para una biografía* [1971], *Procedimientos narrativos* [1972], *Muestra de los procedimientos narrativos y de las actitudes sentimentales que habitualmente comportan* [1976], *Muestra, corregida y aumentada, de algunos procedimientos narrativos y de las actitudes sentimentales que habitualmente comportan* [1977], and *Prosemas o menos* [1984]), he moved from poetry based on a fusion of personal and universal history and the experiences of everyday life into the realm of literary games and what he calls "temas intranscendentes." Unlike his earlier works, these books do not primarily mirror personal history or events in the world but rather tend, as he suggests, toward jokes, verbal play, and parody. He speaks of the books of this period—*Breves acotaciones para una biografía, Procedimientos narrativos,* and the two editions of *Muestra*—in the following terms:

> En cierto modo, estaba tratando de iniciar la escritura a partir no de experiencias, sino de esquemas, aunque no he podido—ni querido—evitar casi nunca que los esquemas se llenasen con mis experiencias.[7]
>
> [In a certain way, I was trying to start writing by drawing from a schematic framework rather than from experiences, although I have almost never managed, nor wanted, to prevent my schemes from filling up with my experiences.]

González views his change of poetic orientation as a way of converting his critique of society into a critique of language and of his own powers of expression. He comments as follows on the period of his transformation: "En aquellos años personalmente—y objetivamente—difíciles, cuando la esperanza en un cambio durante mucho tiempo deseado se había convertido primero en impaciencia y luego en decepción, nada se me presentaba más inútil y más ajeno a los actos que las palabras"[8] [In those years, which were difficult from a personal—as well as objective—perspective, when hope for a long-desired change had turned first to impatience and then to disappointment, nothing seemed to me more useless nor more removed from deeds than words].

Although González attributes the shift in his poetic stance to frustration at what he viewed as the absence of political change, his questioning of the utility of words was symptomatic of much more generalized dilemmas that underlay many of the intellectual discussions of the period during which he developed his new style. His disillusionment with the word parallels the reaction of other midcentury writers to what are viewed as the unspeakable horrors of our times. As George Steiner points out in an essay dating from 1966 and thus contemporaneous with González's period of transition: "The question of whether the poet should speak or be silent, of whether language is in a condition to accord with his needs, is a real one. 'No poetry after Auschwitz,' said Adorno, and Sylvia Plath enacted the underlying meaning of his statement in a manner both histrionic and profoundly sincere."[9] Though González did not choose the silence that for Steiner is one of the poet's possible responses to totalitarianism and inhumanity, he moved, as he himself puts it, toward an "antipoesía" [antipoetry], the roots of which are to be found in "cierto rencor frente a las «palabras inútiles»"[10] [a certain rancor toward "words and their uselessness"].

Despite González's insistence on the political roots of his flight from transcendent themes toward gamelike and schematically based poetry, the new directions his work took in the middle sixties were very much in keeping with widespread artistic and critical trends, not all of them directly related to politics. This period, in fact, saw the flowering of many aesthetic ideas that had been germinating for decades. González's skepticism regarding attempts to state meaningfully any consciously held worldview parallels certain structuralist and poststructuralist leanings, such as the loss of faith in individual consciousness as the center and origin of the literary work or the devaluation of the signified in favor of the play of the signifier. The poet's shift reflects the influence of the postmodern sensibility emerging around him. This new orientation abandons the sometimes utopian projects of modernism, substituting an insistent self-referentiality for the modernist "formal-expressionist aesthetic"[11] and replacing modernism's epistemological bent with an ontological questioning.[12] González's second period embodies as well the indeterminacy that Marjorie Perloff identifies as a significant characteristic of contemporary poetry. In her book *The Poetics of Indeterminacy: Rimbaud to Cage* (1981), Perloff describes poets of indeterminacy as tending toward "unmediated presentation" and toward works of enigma in which association and poetic surface override the communication of an epiphany or higher reality. In one of these poets, David Antin, she detects an "increasing distrust in the image as an embodiment of personal emotion."[13] González, as he evolves poetically, writes more and more poems that not only could be considered examples of postmodern verse but could be included in Perloff's category of works of indeterminacy as well.

González, then, participated in a generalized movement among thinkers and literary critics toward a stance critical of language and reason. His works increasingly came to reflect the postmodernist awareness of the challenge the power of language poses to the notion of representation.[14] Significantly, too, his flight from transcendent themes toward schemes and games and his growing doubts about the value of trying to articulate a consciously held worldview coincided with his own integration into an international academic community at a moment when literary theory had assumed center stage in intellectual arenas. In 1970, when he lectured in the United States for the first time, intellectual debate over problems of language had begun to intensify. The belief in the human ability to shape language in order to express preexisting thoughts and experiences was being called into question and critical focus had shifted from the text as object to the strategies and pleasures of the reading process. Though he disavows the influence of critical theory on his works,[15] González has continued to be exposed to critical thought on an international level, having divided his time, from 1972 on, between teaching at American universities and visits to Spain and Mexico.

Thus González's loss of faith in his own words was not only a result of self-effacing behavior learned in childhood and of political disillusionment suffered later but was also a reflection of general trends among intellectuals, many of whom had begun to question the existence of knowledge "which one can acquire in some tangible or permanent way."[16] Moreover, he was not alone among Spanish poets in doubting the utility of words during the period of transition from the sixties to the seventies. Fanny Rubio and José Luis Falcó have detected similar preoccupations in many of the younger Spanish poets who emerged during the seventies, citing as decisive their growing awareness of new developments in linguistics, semiotics, and psychoanalysis. In poets born after the Spanish Civil War, Rubio and Falcó frequently discover attitudes of skepticism toward the "valor activo de la palabra poética" [active value of the poetic word] and of the "inutilidad de la literatura" [uselessness of literature]. And in statements by a number of poets represented in José Batlló's 1974 anthology, the two critics find poetry treated almost as a kind of linguistic free play. Guillermo Carnero speaks of

1 / INTRODUCTION

"el propósito de restaurar la primacía del lenguaje" [the aim of restoring the primacy of language], while Eugenio Padorno conceives poetry as a linguistic adventure. The loss of faith in "el valor activo de la palabra poética" has led many of these poets, according to Rubio and Falcó, to cultivate self-reflexive verse or metapoetry, a tendency particularly acute in Gimferrer and Carnero.[17] This atmosphere of decreasing confidence in the poetic word has had clear repercussions in González's work.

With its turn toward play and nonsense, González's second period thus coincided with the assimilation of important international artistic currents by a broad panorama of Spanish poets. Significantly, Rubio and Falcó affirm the influence of semiotics in Spanish poetry anthologies as early as 1971, the same year in which González published the first book he characterizes as written in his new mode, *Breves acotaciones para una biografía*. Yet despite similarities, González differs from the *novísimos* [very new ones], as the poets emerging around 1970 were sometimes called, in his cultivation of what he terms *nonsense* and in certain ways has taken care to dissociate himself from them. He initially attacked their works as frivolous and later decried their willingness to ignore in their writing that Franco had ever existed.[18] He, on the other hand, turned to linguistic play only after exhausting efforts to put his talents at the service of change. Furthermore, his gesture renouncing the hopeful tenets that words are useful and the poet's job full of purpose implied frustration and concern rather than evasion. The difference between his stance and that of the *novísimos* illustrates Carlos Bousoño's observation that instead of constituting strictly separated generations, poets of different ages respond to the same stimuli from the present, but from the perspective of their own generation.[19] Thus in a roundabout sense even González's ludic texts express the poet's conception of his works in terms of the sociopolitical conditions of his times. Nevertheless, in his second period he is more apt to allow himself access to playful, gratuitous modes of expression that lead to successful experiments with new types of poetry. From the rational witness in the service of change described by Emilio Alarcos Llorach, González becomes a medium for language and a creator of magic through play. He becomes a postmodernist, albeit a humanistic one (as Silvio Gaggi describes John Barth).[20] González's poetic reorientation in midlife reflects a vitality and capacity for renewal that for a student of human development such as Erik Erikson would distinguish him from others less able to find fresh sources of inspiration and creativity at the age of forty-five or fifty.

Thus González's works have been divided—by the poet himself as well as by some critics—into two distinct periods that coincide with two divergent conceptions of poetry and its function. (Patrick Josef LeCertúa speaks of poetry of "experience" versus that of "experiment.")[21] Alarcos Llorach's 1969 study, departing from the premise of poetry as testimony and from the critical notion of form following content, might be seen as the critical counterpart of González's first period. My study is an assessment—in line with selected critical essays published by other critics in the 1980s and to which I refer—of González's second, more ludic, period, as well as a retrospective examination of the relationship of this poetry to his early works, to his history of political and existential witnessing.

I base my study of González's evolution on what might be termed postmodern critical foundations: the notion that literary works do not spring from the author as rational source but rather from a complex web of historical, literary, linguistic, and intellectual realities in which the author is enmeshed and reader/audience/critic is also implicated. I view both González's early political and existential works and his later ludic poems as born from the play of preexisting discourse. I study the full unleashing of this play, its results and effects, in González's later period, examining his manipulations of genres and literary tradition, his games with words, and the nonsense he creates through violating logic, combining incompatible spheres of discourse, and juggling boundaries. I relate González's ludic poetry to trends in contemporary art, taking into account the theories of postmodernism that have proliferated in the last few years. I thus suggest that González be viewed not just in terms of what has been called the "second postwar generation" (and in terms of social poetry that developed into what Debicki aptly calls "poetry of discovery") but as a writer who entered the seventies in a state of crisis and development.

In presenting such a study, based on a schematic division of an author's work that he himself recognized and propounded, one caveat is necessary. González, like the "novísimos" as Biruté Ciplijauskaité describes them, has a view of his works very different from Jorge Guillén's vision of "la Obra"[22] [the Oeuvre]. González's works do not obey a totalizing authorial conception, nor has he ever reordered them to create a coherent poetic universe. As he states, "[Y]o no escribo libros, sino poemas"[23] [I don't write books; rather, I write poems].Thus there is much overlap between the early and the late González, with wordplay and manipulations of logic present from the beginning, and straightforwardly elegiac and amorous poems appearing throughout his oeuvre. The speech with which González accepted the Príncipe de Asturias Prize in 1985 synthesized his poetic personality. His statement on that occasion reflected a postmodern view of the poetic act as a collaborative encounter between the writer's words and the readers' experience, an ongoing event in which readers bring to life the otherwise meaningless writings that the poet has put on paper. At the same time he managed to capture a sense of solidarity and human community compatible with his social period:

> [S]iempre he sostenido que los poetas no existen, salvo en la lectura. Si hablase como poeta les hablaría, en mi opinión, desde la nada. El poeta Angel

1 / INTRODUCTION

González, si es, estará en los libros como una posibilidad, como una propuesta al lector que será quien, en último extremo, decida su existencia o su inanidad. Aquí está, tan sólo, el hombre que ha tramado las palabras que le dan vida al poeta, palabras insuficientes en sí mismas, que no tendrían sentido sin el concurso de los otros. Y ésa es una de las grandes lecciones que, a mi modo de ver, se desprenden de la poesía. Porque nuestra forma de ser, lo que efectivamente somos, depende de los otros más de lo que habitualmente pensamos. Nadie, y esto es muy evidente en el caso de los poetas, puede existir sin los demás.[24]

[I have always maintained that poets don't exist, except in the reading process. If I spoke as a poet, I would speak to you, in my opinion, from nothingness. The poet Angel González, if he exists, will be in books as a possibility, as a proposal to the reader who will be the one who in the final analysis will decide on his existence or his emptiness. Before you now stands only the man who has put together the words that give the poet life, words insufficient in themselves, which would have no meaning without the assistance of other people. And that is one of the great lessons that, as I see it, come out of poetry. Because the way we are, in fact what we are, depends on others more than we tend to think. No one, and this is very evident in the case of poets, can exist without other people.]

Keeping in mind this idea that the reader is a collaborator, without whom the poet would not exist, and considering as well John Wilcox's demonstration, in his book on Juan Ramón Jiménez, of the range of readings to which a body of poetry can legitimately give rise, I approach my study as a collaboration between what González has identified as his ludic texts and my own sensibilities as a reader armed not only with my own particular fund of cultural knowledge but with certain postmodern critical conceptions and presuppositions as well. I believe such an approach is amply justified in dealing with González's poetry, whose complex conceptual base often requires considerable reflection on the reader's part in order to be fully appreciated.[25] His colloquial language and themes can be deceptive, and the multiple refractions of his work have led Douglas K. Benson to the apt description of his poetry as quicksand.[26] My work is a record of the particular textual snares into which his poetry has lured me over a period of many years.

Chapter 2 of my study traces González's poetic roots from childhood through early adulthood and surveys his subsequent career as a writer. Here I examine his developing poetic philosophy, the changing critical responses to his works, and his exposure to major intellectual and artistic trends. In chapters 3 and 4, I begin analyzing specific poems, comparing the irony and satire of González's first period with the indeterminacy, collage, fragmentation, and defamiliarization (variants of postmodern experimentalism) of his later works. In these chapters I discuss González's evolution from a committed political poet to one who believes words are useless. I suggest, however, that this evolution is fraught with paradox and complication. Like the early imitative love poetry that he wrote to evade an inhospitable environment, his earliest political works—written in coded language intended to be understood by his politically initiated opposition cohorts—often entail a certain loss of speech, a silencing of his voice brought on not just by censorship but also by a state that Paul Ilie has termed "inner exile."[27] The more explicit and direct political expression through which he reclaimed his voice in the early sixties soon gave way to the loss of faith he links to the work *Tratado de urbanismo*. Paradoxically, however, this loss freed González to write the ludic works of his second period, which constitute his least purposeful but richest poetry. His move from purposefulness to play does not mean, nevertheless, that politics do not continue to underpin his poetry. Some works that he intended as pure play, for example, turned out to embody political issues of crucial importance at the moment when they were written. His entire second period can in fact be interpreted as one writer's response to the "*crisis intensísima de la razón racionalista*" [very intense crisis of rationalist reason] that according to Carlos Bousoño led Spanish poets of the seventies, including González's younger contemporaries, to embody their loss of faith in poems that perform a radical critique of institutions, conventions and language.[28]

Chapters 2, 3, and 4 set the stage for a discussion of González's ludic poetry in chapters 5 through 8. Chapters 5 and 6 apply Bousoño's notion of a crisis of reason to González's poetry. In chapter 5 I examine his inversions of and play with logic and in chapter 6 his playful juxtaposition of incompatible spheres of discourse. (Much of the theoretical foundation of this section comes from Susan Stewart's book on nonsense.) As these two chapters show, González early on in his career as a poet demonstrated a tendency toward conceptual play. The questioning of Aristotelian logic that for some theorists is fundamental to postmodernism[29] was one of the earliest hallmarks of the ludic in González's poetry. In the seventies, his poetry flourished when he could use his sensitivity to logic and to categories of discourse to enter fully into the contemporary dialogue regarding the origins and limits of art. Chapters 7 and 8 explore González's ludic poetry as a critique of traditional views of the literary word. The first of the two chapters examines the poet's play with literary traditions. Here I discuss the poet's increasing tendency to write poems that call attention to themselves as texts. Among other poetic conventions, I examine in particular the poet's reworking of the elegiac and pastoral traditions, showing how he emphasizes poetic surface and undermines the mimetic dimension of speaker experience by highlighting his texts' debts to literary convention. In the final chapter, I continue to examine González's conceptual poetry by analyzing his poems about poetry and poets. I return in a sense to the political, probing the ideological presuppositions latent in his portrayal of himself, of other poets, and of poetry itself. In addition, I trace the shift in his work from a purposeful anti-aestheticism to a more playful manner of demystifying the poetic process. Finally, my conclusion briefly relates González's evolution to some of the premises of international postmodernism.

2
Roots and Connections: The Genesis of *Palabra sobre palabra*

> La Historia de la poesía, la Historia de la literatura, no es más que un fragmento de la Historia, que siempre es del hombre [The History of poetry, the History of literature, is no more than a fragment of History, which is always that of human beings.]
> —González, "Poesía y compromiso" [Poetry and commitment]

> El poeta no es . . . quien escribe el poema, sino el que queda escrito, lo que es leído: su leyenda; una apariencia, una aparición que sólo se materializa en la fantasía del lector. Su existencia es precaria; depende de los otros. El poeta vive en la lectura igual que los fantasmas habitan en el miedo [The poet is not . . . the one who writes the poem, but the one who is written, that which is read: his legend; an appearance, an apparition that only materializes in the reader's fantasy. The poet's existence is precarious; it depends on other people. The poet dwells in the reading process just as ghosts inhabit fear].
> —González, "Sobre poesía y poetas" [On poetry and poets]

In a statement titled "Poesía y compromiso," published in *Poesía última* [Latest poetry] in 1963, Angel González expressed a strong belief in poetry's link to history and to the poet's particular moment in time and space.[1] This sense of history results in a certain rootedness, geographical as well as genealogical, that appears in all González's poetic periods and extends both to poems with public, political themes and to those with a more personal, private focus. Much as lengthy stays in Madrid and in the United States did not dilute the deep ties to Asturias he inherited from his grandfather,[2] so too the physical separation of death does not prevent him from connecting, in his poetry, with long-dead relatives. An awareness both of González's family background and personal trajectory and of the broader historical setting for his life is indeed a prerequisite to understanding all his works. Such biographical and historical background aids in assessing not only his elegiac and amorous poems and the "social" poetry he wrote under the aegis of *engagement* but also the more ludic verses of his second period, which he claims to have created as gratuitous play after renouncing all faith in the utility of words.

In keeping with González's essential sociability and communicative openness, he has provided considerable insight into his background through various interviews. Born in Oviedo in 1925, he was the fourth child and third son of María Muñiz and Pedro González Cano. In references to his background he suggests that his own pedagogical affinities were part of a family heritage; both his father and maternal grandfather were educators. His father, though born into what González describes as "una familia campesina muy pobre"[3] [a very poor rural family], pursued a teaching career due to a knee injury that had left him unfit for strenuous labors in the country. González Cano's intelligence was evident, for after studying in Oviedo he was chosen to continue his training in Madrid. His work there, made possible by the Krausist-inspired Junta para la Ampliación de Estudios [Commission for Extended Education], brought him into contact with the movement of progressive intellectual renewal that was flourishing in Spain at the time.

González Cano's studies also prepared him to return to Oviedo as a professor of pedagogy in the Normal School. There, in addition to embarking on a successful career, he met and married the school director's daughter, María Muñiz, with whom he eventually had four children. His life abruptly ended some twenty years later, before his youngest child Angel's second birthday, after a surgeon friend convinced him to have what his son later described as "una operación innecesaria" [an unnecessary operation] to correct a slight limp.[4] Though the family tradition of involvement in education would influence Angel González, ultimately surfacing, for example, in the overtly didactic frame of *Grado elemental*, the poet never really knew his father. More than ten years younger than his two brothers and one sister, Angel was raised principally by three women: his mother, his sister Maruja, and the Aunt Clotilde who would later appear in the poem "Así parece" [So it seems]. González, then, exemplifies what Juan García Hortelano diagnoses as an unusual degree of feminine influence on his generation.[5]

The poet's early loss of direct contact with his father seems not to have prevented him from assimilating certain ideological and personal values that the older man had evidently possessed and which were probably transmitted to him through the surviving family members—the women just mentioned and the two brothers who had reached adolescence before González Cano had died. Though his descriptions of his father's character are based largely on impressions gleaned second hand, the poet nevertheless convincingly suggests that the personality and strong convictions of González Cano influenced him as profoundly as they did the older children. Evidently outspoken on political and religious matters, González Cano was an "agnóstico declarado y republicano fervoroso con ribetes volterianos" [avowed agnostic and fervent Republican with Voltairean tinges]. According to the poet, his father's links to the progressive, liberal school, the Institución Libre de Enseñanza, had left their mark in a certain "puritanismo" [puritanism], in an austerity bordering on asceticism, and in a strong ethical sense that demanded consistency between actions and beliefs. The poet's characterization of his father's republicanism as constituting "todo un escándalo en los años veinte" [a real scandal in the twenties] suggests that González Cano's liberalism at times called attention to the family. Nor did González Cano bother to hide his leanings toward secularism, which according to his son he espoused as a moral duty: "Era un hombre muy laico, y no lo ocultaba: lo asumía como una posición moral"[6] [He was a very secular man, and he didn't hide that fact: he accepted it as a moral posture].

The premature death of his father left Angel González's mother as the indisputably central figure of his childhood. He describes her in the extraordinarily loving terms that follow:

> Si prescindimos de los veinte años que, más o menos, duró su matrimonio, la vida no fue precisamente amable con María Muñiz, mi madre. La orfandad, la temprana viudez, el fusilamiento de su hijo mayor durante la guerra civil, son los desastres más sobresalientes de toda una cadena de catástrofes que ensombrecieron su existencia desde los primeros días de su infancia. Nada fue capaz, sin embargo, de alterar la dulzura de su carácter ni su espíritu amoroso, liberal y comprensivo. Las adversidades revelaron en ella una admirable capacidad, que yo no dudo en calificar de heroica, de reacción ante el infortunio. Inteligente, sensible y abnegada, a mi madre le debo yo varias veces la vida y otras cosas que, contando ya con el hecho primario y azaroso de la existencia, se nos revelan muchas veces como más importantes que la misma vida.[7]

> [If we ignore the twenty years, more or less, that her marriage lasted, life was not exactly kind to María Muñiz, my mother. Orphanhood, early widowhood, and the execution by shooting of her oldest son during the civil war are the most salient disasters of a whole chain of catastrophes that cast a shadow on her existence from the earliest days of her childhood. Nothing, however, could alter the sweetness of her character nor her loving, generous, and understanding spirit. Adversities brought out in her an admirable capacity, which I don't hesitate to call heroic, for responding in the face of misfortune. To my intelligent, sensitive, and self-denying mother I owe not only my life several times over but other things that, given the fundamental and precarious fact of existence, we often come to understand as more important than life itself.]

Though endowed with what the poet terms "una especie de idealismo de raíz cristiana" [a kind of idealism rooted in Christianity], María Muñiz also

2 / ROOTS AND CONNECTIONS

maintained a certain fidelity to her husband's beliefs, sending Angel, for example, to public school while other middle-class children attended private ones.[8] Clearly, even after González Cano's death, the family stood out because of their beliefs, a fact they would feel more intensely after the outbreak of the civil war.

The childhood that Angel González recalls as happy and normal transpired, nevertheless, against a backdrop of violence that would directly affect his family. In a 1985 interview with Miguel Somovilla he remembers some of the events of that period which several years earlier he had declined to recall as too painful.[9] González Cano's sense of ethical responsibility and his outspoken liberalism had not only made a lasting impression within the family circle but had also aligned the family publicly with the Left and surely must have contributed to the activism of Angel's brother Pedro, a militant socialist who participated in the significant October rebellion of Asturian miners.[10] The family heritage was probably responsible as well for the cruel reprisal against Angel's other brother Manolo, who at the outbreak of the war had returned home on vacation from his engineering studies in Barcelona.

Angel González has described his mother's concern for her son's safety at this critical time, despite Manolo's lack of political involvements:

> Todo el mundo sabía que aquélla, la nuestra, era una casa de liberales, con tendencias de izquierdas, aunque nadie, salvo mi hermano Pedro, tuviera militancias determinadas ni actividades políticas. La aureola, además, ya nos venía de atrás: enlazaba con el republicanismo de mi padre. Así que mi hermano Manolo, que había venido de Barcelona, no salía de casa. Ya intuía lo que podría ocurrir y tenía miedo, y mi madre más. Por eso prefería que nadie lo viera, que la gente pensara que aún seguía en Barcelona.[11]

> [Everyone knew that our house was a home to liberals, with leftist tendencies, although no one, except my brother Pedro, had any particular affiliations or engaged in political activity. Our aura, moreover, was something we had acquired in the past: it was connected to my father's republicanism. So my brother Manolo, who had come from Barcelona, never left the house. He already sensed what could happen and he was afraid, and my mother was even more so. For that reason she preferred for no one to see him, for people to think he was still in Barcelona.]

Though Manolo had no "prioridades políticas" [political priorities], according to the poet, he was fingered for execution after applying for and receiving a safe-conduct to leave Oviedo, then under siege, to seek employment and the protection of a friend's family in León. As his own family learned only later, his executioners, to avoid the unpleasantness of murdering the son of a well-known local family in Oviedo itself, waited instead until his bus stopped in Salas, forty-five kilometers away, where they arrested him and shot him later that night. Not hearing from him right away, the family attributed his silence to wartime disruptions of the postal service. They did not suspect the brutal truth until they received a letter from a witness to his detention—a woman acquaintance who had been traveling on his bus that day and who wanted to inform them of what she had seen. Angel González's description of his mother's subsequent attempts to find out what had happened to her son, though understated, is wrenching, and his account of his own role as the family errand boy, who at eleven or twelve had to break the news of the tragedy to his mother after the local priest finally got word confirming the event, underscores the heartbreak of this period:

> [E]l párroco de San Juan . . . nos prometió escribir al cura de Salas para conocer lo ocurrido. A partir de ese momento, yo iba todos los días a casa de don Belarmino, el párroco, para saber algo. Pero las noticias nunca llegaban, hasta que un día sí se recibió una carta. Recuerdo perfectamente lo que decía: «El joven por el que usted se interesa salió de la cárcel de Salas en la noche de tal día, con rumbo desconocido», lo cual era muy claro. Yo tuve que subir hasta casa con esa carta. Fue uno de los paseos más largos de mi vida. Yo a mi hermano lo sentía, como es lógico, pero muy relativamente. A quien yo sentía era a mi madre.

> [The St. John's parish priest promised us he would write the priest at Salas to find out what had happened. From then on, I went every day to the house of Don Belarmino, the priest, to see what I could learn. But the news never came, until one day a letter did arrive. I remember perfectly what it said: "The young man you have inquired about left the Salas jail on the night of such-and-such a day, destination unknown," all of which was very clear. I had to walk home with that letter. It was one of the longest trips I ever took in my life. I felt bad about my brother, naturally, but in a very relative sense. The person I felt bad about was my mother.]

Still further difficulties ensued; the family was plunged into destitution, at war's end, when special widow's assistance provided by the teachers of Asturias was cut off and Angel's sister Maruja was deprived of her teaching post. (Her eventual reinstatement was conditional upon her acceptance of a position outside Asturias for a period of some years.) Clearly, the violence and privation that affected many Spaniards during the war and postwar years touched González's family and, it would seem, were exacerbated, in their case, by their liberal reputation.[12]

The early experiences that Angel González recalls, and the values and beliefs he absorbed in his family, have without a doubt shaped his adult response to his work and to his environment. Many of the ways in which he has characterized himself in interviews, as well as his poems themselves, which he has repeatedly insisted are based on specific personal experiences, can be seen to grow out of his past. He admits to a basic timidity, which he has sometimes attributed to his mother's fear that his behavior might attract too much attention in public.[13] His portrayal of his father's republican leanings as scandalous further suggests that he felt, and was marked by, an atmosphere of suspicion and intolerance. But his remarks about his mother frequently reveal as well a profound sense of responsibility toward her, a deep concern quite understandable in the light of certain familial facts—first, the early death of her husband, and secondly, Angel's presence in the home when one older brother was at war and the other had died. (His devotion, moreover, continued until her death; he remained in Spain throughout the sixties because she was not only elderly but also "muy asustada por la inminencia de la muerte, de manera que yo nunca había podido moverme por el mundo con cierta libertad" [very frightened by the imminence of death, so I had never been able to move about in the world with any degree of freedom].) Alongside profound admiration and gratitude, he has expressed a certain fear of not having lived up to all that she deserved in a son. Or, as Miguel Somovilla puts it, "Doña María ha significado tanto para Angel González que el poeta transmite la sensación de que aún no ha saldado su *deuda* con ella, ya fallecida. Perdura en él un cierto temor a *defraudarla*" [Doña María has meant so much to Angel González that the poet conveys the sensation that he has not yet paid his debt to her, though she is now dead. A certain fear of *disappointing her* still lingers in him]. This sense of responsibility, combined with the moral austerity of his father's ideological bent, was perhaps what led him to develop the internal self-censor that he characterizes as a severe priest within him: "Muchas veces ese *cura* . . . me echa tremendas riñas y en más de una ocasión estuvo a punto de destruirme, de acabar conmigo. . . . [E]se cura . . . me ha atormentado mucho, y aún sigue"[14] [Oftentimes that *priest* scolds me terribly and on more than one occasion he was about to destroy me, to finish me off. . . . That priest has tormented me a great deal, and he continues to do so]. González's periodic espousal of a model of service and utility in poetry may be a result of both his sense of responsibility to his mother and the family tradition of commitment to constructive and ethical positions, factors that on a more fundamental level have no doubt fueled his dedication to creativity and productive effort.

As his family struggled to recover from the harsh blows dealt them by the war, Angel González gradually returned to a normal pattern of life, pursuing his secondary education as well as important friendships. Finishing his studies at the Colegio Fruela, he decided, for practical reasons, to study law at the University of Oviedo, a plan he had to revise at age nineteen when diagnosed with tuberculosis. During the three ensuing years of isolation and repose in the mountains of León, he nevertheless managed—out of the desire to become a wage earner and thus to help his mother—to keep up with his class by studying law books on his own, despite his rapidly growing disenchantment with legal studies. In this period of enforced idleness, he also had time to explore the poetry of Juan Ramón Jiménez, Pablo Neruda, and members of the generation of 1927 and to discover, through hesitant exploration, his own literary vocation. Returning to Oviedo, he dutifully finished law school, though by now, according to his own admission, he was spending more time on his poetry than on his studies.[15] Around this time he began to familiarize himself with the poets of the first postwar generation—Hierro, Otero, and others—while continuing to read Neruda and acquainting himself with Vallejo's works as well.[16]

The more than twenty years that González spent in Spain following his graduation from law school represent a further installment in his struggle with his own historical reality. His personal inclinations now made a legal career seem out of the question. Yet González's flirtation in the early 1950s with what seemed to him a much more attractive pursuit— journalism—did not meet with success, whether because of the scarcity of opportunity in a culturally impoverished post–civil war Spain, or because of a climate inhospitable to his own intensifying political rebelliousness (which included active participation in Communist Party activities). Though failing to culminate in a new career, his journalistically oriented experiences were, nevertheless, important ones. They included a stint as a music critic in Oviedo; a short course in Madrid that conferred on him official status as a journalist; the publication of several interviews and articles; and, above all, incorporation into literary and artistic circles in Madrid.

It is during this period that González renewed contact with a childhood friend from Oviedo who was to play a significant role in his decision to pursue a literary career—Carlos Bousoño. Favorably impressed by the poems González showed him (perhaps in part because the existential tone of some of them coincided with that of his own poetry at the time), Bousoño introduced him to Vicente Aleixandre, who likewise became an indispensable source of critical advice and kindly support. (It was Aleixandre, in fact, who encouraged González to submit the manuscript of *Aspero mundo* to be considered for the Adonais Prize, for which it became a runner-up in 1955.)[17] During this period, González began serving as a government bureaucrat in Seville, but he soon took a leave of absence to work for a year in Barcelona as an editorial assistant. There, he came into contact with talented young writers—Carlos Barral, José María Castellet, Juan Goytisolo, Jaime Gil de Biedma, and others—and forged new associations that led eventually to the publication of his second book in the "Colección Colliure" [Colliure Collection]. Inclusion in the group of twelve authors planned for the "Colliure" project was, as González states, "una especie de presentación en sociedad del grupo literario capitaneado por Barral"[18] [a kind of debut for the literary group headed by Barral]. By this time González's identity as a member of the second postwar generation was becoming firmly established.

In the mid-fifties, as Angel González entered his thirties, he made a provisional peace with economic necessity and with the limited opportunities available to him. He resigned himself to returning to the career in civil service to which he had gained access through a state exam (the "oposiciónes") and which he had initiated earlier in Seville. For almost two decades, until 1972, González combined a kind of underemployment at modest pay—a routine, undemanding position as a Ministry of Public Works functionary—with the pursuit of his literary career and his friendships. He perfected as well what has become his somewhat legendary prowess as a tireless and committed "noctámbulo," devoted to nocturnal wanderings in the company of friends, thus unleashing the Dionysian side of himself that the priest within him at times has attempted to suppress.

During the long years González spent in Madrid, his poetic career gradually took a shape that opened unforeseen doors and eventually allowed him to abandon humdrum bureaucratic employment for a career in college teaching in the United States. His stint in the Ministry of Public Works saw many milestones. In addition to being a finalist for the Adonais Prize, and to making his debut, with *Aspero mundo*, as a publishing poet, he was featured in José María Castellet's important 1960 anthology, *Veinte años de poesía española* [Twenty years of Spanish poetry]. (This latter inclusion he has candidly and modestly attributed to his contacts in Barcelona.)[19] By 1963, he was among five standard-bearers of the new Spanish poetry to be anthologized in *Poesía última*. During the following six years, he completed the works that belonged to what he has characterized as his first phase. The period culminated in an edition of his complete works up to that time (*Palabra sobre palabra*, 1968) and in the appearance of a well-received critical book about his poetry, Emilio Alarcos Llorach's *Angel González, poeta (Variaciones críticas)* [The poet Angel González (Critical variations)] (1969).

González's introduction to his 1980 retrospective collection, *Poemas: Edición del autor*, along with various interviews and statements of his poetics dating from his early years as a writer, illuminates the works of his first period and the intentions behind them. His early collection *Aspero mundo*, published by Adonais and containing a total of thirty-eight poems, emerges as more existential than social and, as the poet has observed, too pessimistic to be a text characteristic of classic social realism[20] (or as Juan García Hortelano would term it, socialist realism). The book does, however, maintain its sense of human solidarity and a historical rootedness in time and place. For González himself, *Aspero mundo* functioned in a way that exemplifies the generation's oft-invoked conception of poetry as "conocimiento" [knowledge or discovery]; through the deep disillusionment he himself detected in the book, the poet was led to an awareness of his own despair. His readings, at the time, of such poets as Celaya, Hierro, and Nora convinced him, nevertheless, that this despondence was part of a collective experience rather than a purely individual phenomenon.[21]

If *Aspero mundo* is not a work of social realism, González's two subsequent volumes—*Sin esperanza, con convencimiento* (1961) and *Grado elemental* (1962)—do place him squarely in the current of social poetry that, rightly or wrongly, has frequently been associated with his generation. For González, *Sin esperanza, con convencimiento* corresponds, despite some continued pessimism, to a period of relative optimism and faith in social realism.[22] *Grado elemental*, on the other hand, he describes as didactic and parodic and more critical than testimonial in nature.[23] But in general terms, these two books, which contain such acerbic poems as "Discurso a los jóvenes" [Oration to the young] and "Entreacto" ["Intermission" (DDW)] from *Sin esperanza, con convencimiento*, or "Estío en Bidonville" ["Summer in the Slums" (DDW)], "Perla de las Antillas" [Pearl of the Antilles], and "Alocución a las veintitrés" [Address at the eleventh hour] from *Grado elemental*, establish González's reputation as a social and political poet.[24] An *ars poetica* from the period, "Poesía y compromiso," perhaps reflecting in its title the Sartrean influence González has referred to elsewhere,[25] states González's belief that poetry should be rooted in a particular historical moment and addressed to the poet's contemporaries. Polemical in tone and at a great remove from any sense of art as play, the essay reveals an idealistic belief in the need for poetry to serve humanity through expressing and confronting the serious problems facing the poet's society at a given moment in time. González here calls for "la poesía crítica" [critical poetry], which he describes as "expresión de una actitud moral, de un compromiso respecto a las cosas más graves que suceden en la Historia que, de alguna manera, estamos protagonizando" [The expression of a moral attitude, of a commitment toward the most serious things that are happening in the History that, in some way, we are acting out]. Though he rejects the idea of the "poeta mediatizado," one dominated by ideology, he insists that "lo que le preocupa, lo que le angustia o lo que le amenaza [al hombre]" [what concerns, torments, or threatens (human beings)] be included in poetry to avoid its being confined to "la *tierra de nadie* de la frivolidad"[26] [the no-man's-land of frivolity]. He thus assumes an ethical position of service and expresses his belief in the ability of the individual to affect society positively.

In the ensuing several years, González maintained his view of poetry as fulfilling a social function and, as later statements suggest, he has never lost respect for such a position.[27] His optimistic espousal of such a point of view, however, gradually assumed a less emphatic tone, and eventually, he has said, he lost faith altogether. In 1965, if his subtitling a statement of his poetics "Defensa de la poesía social" [Defense of social poetry] means anything, he had gone on the defensive, but he still affirmed his faith in "esa poesía crítica que sitúe al hombre en el contexto de los problemas de su tiempo, y que represente una toma de posiciones respecto a esos problemas. Más que posible," he says, "esa poesía me parece inevitable"[28] [that critical poetry which situates human beings in the context of the problems of their time, and that represents taking a stand with regard to those problems. That poetry seems to me to be not merely possible, but unavoidable]. By 1968, however, he was expressing in more measured terms his enthusiasm for the label "social poetry" and for what it represented, stating that such a label, when applied to him, "nunca me molestó demasiado" [never bothered me too much]. At this juncture, while he still saw a possible importance for society in the poet's work, he was forced to recognize certain limitations: "En la hora actual, la poesía, acentuando sus posibilidades ideológicas, podría desempeñar un papel clarificador y ético—en el más amplio sentido de las palabras—. La contradicción reside en el hecho de que la poesía es un arte demasiado minoritario, hoy, para cumplir esa función"[29] [By stressing its ideological possibilities, poetry could play at the present time a clarifying and ethical role—in the broadest sense of those terms. The contradiction lies in the fact that poetry today is too much of an art for the few to fulfill that function].With these words González hits upon one of the conflicts of his generation: the desire to create finely wrought works of art, on the one hand, but to write for humanity as a whole, avoiding elitism and escapism, on the other. Yet even at the height of his cultivation of social realism, González's poems often (in fact, more often than not) strayed from social and political themes. *Sin esperanza, con convencimiento,* as he himself points out, is dominated by the theme of time, with poems on other subjects, "el amor, el sentido—o la falta de sentido—de la vida, la esperanza y la desesperanza, la Historia" [love, life's meaning (or lack of meaning), hope, and despair, History], also interspersed. The next several books—*Grado elemental, Palabra sobre palabra,* and *Tratado de urbanismo*—continued to explore these themes, with love poetry, González notes, occupying more space, except in *Grado elemental,* than social criticism, and forming the totality of the initial *Palabra sobre palabra* (1965). If González was quick to condemn frivolity in art during this period, his ludic side nevertheless found an outlet of sorts in the satisfying game he played of fool-the-censor. His use of irony, on the other hand, may at times have been a form of self-containment, of ascetic avoidance of self-indulgence, expressing the "priest" within him, a way, as he has stated, of distancing himself from painful circumstances, of protecting himself from overly high hopes, and of avoiding both self-pity and grandiosity.[30]

Francisco Ribes's introduction to *Poesía última* (1963) provides a generational context for González's defense of "la poesía comprometida" [poetry of commitment] yet in some senses tempers the picture of González's combative stance. Citing Antonio Machado's definition of poetry as "palabra en el tiempo" [the word in time], Ribes suggests that the poets included in his anthology, using themes that provide "un espejo de su tiempo" [a mirror of their times], struggle with poetry as "conocimiento" but also as "comunicación" [communication]. For these writers, poetry becomes "un modo de más conocer para mejor comunicar"[31] [a way of knowing more in order to communicate better].

González closed his first cycle of works (which Miguel Somovilla sees as constituting, in reality, just one book)[32] with *Palabra sobre palabra* —a collection of five love poems—and with *Tratado de urbanismo*. In titling this latter work, González voiced distaste for what he saw as the no longer relevant dependence on rural imagery in much of the poetry of the period.[33] Some of the poems he included express traditional lyric emotions—nostalgia, anguish, despair, and frustration—but have unconventional urban settings. In "Parque con zoológico" [Park with zoo], he contemplates humanity's fall from grace in an imitation paradise, the modern zoo; in "Chatarra" [Scrap iron], he sets a ruin poem in an automobile graveyard. Other poems address such social and political questions as inequality ("Zona residencial" [Residential zone]), economic and sexual exploitation ("Los sábados, las prostitutas madrugan mucho para estar dispuestas" [On Saturdays, the prostitutes get up very early in order to be ready]; "Evocación segunda" [Second evocation]), repression ("Inventario de lugares propicios al amor" ["Inventory of Places Propitious for Love" (DDW)]), bourgeois conformity ("Lecciones de buen amor" [Lessons in good love]), materialism ("Civilización de la opulencia" [Civilization of opulence]) and violence ("Ciudad cero" [City zero]; "Primera evocación" ["First Evocation" (DDW)]). The work contains a middle section that deliberately turns away from social critique, though (despite the poet's intent) its final poem turned out to be one of his most political.[34] This volume—plus such signs of recognition as the publication of his complete works up to 1968 and Alarcos's book-length study of his poetry in 1969—brought to an end González's first poetic stage.

By a neat coincidence, it seems, Alarcos Llorach's critical study came at just the right time to elucidate the various books that make up González's first period. Yet perhaps this dovetailing of poetic and critical activity was not entirely coincidental after all. The writing process does not take place in a vacuum but rather is shaped by an audience, both intended and real. The progressive development of writers depends at every step on the reception they receive, making the critic no more parasitic than the writer, something González has implicitly acknowledged more than once, most notably in the speech he delivered when granted the Príncipe de Asturias Prize in 1985.[35]

An examination of Alarcos's critical premises in the light of González's authorial ones reveals the usual unstated relationship between poets and the intellectual context in which they operate. As I suggested earlier, González based his poetics, during his initial creative period, on an ethical commitment—on his belief that authors must take a stand regarding problems in their societies and that through precise, accurate choices of words they can communicate coherent positions to their contemporaries. In this early stage, the poet rejected purely aesthetic aims, revealing his belief in purpose and utility in art. Criticizing the author who expresses a merely individual perspective or even seemingly timeless realities,[36] he insisted on the individual's link with collective humanity. His point of departure, nevertheless, was a humanistic faith in the individual authorial consciousness and in reason as a basis for the point of view a writer will express. This substantive view of poetic language—as capturing a preexisting content—carried over into his second period, still appearing in his 1978 reference to "la búsqueda de la palabra poética exacta, justa, precisa, a la vez que imaginativa"[37] [the search for the exact, correct, precise, and at the same time imaginative, word].

In Alarcos's book, a substantive view of poetic language such as the one detected in González's statement is fundamental. Characterizing González's poetry as portraying a desolate world in which love and solidarity provide positive notes, Alarcos affirms the poet's belief in the possibility of a better future for humanity. He describes González as "racional, intelectual y vigilante" [rational, intellectual, and vigilant] and as one who thinks that art should serve society. He speaks of González's "mesura" [moderation] and "contención" [restraint], which along with his reading of the title *Palabra sobre palabra* as a representation of the poet-artificer constructing a poetic edifice out of bricks, suggests authorial volition and control. But most telling are his own division of the book into two sections, the first outlining content, the second form, and his belief in the imperatives that "todos los contenidos que quiere comunicar el poeta se manifiesten con una expresión precisa, y que ningún elemento de la expresión sea mero relleno, vacío de contenido" [all the contents that the poet wants to communicate should manifest themselves with a precise expression, and that no element of the expression should be mere filler, void of content]. Envisioning a "perfecta adecuación de la expresión al contenido" [perfect tailoring of expression to content], Alarcos understands form as following intentions, and meter as forever subjugated to the ideas the poet wants to express: "La atención primordial del poeta al ritmo del contenido le obliga a forjarse una expresión rítmica particular que no traicione a los contenidos que se manifiestan" [The poet's primordial attention to the rhythm of the content obliges him to forge a particular rhythmic expression that won't betray the contents that are being revealed]. Conceiving the poet's language as a kind of lapidary form designed to communicate a fixed meaning, Alarcos views González's adjectives as agents of precision. He interprets such ordering expressions as "pero" [but], "sin embargo" [nevertheless], or "en suma" [in sum] as serving González's rationality and considers the portrayal of thought processes, in the poem "Cumpleaños" [Birthday], as serving content by showing that "las vivencias comunicadas no son simples intuiciones, sino que han sido pasadas por el filtro tranquilo de la mente, que han sido contrastadas por el fiel de la razón" [the lived experiences communicated are not mere intuitions but instead have been passed through the calm filter of the mind and weighed and measured by the controlling force of reason]. Alarcos recognizes González's irony but interprets it as the poet's way of sweetening the medicine of his serious message by provoking a smile.[38] Though he touches on some techniques that point to the disaggregation of the poetic text (parentheses or multiple perspectives, for example), he tends to dismiss their destabilizing effect by interpreting them as subordinate to coherent content and poetic aims. When a poem appears that could be read as dialogic or indeterminate, Alarcos sees not a problematic text but González's presentation of a reality that is multifaceted. An example of Alarcos's approach is his interpretation of González's use of a footnote in the poem "Lecciones de buen amor."[39] Instead of considering the note as an antipoetic device that plays on the lyric genre or as a disturbance of the convention of the poem as a construct complete in itself, Alarcos views its use as serving communication by allowing the poet to avoid a parenthetical interruption that would have been too long.[40]

The poetry of González's first period, then, was written—in vastly simplified terms—under the assumption that art should serve society. It was read, at least by Alarcos, through conceptions of art that go back to Enlightenment premises of artistic form at the service of the poet's intentional content (though seeds of González's later, Dionysian tendency to take refuge from his own desolation in unsanctioned and irrational activities do appear and were acknowledged by Alarcos). Even the irony of this period, though González recognized its ability to counterpose two opposing positions, had its practical end—the deceiving of the government censors. González himself—revealing the rational side Alarcos stresses—describes his transition to his second period, a change that he identifies with *Tratado de urbanismo* (appropriately called a "fulcrum" by LeCertúa).[41] With this volume, written during what might be seen as a period of political stagnation and personal crisis, he renounced his faith in words. Calling words useless, he continues as follows:

> Mediada la década de los 60, la inmutabilidad (más aparente que real, contempladas las cosas desde hoy) de una situación a la que yo no veía salida, me hacía desconfiar de cualquier intento, por modestos que fuesen sus alcances, de incidir verbalmente en la realidad.[42]

[Halfway through the decade of the sixties, the immutability (more apparent than real, if things are viewed from today's perspective) of a situation from which I could see no escape made me suspicious of any attempt, no matter how modest its scope, to penetrate reality with words.]

It is at this juncture that González turned to fragmentation, nonsense, jokes, and verbal play. As he abandoned the testimonial mode and (as Carnero phrases it) turned toward language that is "menos instrumental"[43] [less instrumental], he tended toward a new view of his relationship to the poetic speaker, which he expressed in 1985 as follows:

[S]é que quien habla en mis poemas es un personaje de ficción, que trata vanamente de imitarme, que intenta incluso hacerse pasar por mí mismo, disfrazándose con mis trajes. La ironía me sirve para marcar la distancia que me separa de él. A veces trata de engañarme también a mí, pero no lo consigue nunca; sé que su verdad es el reverso de mi mentira, y yo lo trato como a uno de esos muñecos de magia negra, a quienes los brujos clavan alfileres para producir dolor en sus enemigos. Lo que ocurre es que, en vez de clavarle alfileres, yo se las quito.[44]

[I know that he who speaks in my poems is a fictional character, who tries in vain to imitate me, who even tries to pass for me by disguising himself in my clothes. Irony allows me to mark the distance that separates me from him. Sometimes he also tries to deceive me, but he never succeeds; I know that his truth is the reverse of my lie, and I treat him like one of those dolls in black magic, which the sorcerers stick with pins in order to cause pain in their enemies. What happens is that instead of sticking pins in him, I pull them out.]

Ironically, by the time González's discouragement at Franco's continuation in power had led him to adopt new gamelike poetic styles in disillusionment with the power of words, the dictator had already begun to loosen his grip. This fact, along with Spain's economic boom, had caused the opposition's focus and sense of purpose to waver. But though this relaxation apparently left less to react against, there was no prospect of immediate change on the horizon to absorb the opposition's critical energies. Nevertheless, as he moved into his second phase, González experienced a freedom from historical exigencies that he eventually described as follows:

Poesía social, civil, comprometida, crítica. . . . Esas eran las tendencias que dominaban en el ambiente literario—y no sólo en el de España—cuando comencé a publicar mis poemas. Por entonces, la guerra estaba aún muy próxima. . . . La dictadura era, además, una realidad . . . agresiva. . . . No . . . porque quisiese transformar el mundo—algo que, por supuesto, también quería—, sino porque tenía que clarificarlo ante mí mismo, . . . comencé a . . . contar mi historia dentro de la Historia. . . .

Todo ha cambiado mucho, por fortuna, desde entonces. La Historia es ahora, para mí, un habitáculo menos envolvente, menos abrumador, que me permite moverme con una libertad que antes desconocía.[45]

[Social poetry, civil poetry, committed poetry, critical poetry. . . . Those were the tendencies that dominated literary circles—and not just in Spain—when I began to publish my poems. At that time, the war was still very recent. . . . The dictatorship was also an aggressive reality. . . . Not . . . because I wanted to change the world—which of course I did also want to do—but because I had to explain it to myself, . . . I began to . . . tell my own story within History. . . .
Fortunately, everything has changed greatly since then. Now history is a less gripping, less overwhelming dwelling place that permits me to operate with a freedom previously unknown to me.]

In addition to politically linked motives for change, there were certainly artistic ones. If *Tratado de urbanismo* exhibits signs of a threshold of intellectual crisis and change, it was written in a context of experimentalism that traversed Hispanic literature and international art circles at this time. A similarly transitional work in the Spanish novel, Juan Goytisolo's *Señas de identidad*, had come out one year earlier, in 1966. At about the same time, Juan Benet—for whom the anecdotal element of a novel "se ha transformado en un medio con el que poner de manifiesto una prosa perfecta, última meta del escritor" [has become a means through which to display a perfect prose, the writer's ultimate goal] and who is thus at a far remove from "la literatura 'comprometida'"[46] [politically committed literature]—published his first narratives. During this period, the model of poetry capturing reality in words was challenged by works in which language takes on a life of its own and by the experimentalism that now might be associated with the postmodern sensibility. The change González underwent at this time certainly reflected, on an individual scale, more generalized tendencies in the poetic panorama of Spain. For José Luis García Martín, almost all of González's generation experienced in this period a similar poetic crisis based on "[u]na falta de fe en la eficacia social de la palabra poética, en su capacidad para transformar el mundo"[47] [lack of faith in the social effectiveness of the poetic word, in its capacity to transform the world]. Fanny Rubio and José Luis Falcó, likewise, refer to the crisis that had overtaken González's generation by this time: "Durante la década de los sesenta habíamos asistido a un doble fenómeno de consolidación y de cansancio. Consolidación de la segunda promoción de postguerra; . . . y cansancio hacia esa misma estética dominante (por todos conocida bajo el confuso rótulo de *realismo*), y que comenzó a dejarse sentir dentro de la misma promoción del 60" [During the sixties we had witnessed a double phenomenon of consolidation and of fatigue. Consolidation of the second wave of postwar writers; . . . and fatigue toward that same dominant aesthetic (known to everybody by the confusing label of *realism*), which began to be felt among the same group of writers of 1960]. Like *Tratado de urbanismo* for González, José Batlló's *Antología de la nueva poesía española* [Anthology of the new Spanish poetry] (1968) is for Rubio and Falcó a work that bridges two periods. The book, they say, "con el tiempo adquirió un especial significado: el de constituirse en puente entre dos maneras distintas de enfrentarse al hecho poético, entre dos concepciones diferentes de lo que «es o debería ser» la poesía" [with time acquired a special significance: that of a bridge between two distinct ways of approaching the phenomenon of poetry, between two different conceptions of what poetry "is or should be"]. Included in the anthology (analogous to certain poems from *Tratado de urbanismo*) were works by younger poets (Pedro Gimferrer, José Miguel Ullán, and Manuel Vázquez Montalbán) that heralded a new style and a new "generation" that, as Rubio and Falcó state, made its first appearance as such two years later in José Castellet's *Nueve novísimos poetas españoles*. It is no coincidence that the common threads Rubio and Falcó find in the *novísimos*' statements of their *ars poetica*—"el sentimiento de inutilidad de la literatura, de la poesía, la pérdida de la fe en el valor activo de la palabra poética"[48] [the sense of the uselessness of literature, of poetry, the loss of faith in the active value of the poetic word]—correspond to González's description of what he was going through during this period. González, it is true, did not accept wholesale the premises of the *novísimos* and in fact strongly objected, initially, to their supposed aestheticism. Even in 1978, long after entering his second, less socially committed phase, he rejected their "pretendida destrucción del lenguaje" [attempted destruction of language] and echoed his earlier sentiments,[49] defending Celaya's view of poetry as "un arma cargada de futuro" [a firearm loaded with the future] as not precisely true but not entirely false either.[50] But by the early seventies González undoubtedly experienced skepticism regarding words coinciding with reality, as he explicitly pointed out later.[51] This was precisely the message of the burgeoning tide of critical thought that viewed literary works from an intertextual perspective, considering poetic texts as Northrop Frye did, not as mirrors of external reality, but as constructs that "can only be made out of other poems."[52]

Though the real explosion of critical theory, and of the poetry of the *novísimos* as well, would take place a little after the publication of *Tratado de urbanismo*, nevertheless the effects of new ideas that were to challenge traditional notions of reading and writing were beginning to be in the air at the time the book was written. The sixties are cited as a decade of "profound change and disquiet" by, for example, literary theorist Hazard Adams.[53]

González's experience of a decade of global intellectual crisis coincided, furthermore, with a period of some personal upheaval and change. In his interview with Federico Campbell published in *Infame turba* [Infamous horde] in 1971, significantly titled "Angel González o la desesperanza" [Angel González, or despair], undercurrents of depression appear. González speaks of his congenital pessimism and of his own insecurities, and when asked about literary criticism, which at this time was acquiring increasing importance as a discipline, he confesses his deficiencies in the area of foreign languages, as well as his ineptitude for critical reading: "[S]iempre fui pesimista"; "Soy incapaz de publicar un texto antes de que alguien lo lea"; "[E]scribir un poema me produce cierto entusiasmo. Cuando está terminado me produce desilusión, casi asco físico"; "[S]oy muy refractario a la lectura de textos críticos. . . . [Y]o leo muy mal el inglés. He leído muy poco en idiomas extranjeros. . . . [S]oy también muy mal lector de textos teóricos"[54] [I was always a pessimist. . . . I'm incapable of publishing a text before someone reads it. . . . (W)riting a poem produces a certain enthusiasm in me. When it's finished I feel disillusionment, almost nausea. . . . I'm very resistant to reading works of criticism. . . . I read English very badly. I have read very little in foreign languages. . . . I'm also a very poor reader of theoretical texts].

In this interview González speaks of his own past with a bitterness unusual for him. He tempers his usual praise for his mother by maintaining that his sense of disillusionment and failure had roots in his early childhood. He avoids recalling too-painful memories of the war years: "Prefiero omitir detalles molestos hasta en el recuerdo" [I prefer omitting bothersome details even in remembering]. He portrays himself and his generation as pushed aside and their talents wasted:

> La historia de España no es una historia cómoda: deja muy poco margen a la esperanza y al optimismo. De todas formas, yo tengo fe y optimismo en la buena marcha, a la larga, de las cosas. Pero mientras las cosas se arreglan o no se arreglan, lo que quedó inutilizado y perdido ha sido mi vida, es mi vida y la de muchos de mi generación.

> [The history of Spain is not a comfortable history; it leaves very little room for hope and optimism. In any case, I have faith and optimism that things will go well in the long run. But while things are either getting fixed or not getting fixed, what was wasted and made useless was my life, my life and that of many in my generation.]

He views both his employment and Madrid, where he lived at the time, in a negative light, much more so than later on after residing in the United States: "Para mí Madrid es una ciudad particularmente desagradable. Una de las razones es que trabajo aquí, que estoy lleno de obligaciones desagradables; otra es el planteamiento urbanístico catastrófico de la ciudad"[55] [For me Madrid is a particularly disagreeable city. One of the reasons is that I work here, that I'm full of disagreeable obligations; another is the catastrophic

2 / ROOTS AND CONNECTIONS

way the city has been developed]. The interview in short conveys a definite malaise, and it is therefore not surprising that González made striking changes after this period. Perhaps it is significant that the death of his mother had occurred in 1969—two years prior to the interview—and that he himself was approaching the age his father had attained at the time of his death. Some of the weight of responsibility toward his mother and toward the high ideals of his father's derailed destiny may have been lifted, allowing him to seize new opportunities in America when they arose. And while he has described his turning to humor and irony as a way of coping with the frustrations of the period (a use for humor proposed by Freud), he may also have developed his playful side in a kind of liberation from family scripts that emphasized service.

For whatever reasons, González's life took new directions after this period that, happily, led him to what he has described as "la mejor época de mi vida"[56] [the best period of my life]. By 1970, opportunities to travel in the United States, Mexico, and Venezuela presented themselves, and in 1972 he was invited to spend five months as a visiting professor in New Mexico. After a two-month visit to Venezuela, a month in Chile, and several weeks in Argentina, he returned to Spain prepared to experiment with a life devoted exclusively to writing. Nevertheless, statements he made to Ana María Moix during the interim period between his first stint in America and his more definitive incorporation into American university life the following fall reveal the difficulty he had in establishing a productive daily routine in Madrid in the face of the constant pull of his friends:

> Me levanto tarde, casi nunca antes de las doce, y muy cansado. . . . No me gusta comer fuera porque salir puede estropearme el día: puedo encontrar a algún amigo, empezar a hablar, liarme a tomar copas, en fin, el desastre. Antes de comer, intento ponerme a trabajar, generalmente con poco éxito. Después, ya por la tarde, sí, trabajo. . . . Si puedo resistir la llamada invitándome a salir a cenar, me quedo en casa, ceno poco, me acuesto y leo. Si no resisto la llamada, es peor: me acuesto a las cinco de la madrugada y el día siguiente queda borrado en sueño, cansancio, alka-seltzer, etc. . . . y mala conciencia, sí, mala conciencia por no haberme quedado en casa.[57]

> [I get up late, almost never before noon, and very tired. . . . I don't like to eat lunch out because going out can ruin my day: I might run into a friend, start talking, get involved in having a few drinks, in short, a disaster. Before lunch, I try to get down to work, generally with little success. Later, in the afternoon, I do indeed work. . . . If I can resist the telephone call inviting me out to dinner, I stay home, eat a light supper, and go to bed and read. If I don't resist the call, it's worse: I get to bed at five A.M. and the next day is a blur of sleepiness, fatigue, Alka-Seltzer, etc. . . . and a guilty conscience, yes, a guilty conscience because I didn't stay home.]

Thus he wavered—both in his choice of employment and in the structure of his days—between duty and freedom from responsibility. The view of art that he expressed at this time reveals the evolution he had undergone since his early expressions of commitment to social poetry: "[P]ara mí el arte debe responder a un sentimiento lúdico"[58] [for me art should respond to a sense of play]. This philosophy is the basis of much of his most successful later poetry. He continued to evolve in this direction, by 1983 referring to his poems as products not of inspiration but of "ocurrencias" (one meaning of which, significantly, is "joke"), and emphasizing the gratuitous nature of the poetic game, which begins with "palabras que se te ocurren al margen de tu voluntad"[59] [words that occur to you outside of your will].

The ludic strand in González's poetry obviously corresponds to a fundamental aspect of his personality. He has repeatedly expressed his preference for people over literature (as in the Moix interview). His assiduous dedication to spontaneous social interactions and to the company of friends, especially during nocturnal sorties, is well known: "En Madrid había muchos bares abiertos toda la noche y era muy agradable prolongar la convivencia, la conversación, la tertulia con amigos a lo largo de toda la noche. Yo lo hice así durante muchos años y eso se acabó convirtiendo en un hábito"[60] [In Madrid there were many bars that were open all night and it was very pleasant to prolong the camaraderie, the conversation, the socializing with friends throughout the whole night. That's what I did for many years—it ended up being a habit with me]. That his sociability has served a Bacchic function, becoming a way of letting go of inner strictures, seems clear from statements in which he himself notes his Apollonian/Dionysian nature. He has spoken openly of the congenital timidity, that—like his priest-driven seriousness and rational, responsible nature—he has overcome at times through drinking. He has referred as well to his tendency to value the irrational and magical events that sometimes happen late at night: "[D]e noche ocurren cosas más sorprendentes, tal vez por la intervención del alcohol. Suceden hechos insólitos, a veces mágicos, que de día no suelen ocurrir"[61] [At night things that are more surprising happen, perhaps through the intervention of alcohol. Unusual things occur, sometimes magical ones, that normally don't take place in the daytime].

Shortly after his interview with Moix, he returned to the University of New Mexico as a regular faculty member. Though in subsequent years his absence from Spain has provoked numerous expressions of nostalgia, the combination of winters in the United States and summers in Madrid has offered change and variety. González has later spoken more fondly about life in Spain than in *Infame turba*. At the same time, he has expressed an objective appreciation for the stability his American situation has offered him.

Life in the United States, despite many deficiencies for a Spaniard accustomed to the greater possibilities for interaction with a well-established circle of friends in Madrid, has provided an atmosphere in which González could accomplish certain goals that might have eluded him elsewhere. As he has stated regarding New Mexico: "[E]s un poco el puerto donde reposo y descanso" [It's sort of the harbor where I repose and rest]. This harbor has provided, he says, "una cantidad de tiempo libre enorme para hacer mis cosas, e incluso para no hacer nada. Es un tiempo de tranquilidad, de paz. Incluso mi salud física lo agradece" [an enormous amount of free time to do what I need to do, and even to do nothing. It's a time of tranquility, of peace. Even my physical health is grateful for it]. Returning after a stay in Spain, he observed: "En definitiva, que voy por una parte con pena, pero por otra con la misma sensación de quien ve el puerto próximo donde recogerse y refugiarse"[62] [Unquestionably, I'm departing on the one hand with sadness, but on the other with the feeling of one who sees the harbor near where it's possible to take shelter and find refuge]. Both this change of environment and the gradual political transformation of Spain have led him in new poetic directions. Referring to the political situation, he has declared:

> Antes, podía decirse, tendía más a una poesía de compromiso ciudadano y ahora veo que, sin que haya abandonado aquellas actitudes, el compromiso no es tan esencial. Al alcanzarse una situación política de libertades públicas, no se le exige el compromiso al poeta ni el poeta se lo exige a sí mismo, y por esto puede dedicarse a elaborar una obra más propia, más privada, más personal. Al cambiar la situación cambia un poco la actitud del poeta.
>
> [Before, one might say, I tended more toward a poetry of civic commitment, and now, without having given up those earlier attitudes, I see that the commitment is not so essential. When a political situation allowing public freedoms is reached, political commitment is not demanded of poets nor do they demand it of themselves, and for that reason they can devote themselves to fashioning a more private, personal work, one that's more their own. When the situation changes, the attitude of the poet changes somewhat.]

Simple distance from Spain, moreover, gave him a new perspective; he adds that residence in the United States "Me proporcionó una temática nueva y me incitó a tratar algunos temas que hasta entonces no había tratado. Con el distanciamiento creo que mi obra se hizo más personal"[63] [It gave me a new subject matter and inspired me to treat some themes that until then I hadn't treated. With the separation I believe my work became more personal].

After leaving Spain for America, González wrote two books of literary criticism, one, on Juan Ramón Jiménez, published in 1973, and the other, on Antonio Machado, first published in 1980. This second book was conceived, he says, in a period of "ocio forzoso"[64] [involuntary idleness]—a semester of unemployment during his early stage as a visiting professor in the United

States. The first five or six years of this American period also saw the publication of innovative work in the form of *Procedimientos narrativos* and of *Muestra* in its first and second versions. These volumes, with their self-referential, ludic qualities and their foregrounding of poetic artifice, consolidate the postmodern leanings that González will continue in subsequent poems. His voluntary exile, then, like the earlier, involuntary one in Páramo de Sil, provided not only time but also a challenge in the absence of familiar props, resulting in the germination of new creative forces.

González's stay in the United States and his successful incorporation into American academic life have resulted additionally in intensifying interest in his work within the American critical community. Upon arriving at the University of New Mexico, he became the subject of a doctoral dissertation there, with others eventually following at other universities. More importantly, a number of innovative and rigorous critical studies, incorporating recent developments in literary theory, have reinforced and mirrored the experimental ludic qualities characteristic of this second period. In 1977, a bilingual anthology of González's poems, translated by Donald Walsh, was published by Princeton University Press. Several years later, Andrew P. Debicki, in his book on poets of the fifties, *Poetry of Discovery: The Spanish Generation of 1956–1971*, analyzed González's reformulation of familiar clichés. Douglas K. Benson has examined irony and parody in González, and Nancy Mandlove and Margaret H. Persin, among others, have approached his poetry using fresh and incisive critical tools. Studies on González, as well as interviews and reviews, have proliferated on both sides of the Atlantic, becoming approximately four times as frequent after 1970 as before. In a review published in Spain in 1976, Guillermo Carnero expressed enthusiasm for the "vitalidad" [vitality] and "renovación" [renewal] he had discovered in *Muestra*.[65] His reaction is similar to the interest in González found among innovative American critics.

By 1984, a series of events had begun to crown the previous thirty years of poetic development. In the United States, González's works received two tributes from the academic community: one, a special session of the 1984 Modern Language Association devoted to his works, and the other, a symposium in his honor in January of 1985, sponsored and underwritten by the University of New Mexico. In Spain, the recognition—practically simultaneous—was more resounding; in June of 1985 González was declared the winner of the important Príncipe de Asturias Prize. This new honor led to the publication of two homage volumes, *Angel González: Verso a verso* [Angel González: Line by line] (1987), published by the Caja de Ahorros de Asturias [Savings Bank of Asturias], and a special issue of the Asturian literary magazine *Luna de abajo* [Low moon], both of which contain critical studies as well as personal testimonials by friends. Thus while the fifteen years that elapsed between *Aspero mundo* and González's first trip to the United States saw a steady consolidation of his works and reputation, the next fifteen brought real recognition.

If González, in comments, has returned time and again to the primacy of life over literature and to the importance of literature based on actual experiences, and if in his personal life he has at times had to struggle to balance his vital impulses with the need for tranquility to work, the two opposing veins come together almost inseparably in the homage paid to him by friends and admirers. In addition to considering his poetry, the statements of many of his contemporaries reveal genuine enjoyment of his success as they testify over and over to the warmth of his personality and to his vitality. The following words of Jaime Gil de Biedma are typical: "En cuanto amigo y en cuanto lector, agradezco sobre todo la sólida capacidad de simpatía humana que he encontrado siempre en él y en sus poemas"[66] [As a friend and as a reader, I especially appreciate the solid capacity for human sympathy that I have always found in him and in his poems]. Not to be forgotten, finally, is the important role love relationships have played in González's life. "Yo no recuerdo ninguna etapa de mi vida, desde que soy joven, en que no estuviera verdaderamente enamorado y ligado a una mujer" [I don't remember any period in my life, from the time I was young, when I haven't been truly in love and involved with a woman], he states. He speaks of "cuatro historias de amor muy importantes en mi vida" [four very important love stories in my life], but with a certain characteristic reticence, he does not elaborate upon them. What he does mention is his relationship with his longtime companion Susana Rivera, to whom he has dedicated *Prosemas o menos* and *Palabra sobre palabra* (1986), and of whom he has stated: "Para mí su compañía y su presencia son algo fundamental en este momento"[67] [Her company and her presence are something fundamental to me at this time].

As I have tried to suggest in providing an overview of his development, González's responses to changing aesthetic currents have resulted in a complex body of work more in line with international postmodernism than with the existential and social trends he was originally associated with in Spain. Overall his work reflects many elements that theorists of postmodernism have identified as characterizing the art and literature of recent decades. González clearly partakes of a generalized disillusionment with what Silvio Gaggi has termed the "ambitious and sometimes utopian aims" of modernism.[68] The ludic experimentation that figures so prominently in his works must be seen as an outgrowth of this disillusionment. But as Gaggi points out, postmodern artists do not necessarily reject modernism completely. González, even while developing a body of poems that reflect constant change, has maintained an underlying line of constancy in his interests and concerns that is evident even in his most recent poetry. The five poems included in the volume of critical studies on his poetry edited by Andrew P. Debicki and Sharon Keefe Ugalde in 1991 and incorporated into the fourteen-poem collection *Deixis en fantasma* in 1992 recapitulate much of González's vital experience. In the first of these poems, a tribute to Antonio Machado, appear traces of González's ideological and poetic roots. In the second and third we detect resonances of the poet's struggle with his inner priest and with time and death. In the fourth and fifth, the poet gives poignant testimony to an enduring love that goes far beyond the "este momento" of his understated comment about Susana Rivera. Thus after a poetic trajectory of considerable experimentation and play, he has continued to weave together his thematics of time, politics, love, ethics, and the connectedness between art and life. As the following chapters show, González carries postmodernist experimentation to great lengths. But like John Barth and John Fowles as described by Silvio Gaggi, he remains a "humanistic postmodern,"[69] never losing his humanistic grounding completely, a fact that must be borne in mind as we undertake the analysis and assessment of his poems.

3
The Poetry of *Engagement*: From Inner Exile to Expressive Freedom

> [S]i el artista ha de ser libre para todo, menos para comprometerse, ¿para qué le sirve la libertad? . . . En rigor, el compromiso es un acto de libertad, un acto libre [If artists are to be free to do anything, except to commit themselves politically, what good to them is their freedom? . . . In truth, commitment is an act of liberty, a free act].
> —González, "Poesía y compromiso" [Poetry and commitment] (1963)

> [P]ara mí el arte debe responder a un sentimiento lúdico [For me, art should respond to a sense of play].
> —González, "Veinticuatro horas" [Twenty-four hours] (1972)

González's turn from *engagement* to poetic play is amply illustrated by these two quotations, published, remarkably, within ten years of one another. But in spite of the fact that his life, his works, and many of his public statements point to a clear pattern of change and development, nevertheless the two staples of his poetic personality—politics and play—represent not two totally opposite poles but two elements in complex interrelationship. The tension embodied in González's poetry between the assumption that words have a definite utility and the premise that art is primarily gratuitous and playful reenacts and echoes important segments of critical debate within the twentieth century.

The utility that González sought in his first period but eschewed in later works has been debated as a legitimate aim of literature since early in the century, definitions of literature itself having sometimes even turned on the usefulness of words or its absence. Russian formalist ideas of the word as an "autonomous source of pleasure" have in recent years resurfaced in Michael Riffaterre's distinction between tropes in nonliterary language, used only to persuade, and those in literature, which exist as functions of literariness.[1] Such views imply an intrinsic split between literature, on the one hand, and words used for practical ends, on the other. Opposing points of view, described by Fredric Jameson, have posited that language and politics are in some senses virtually inseparable, that literary works embody conscious and unconscious ideological biases and in fact are instruments of class domination.[2] But if this latter perspective makes it difficult to argue that any given literary text is totally free of political meaning, awareness of the complexity of language in literature makes it equally difficult to imagine a text in which utility, purpose, and connectedness with the body politic do not coexist with gratuitous and ludic elements. As language unfolds, structures that emerge from both the conscious and unconscious mind are projected as on a screen. At the same time, words in their slipperiness take on a life of their own, playing with and off each other. As Susan Stewart demonstrates, art and play have in fact long been closely linked by aestheticians and have much in common. But even the question of whether play itself has social utility has become a topic of ongoing debate.[3] González's evolution from politics to play thus reflects one of the fundamental critical issues of Western thought in our times. Yet to understand his development fully, we must consider the specific Spanish atmosphere in which his ideas evolved. We must take into consideration especially a long-standing debate in Spain: the dispute over "pure" and "impure" poetry. This debate is emblematized in the contrast between Juan Ramón Jiménez and Blas de Otero, who dedicated and directed their poetry to "la inmensa minoría" [the great minority] and "la inmensa mayoría" [the great majority], respectively. González, whose taste for poetry grew in part out of readings of Jiménez, has never completely stopped writing poems that in many ways share the modernist aesthetic of transcendence, immanence, and formal beauty (as such poems as "Crepúsculo, Albuquerque, estío" [Twilight, Albuquerque, summer] or "Crepúsculo, Albuquerque, otoño" [Twilight, Albuquerque, autumn] in *Prosemas o menos* demonstrate). Nor has he stopped expanding his own technical repertoire. Yet an opposing current of thought, critical of what was perceived as "pure" poetry, must be viewed as a more fundamental formative influence on González. This current, which included such major writers as Miguel de Unamuno and Antonio Machado, prefigured many of the attitudes of González and other postwar social poets. Machado's particularly potent influence, given González's liberal background and his family's association with the progressive ideals of the turn of the century, should come as no surprise. In his commentaries on poetic developments in Spain, Machado opposed pure poetry and automatic writing, as Guillermo Carnero notes, and he criticized younger poets for creating works lacking emotion and connection to the society in which they arose. Machado believed strongly that poetry should be rooted in time and place. In Carnero's words, moreover, he was "poco amigo del perfeccionismo verbal, partidario de los valores coloquiales y contenidistas del lenguaje, y enemigo de una literatura de vanguardia carente de dimensión emotiva y de experiencia vital"[4] [a man little drawn to verbal perfectionism, an advocate of the colloquial values of language and of the latter's ability to express content, and an enemy of an avant-garde literature devoid of the emotive dimension and of life experience]. Parallels to these attitudes in González's works are not hard to find. González's colloquialism and *engagement* come immediately to mind, but even his early, imitative love poems follow a model of poetry as an expression of emotional intimacy. (Not surprisingly, Machado and González share a taste for Bécquer.) It is not illogical, then, to view Machado as one of González's poetic fathers, in terms of poetic values.[5]

In keeping with González's identification with Machado and with a current opposing pure poetry, we find poems throughout *Palabra sobre palabra* that ridicule the creation of elaborate poetic artifices and decry the obsessive search for beauty at the expense of awareness of human suffering. González's colloquial language, sometimes even vulgar and shocking, and his directive against purity—"Mantén sucia la estrofa. / Escupe dentro" [Keep the stanza dirty. Spit in it]—recall the rhetoric of prewar debate, in which purists recriminated their opponents for using such terms as "cloaca" [sewer], "estiércol" [manure], "mierda" [shit], and "ramera" [whore], while the latter in turn decried the icy sterility of their adversaries. As Carnero makes clear, those opposed to "pure" poetry frequently considered emphasis on form inimical to human values.[6] González, in addition to incorporating a certain anti-aestheticism into his own poetry, initially criticized younger poets—the *novísimos*—for ignoring political realities, for glorifying luxury, and for experimenting excessively with technique.[7]

González's sense of ethical commitment as a poet was further reinforced by the Marxist and existentialist leanings of many of his contemporaries. Sartre's belief that we create ourselves through the way we live and his advocacy of responsibility without illusions[8] no doubt influenced González's stance, as did the poet's association with those dedicated to forging social change through poetry. Yet the simplistic view of poetry as a social tool, as "un arma cargada de futuro" in the words of González's friend and fellow poet Gabriel Celaya, was eventually undermined, ironically, by meager results. Perhaps more importantly, new viewpoints, which conceived art as embodying social structures regardless or even in spite of the author's goals and intentions, were emerging. The model of words as capturing a preexisting content (which, as we saw in chapter 2, informed Alarcos Llorach's study of González) was being replaced by a growing recognition of the limitations of individual consciousness and of reason. Models of individual enmeshment in larger systems had begun to undermine the authority of politically committed art.[9] Artistic and linguistic self-consciousness had begun to make all ideologies suspect, and awareness of the complex relationship between the individual and broader social structures made the premises of traditional humanism more and more problematical.

The pattern of González's evolution—early lyrical games that bore little relationship to his own circumstances and that he wrote without intending to publish them;[10] espousal of an existentialist- and Marxist-inspired poetry of commitment after publishing became a possibility; and, finally, a disillusionment with *engagement* that led him toward gratuitous poetic play—thus reflects his involvement in larger aesthetic currents, particularly the ongoing twentieth-century debate on the nature of art and its purpose. Yet in referring first to his early politically motivated poems and later to his nonsensical or playful works, González has described his poetic evolution as primarily a response to particular political realities in Spain rather than to aesthetic or intellectual trends; he turned to verbal play, he says, through political disillusionment. He also specifically denies that literary theory has influenced his poetry.[11] But in fact González is not immune to the aesthetic trends of the times. As Debicki has noted, he sometimes even cultivates several tendencies at once, making his work difficult to characterize.[12] This multiplicity of voices is due, I believe, to his responsiveness to the changing and conflicting artistic imperatives that have shaped twentieth-century Spanish literature. In his poems, strong purpose can indeed coexist with gratuitous play, social criticism and political commitment with reworkings of traditional lyric forms and themes, and intentional ugliness with aestheticism like that associated with the early Juan Ramón Jiménez. These divergent strands have led critics to differ significantly in their readings of his works. In reconsidering politics and verbal play in his poetry, I hope to reconcile some of these differences, at least in part.

To understand the complex relationship between politics and play in González's work, it is necessary to scrutinize both his early and late poetry and to consider the effect of his changing attitudes toward the utility of words. In his early political poems, González intended to persuade. The tropes he used were chosen to serve the ends of utility and persuasiveness, and they thus fit Riffaterre's description of nonliterary language as words meant to convince. González has commented that because his main audience consisted of those who already shared his convictions, little actual convincing may have been going on. Yet his belief that, even for those readers, his poetry served a purpose of reinforcing and strengthening previously held notions[13] underscores his confidence in poetry as an instrument of persuasion.

González's early social and political poetry directs the reader's attention to an immediate, shared political environment beyond the poem. In this phase, he often relied heavily on irony to allude indirectly to specific political and social realities.[14] The impact of the irony and other techniques of indirection that he used to elude censors depended on their transparency to readers

3 / THE POETRY OF ENGAGEMENT

"in the know," and thus on a body of shared assumptions, values, and knowledge. Somewhat like realistic prose, which disguises the seam between the world inside the text and the world outside it, this early poetry depends on the seamless harmony between the thrust of the poem and the ideology of the readers within González's intellectual milieu, who to appreciate his irony had to be, in a sense, initiates. His use of language cannot be termed straightforward in these poems. He manipulated and juxtaposed meaning systems and, as Shirley Mangini has pointed out, imitated the rhetoric of the Francoist establishment, not with the unconsciousness of earlier social poets but with an ironic self-awareness.[15] Nevertheless, his juxtapositions and adaptations were not meant to disorient seriously or to challenge his intended reader but rather to reinforce common convictions. In Susan Stewart's terms, these poems must be seen as "commonsensical" in their own way, being entirely consonant with a larger system of logical discourse and reference shared with their intended audience.

Guillermo Carnero has suggested that political art requires "fe, programa o enemigo"[16] [a faith, a program, or an enemy]. When González turned away from social and political commitment in the mid-sixties, he did so out of a double loss of faith. On the one hand, he had become disillusioned with Franco's continued hold on Spain, but significantly, too, he has spoken of losing faith in the utility of words. Though couched in negative terms, his new skepticism had a positive side. He began to see tropes and words as liberated from their function as persuasive devices, a fact that allowed linguistic play and humor to develop much further in his works than in the past. Yet as the analysis of specific poems in chapter 3 will show, ideology does not disappear totally from his later works but rather tends either to emerge unsolicited from play that has been given free rein, or to become an implicit corollary of a meta-art that questions power structures through undermining various types of discourse. In this latter phase, his poems become at times indeterminate and multiple-voiced, juxtaposing meaning systems and threatening patterns of common sense. In short, they become a critique of reason and, as Carlos Bousoño suggests in discussing other Spanish poets writing at the same time, a critique of language as an embodiment of power.[17] It seems safe to assume that these later poems offer a more complex challenge to their readers than did the poems González directed at initiates during his early period of communicating a shared vision. Certainly these poems are more engaging for those not directly implicated in the drama of postwar opposition politics.[18]

A close examination of the social and political poems of González's early period of critical intent reveals how his *engagement* and his opposition status affected his work at that time. These poems generally express the leftist opposition politics of the Spanish underground, solidarity with those oppressed by capitalism, and disapproval of writers who turn their backs on society to pursue purely aesthetic aims. The early poems "Me falta una palabra" ["I'm lacking one word . . ." (DDW)] (p. 17) and "Soneto a algunos poetas" [Sonnet to some poets] (p. 44), both from *Aspero mundo*, criticize poetic escapism. In the first text, a self-indulgent speaker-poet attempts to shut suffering humanity out of his consciousness so he can pursue his poetic game. He becomes increasingly irritated with the interruptions of those who clamor for their very subsistence or whose mourning and dying prevent him from finding the special word he seeks. Eventually he declares himself poetically impotent. Implicitly calling into question the search for "una sencilla / palabra que haga juego / con . . ." ["a simple / word that will / match . . ." (DDW)] (he leaves the sentence unfinished), González in this poem censures verbal games. Through his irony, he suggests both the futility of attempting to escape to an ivory tower and the writer's obligation to attend to pressing human problems. This poem, it is clear, continues the long-standing polemic of pure versus impure poetry, described above.

In "Soneto a algunos poetas," González again decries a type of poetic impotence, that of hand-wringing poets who—through fear of the Franco regime?—mask their anguish by writing evasive and perhaps obscure poetry using words the government censors will find unexceptionable. Understood are González's conviction that truly relevant poetry can bear powerful witness and his belief in addressing a collective audience.

As these poems show, González's sense of political commitment was not totally absent from *Aspero mundo*. He has said, in fact, that as soon as publishing became a possibility he began to consider utility a necessary feature of his writing. But not until *Sin esperanza, con convencimiento* did he turn fully to social and politically committed expression. In many poems from this second book González puts into practice what he advocates: responsiveness to social and political reality. According to a discussion between the poet and Tino Villanueva, González's main tools at this time were irony and the "objective correlative," both employed in what Villanueva describes as a "subversive" manner. González himself has reflected that he and his cohorts avoided direct naming not for the aesthetic considerations the Symbolists invoked, but because "estaba prohibido nombrar"[19] [it was forbidden to name]. For whatever reason, nevertheless, the strategies of González and others like him involved trying to convey more than what their words appeared on the surface to communicate.

Critical opinion has been divided on how much to consider González's political purpose in assessing his social and political works. Tino Villanueva is among those who have closely adhered to political interpretations of González's early works. He adopts the position that in these poems González used a kind of coded communication that indirectly expressed the opinions of the opposition group to which the poet belonged. Exemplifying this approach is Villanueva's analysis of "Entreacto." In this poem, he states, the intermission of a play becomes the objective correlative for the peace of early postwar Spain, a period that many leftists at the time viewed as only a temporary lull in a conflict whose final battle was yet to be fought. Villanueva similarly analyzes the indirectness of "Discurso a los jóvenes," whose speaker's exhortation to the young to uphold the traditional power bases of the Spanish Establishment ironically suggests the violently repressive and reactionary nature of the Franco regime.[20] Villanueva's approach to González, in conceiving art as a tool that both reflects reality and creates the conditions for desired change, follows the form/content duality that, as we saw earlier, undergirds Alarcos Llorach's study of the poet. Like Alarcos Llorach, Villanueva measures the success of social poetry by how well form captures content, by "la adecuación o solidaridad entre fondo (el conjunto de ideas, vivencias y sentimientos) y forma (la manifestación lingüística en todas sus facetas)"[21] [the fit or cohesion between substance (the assemblage of ideas, experiences, and feelings) and form (the linguistic expression in all its facets)]. This formula allows for a definition of "fondo" [substance] that includes González's interpretation of his society as well as his hopes for the future. The future that the poet expected and desired to bring about in such poems as "Entreacto" was an agenda shared with his cohorts but one that historical developments would show to be wishful thinking: Franco continued in power, despite expectations that he would fall. Nevertheless, without faith in the accuracy of the poem's vision of society, and without a purpose that transcended the purely aesthetic, the poem would probably not have been written.

While Villanueva's interpretations, then, turn on a strict correlation to Spanish politics and on a knowledge of the poet's intentions, other critics, rejecting any simplistic division of González's work into less and more "artistic" periods, have framed their discussion of his early works in terms of his complex use of tropes and rhetoric as vehicles for the play of discourse rather than for ideas. Douglas K. Benson proposes multilayered readings of such poems as "El campo de batalla" [The battlefield], from *Sin esperanza, con convencimiento*. He views the poem as misread by critics whose interpretations he terms "straight." He suggests as well that even texts the poet sees as primarily political are "richer and more ambiguous than González will admit."[22] Margaret Persin, similarly, questions the overemphasis on González's themes and "testimonial posture." She explores his poetic texts—even his early ones—as "complex structures, whose artistic devices (such as multiple speakers, apostrophe, and contrasting time frames) involve the reader in a multifaceted artistic and linguistic experience." Her view that the "superficial simplicity of the text's overt message is contradicted by its rhetorical complexity" supports Benson's vision of richness beneath a deceptively simple surface. Persin's illuminating study sees the dialectical relationship between presence and absence as a constant even in González's earliest works. She focuses not on the poet's censorship-induced omission of certain types of explicit content but rather on the poem as process and experience, the role of the reader in completing the text by supplying what is missing, and on the inherent slipperiness of language itself. As she states: "The dialectic of presence and absence, of course, points to the deconstructivist attack on logocentrism and its contention that language itself must accept partial complicity in its failure to communicate unadulterated truth through its structures. A certain linguistic structure can signify one thing, but it can also be coaxed to mean quite the opposite."[23]

Studies such as those of Persin and Villanueva, then, at once contradict and complement each other. Though both critics recognize González's texts as requiring completion by the reader, for Villanueva such completion means apprehending the particular, even topical, content that the form perfectly captures, while for Persin the absent elements in the text point to a multitude of possible meanings that the readers must supply. Juxtaposing the positions of these two critics, however, raises the crucial question of whether the shift González associates with his "loss of faith in words" is real and significant. Does the usefulness he intended in his early poems or the political applicability Villanueva detects in certain works really affect his poetic praxis, making early works fundamentally different from later ones, and if so, how? Or do the complexity of language and intrinsic indeterminacy of literary texts override any political purposes he may have intended? To answer these questions a look at several early poems and differing critical approaches to them may be useful.

The limitations of Villanueva's approach become obvious when we compare his reading of the poem "El campo de batalla" with analysis by other critics. For Villanueva, the text expresses González's vision of the Spanish Civil War from a specific political position. The "poderosos buitres" [powerful vultures] who ascended out of the south, for example, are Nationalist troops, and the ending is a pointed reference to the war as a "contienda todavía no terminada" [struggle not yet finished] (an interpretation that commentary by González, quoted by Villanueva, seems to support).[24] For Villanueva, González's depiction, in the final stanza, of a peaceful wheat field that has obliterated all signs of the earlier battlefield was intended to distract censors from the poem's veiled incitation to continue the fight. But other critics complete the poem in a fashion different from Villanueva's. Like Persin, Benson emphasizes the process of reading and the complexity of González's poetic discourse. This leads him to view certain details differently; the soldiers "pegados a la tierra en paz al fin" [clinging to the ground

3 / THE POETRY OF *ENGAGEMENT*   55

in peace at last], whom the speaker explicitly distinguishes from those who died, have for Benson indeed perished. The various levels he identifies include an antiwar statement, a speaker revealing his own hackneyed antiwar discourse, and a portrayal of life itself as war. States Benson:

> [T]he theme of the work was not a commentary on war as much as it was a commentary on the speaker's tragic role. Like most of us, he can neither help nor escape, yet he feels compelled to participate. He does so by creating combinations of words—his only link to the rest of mankind.[25]

What for Villanueva is discourse that due to censorship must be at times covert in its nevertheless pointed message is for Benson an open text that questions its own discourse at various levels. Can we explain these disparate readings through the inevitable process by which each reader—reading from a specific point in time and armed with particular critical tools—completes a poem in a different way, or does something in the text itself invite confusion? If form were so perfectly matched to content, as Villanueva contends, why do he and Benson see the poem so differently? Can their readings be comfortably reconciled? Are the poems González wrote before he renounced his faith in words just as open as texts as the poems of his second period?

Before attempting to answer these questions, a look at one more critical approach to González's early poetry may be helpful. At the other end of the spectrum from Villanueva, and closer to Benson, lies Persin's analysis of the poem beginning "Si serenases / tu pensamiento" ["If you composed / your thought" (DDW)] (pp. 67–68).[26] Persin shows how through the dialectic of presence and absence González creates a text that, like an Escher print, paradoxically encloses two contradictory visions of reality: a world in which the speaker could be understood, which he might be able to see if calmer; and the inhospitable, alienating environment in which he finds himself. Persin, then, finds a certain indeterminacy in this poem. But by applying Villanueva's approach, we might be able to explain the indeterminacy away, naturalizing the two seemingly incompatible visions expressed by interpreting their very existence as signs of either existential anguish (González has pointed out the large number of existentialist poems in his early books) or of the alienation of a leftist speaker in Franco's Spain. That in his state of excitation he cannot find people who speak his language or understand him might even reflect the censorship-induced isolation that Paul Ilie identifies in *Literature and Inner Exile: Authoritarian Spain, 1939–1975* (1980).[27] The ending—"sigue buscando, muévete, camina" [keep searching, move, get going]—might express the simultaneous discouragement and determination of the title *Sin esperanza, con convencimiento*. The question remains: admitting that heavily contextualized readings of the type Villanueva favors seem somewhat restrictive, are they necessarily invalidated by critics more attuned to the complexities, gaps, and self-undercutting nature of González's language? And do the more open readings run the risk of ignoring some intrinsic limitations in the texts themselves?

"Mensaje a las estatuas" [Message to the statues] (pp. 99–100) from *Sin esperanza, con convencimiento* serves as a fairly typical example of González's intensely political poems. Our analysis allows us to examine the effects of González's aims on his aesthetic product at this stage and to address the questions just posed, as well as others even more important to the overall question of the poles of politics and play in his work: Do his political aims make these early poems qualitatively different from those written in his later, more ludic stage, or is play with language equally evident here? And how important is the recognition of González's specific target to the success of a reading?

"Mensaje a las estatuas" begins with the following apostrophic statement that mirrors both the action of the sculptor (who chisels bit by bit, part by part) and the speaker's act of apprehending the statues he beholds:

> Vosotras, piedras
> violentamente deformadas,
> rotas
> por el golpe preciso del cincel,
> exhibiréis aún durante siglos
> el último perfil que os dejaron:
> senos inconmovibles a un suspiro,
> firmes
> piernas que desconocen la fatiga,
> músculos
> tensos
> en su esfuerzo inútil,
> cabelleras que el viento
> no despeina,
> ojos abiertos que la luz rechazan.
>
> [You, violently deformed
> stones,
> broken
> by the precise blow of the chisel,
> will display for centuries to come
> the last profile that they gave you:
> chests impervious to a sigh,
> firm
> legs that know no fatigue,
> muscles
> tense
> in their useless effort,

3 / The Poetry of Engagement

> heads of hair that the wind
> doesn't disarrange,
> open eyes that reject the light.

"Mensaje" on the one hand continues the dialectic of presence and absence in the context of the boundaries between life and art. Statues—here deformed rocks—resemble living people but in reality lack life. In lines 8–15, vitality is both called forth and dismissed in the "cabelleras que el viento no despeina"—simultaneously hair blown by winds (the winds of time?) and sculptures immune to change. The speaker nevertheless predicts the destruction even of the apparently unchangeable. Echoing biblical images of dust returning to dust, he foresees that the statues will revert to their prior condition of undifferentiated stony matter. In a final image, the sculptures that indeed will fall (instead of mocking time as it seemed at first) mirror what they commemorate even in being subject to destruction and oblivion:

> Hacia la piedra regresaréis piedra,
> indiferente mineral, hundido
> escombro,
> después de haber vivido el duro, ilustre,
> solemne, victorioso, ecuestre sueño
> de una gloria eregida a la memoria
> de algo también disperso en el olvido.
>
> [To stone you will return as stone,
> indifferent mineral, fallen
> rubbish,
> after having lived the hard, illustrious,
> solemn, victorious, equestrian dream
> of a glory erected to the memory
> of something likewise scattered in oblivion.]

"Mensaje" recalls much poetic tradition ranging from the baroque period forward. It evokes treatments of the work of art as an attempt to overcome time and gives the ruin poem the particular twist of placing the perception of decay entirely within the speaker's mind. Its use of apostrophe likewise has many resonances. As Jonathan Culler has shown, the use of apostrophe in poetry raises complex issues, many of which surface in "Mensaje a las estatuas."[28] First of all, in addressing the statues directly, the speaker seems to bring them to life, mimicking the very deception that the poem attributes to them as works of art. Similarly, the apostrophe creates the illusion that, though made of stone insensitive to sound, the statues can hear. The reference to "vuestra / soñada eternidad" [your dreamed-of immortality] endows them with the capacity to dream. These obvious illusions bear out Culler's view of apostrophe as a "sign of a fiction which knows its own fictive nature."²⁹ Here apostrophe, uniting the object of address and the speaking subject within this fiction, draws in as well the poet himself, who like the statues participates in commemoration. The apostrophic address is thus intimately intertwined with the subject matter of the poem.

If we wanted to de-emphasize the directness of González's political message in his works of this period and to stress the openness of even these early poems, we would be tempted to stop here, with a reading that demonstrates the complexity of the poem, its embodiment of paradoxical views of the relationship between art and life. But some of the vocabulary of the text recalls other González poems from this period in which the Franco regime is more obviously targeted. The references to military heroes bring to mind "Discurso a los jóvenes" (pp. 110–12) and "Piedra rota" [Broken stone] (pp. 122–23). These poems link similar martial figures to the power of horses, to equestrian statues, to petrifaction, to violence, and to the rejection of enlightenment. The depiction of a triumphant leader as a living statue, in "Piedra rota," encourages us to follow Villanueva's interpretation of other poems by reading the sculpted figures of "Mensaje a las estatuas" as objective correlatives for the petrified—and for González distasteful—glory of those in power in Spain when the poem was written.

Such a reading activates another function of apostrophe identified by Culler: to permit a speaker, through a relationship with another, to constitute himself or herself. In "Mensaje a las estatuas," the poetic voice defines its disapproval through the manner in which it addresses the statues. Distaste, however, is directed at the statues only in a transparently fictional manner. The word "Mensaje" in the title, furthermore, suggests more immediacy, utility, and practicality than we would expect from a typical apostrophe to a work of art. The term even suggests a coded communication, thus raising the possibility of a covert message, if not to the statues, then to their real-life counterparts—those whom they imitate and commemorate. The poem thus can be viewed as a means of addressing the powers of the Spanish state under Franco and of accusing them of various faults: inhumanity ("senos inconmovibles a un suspiro"), uselessness, ignorance, arrogance, coldness, and disdain (ll. 17–20)—even of being living corpses. The speaker's prediction that the twisted rocks will fall—"caeréis por vuestro peso" [your weight will bring you down]—can be seen as a threat, the double meaning (based on the figurative sense of "caerse de su peso" [to be self-evident]) suggesting a regime vulnerable to its defects becoming known, capable of being broken by "el golpe preciso del cincel" (p. 99) that almost seems to be an undercover reference to the incisive words of poets like González. But though the poet clearly targets the regime, the indirectness of his expression means that the real addressees were his political cohorts. This audience, we surmise, was intended to read between the lines, understanding and enjoying the poem as an indictment, an insult, an aggressive and defiant message to those in power, and a confirmation of their belief that Franco's demise might be imminent. In line with Culler's description, the apostrophe here tropes "not on the meaning of a word but on the circuit or situation of communication itself."[30] The poem, then, has three addressees: spoken to the statues, it directs a covert curse or imprecation at those in power in coded terms aimed at González's cohorts.

Thus "Mensaje a las estatuas" can be read either in more general terms as a metapoetic meditation on the impermanence of glory, or more specifically, as an expression of González's desire to fulfill a political purpose through his poems at a particular moment. The question then arises of how to assess these two divergent possibilities. How integral to the text is the inference that this poem about the perishability of worldly glories has to do with the desired fall of a particular political regime? Does this inference depend too heavily on what we know about the poet beyond this poem? A look at language used in the poem is helpful in addressing these questions. Several details of the poem undermine the validity of reading the text as primarily a meditation on the ravages of time instead of as a specific political exhortation.

Throughout the poem, a series of words with strong negative connotations seems inappropriate for a treatment of the philosophical issue of time's hold on the seemingly immutable. The statues are arrogant and "violentamente deformadas," their effort "inútil." The word "duro" applied to their "ecuestre sueño" adds little life to their description as sculptural signs of impermanence but is expressive when applied to an implacable regime. Instead of creating an aesthetic distance between the statues and what they represent, the poem conflates the two. The statues, like the battlefield in "El campo de batalla," are not identified as particular sculptures but rather remain largely at the level of abstraction, which bolsters the assumption that they serve primarily as objective correlatives.[31] Thus it seems reasonable to conclude that the level on which "Mensaje a las estatuas" refers to statues is indeed subordinated to the political coding of an incitation and a covert insult to the regime. (This is not to say, however, that giving the poem such a function was necessarily a totally conscious procedure on the part of the poet.)

Other political and social poems from *Sin esperanza, con convencimiento* are based on objective correlatives that are not only abstract but are also distorted to fit the situation beyond the poem to which they are intended to correspond. Returning to "Entreacto" (pp. 113–14), we find a poem about Spanish politics, but one that like "Mensaje a las estatuas" is cast into the form of a speaker reacting to a work of art. As González has stated, "[t]odo el esfuerzo al escribir el poema consistió en gran parte en ajustar la alegoría (los datos de una situación teatral posible) para que sirviera también de referencia a la situación española tal como ya lo vivía en torno a 1956 ó 1957. Creo que es una alegoría bastante exacta"[32] [all my effort when I wrote the poem consisted largely of adapting the allegory (the facts of a possible theatrical situation) so that it would also serve to refer to the Spanish situation as I was living it around 1956 or 1957. I believe that it's a fairly accurate allegory]. As with "Mensaje a las estatuas," the poet conflates art and life, imagination and history. Referring ostensibly to the story told in the play ("No acaba aquí la historia" [The story doesn't end here]), he alludes in reality to Spain's recent history. As in "Mensaje a las estatuas," the work of art used as an objective correlative is an abstraction, its links to real life sketchily drawn. The idea of a play is communicated through details that have the feel of theatrical clichés—the audience who knows "el móvil / de la traición y el nombre / de quien la hizo" [the motive / of the betrayal and the name / of the person who did it] the grim-faced gardener who announces, "«Llueve, señores, / llueve / todavía»"[33] [It's raining, gentlemen, it's still raining].

The equation between play and political situation is, however, only partially exact, despite González's confidence to the contrary. As the poem suggests, a terrifying theatrical performance can be punctuated by intermissions in which life and art separate, when "comprobamos / alegremente que todo era mentira" [we merrily confirm that it was all just pretend] but the political pause to which González on one level refers permits no such relief. The text's suggestion that the outcome "está escrito" [is written], while true of a play, is enigmatic if applied to the scriptless historical situation the poet wishes to evoke. Thus elements of the play as objective correlative do not quite fit the political reality to which the poet alludes. Likewise, the description of the play is distorted by the allegory. The sense of tension among the spectators is too extreme for total credibility, given the public's seemingly limitless capacity to absorb violent shocks in art (as recent trends in cinema have once more amply demonstrated). The coded references to the postwar peace in Spain as a truce before hostilities resumed (suggested by such words as "historia" [story, history], "tregua" [truce], "traición" [treason, treachery, betrayal], "desesperación" [despair], "ayer" [yesterday], and "violencia" [violence]) distort the description of theater, which despite its real effects on our emotions does not have the same impact on our lives as a repressive political regime. Significantly, even though González sees the poem as a particularly accurate portrayal of the postwar situation, even a fellow poet sympathetic to his point of view, Jaime Gil de Biedma, did not make the connection González had intended, although he was moved by the poem nonetheless.[34] The jarring notes we observe, and Gil de Biedma's confusion, demand some further explanation. We are led to wonder if the sense of cliché (and even unreality) of "Entreacto" reflects indirectly the poet's besieged condition as part of Spain's underground opposition, a condition that forced him to express himself incompletely and at the same time made collective goals paramount. References in the poem to the inability to express something openly—"disimulan," "ineficaces y tortuosos diálogos / refiriéndose a un ayer" [ineffective and tortuous dialogues / referring to a yesterday], the need for a key ("clave")—seem to support this hypothesis. The poem (like "El campo de batalla" in Benson's eyes) becomes significant for encapsulating problems of the communicative process. To understand the poem in this way, we must consider González's political motives and beliefs. But as Gil de Biedma's reaction proves, González's coded expression veils his intent and distorts his views, making them difficult to identify at times, even to the most sympathetic, informed, and sensitive of readers.

"Discurso a los jóvenes," another well-known poem from *Sin esperanza, con convencimiento*, takes the form of a caricaturesque political harangue by a speaker whose similarity to a Franco regime spokesman is unmistakable. It has been frequently noted that in exalting the regime, this speaker ironically exposes its very defects as the opposition perceived them—violence, repression, mindless devotion to tradition and to rightist power bases. González's poem itself has elements of what the regime is said to want to crush—"lo que florece" [that which flourishes], "lo que se alza" [that which rises up]. Ironically, the poet's voice is indeed partially silenced by the need for indirection and for addressing collective problems. What predominates in the poem, in fact, is vacuous Francoist rhetoric, admittedly manipulated by the poet for effect, along with clichés and abstractions ("los que no buscan / más que luz y verdad" [those who seek / only light and truth]).

Thus González's early political poetry makes us ask whether his devotion to what is of necessity a collective vision or his need to code his language to address his cohorts indirectly co-opts and distorts his voice at times, limiting the expressive and aesthetic possibilities of his work. Were his circumstances, and the sense of urgency and commitment that they provoked, in a sense antithetical to the play of words that is art?

Several arguments might be advanced to counter this view of a fractured poetic voice in González's early works. Circumstances of composition—like the poet's conception of his intent—might be deemed irrelevant. Julian Palley's reference to "Freud's magic writing pad that is literature"[35] suggests one way the poem transcends what the artist intends or has in mind, and the creative readings that have indeed been teased out of these poems confirm Palley's point. Critics' divergent interpretations of poems like "El campo de batalla" can be reconciled by viewing literature as a collaborative effort of poet, reader, and word, as Margaret H. Persin does in the following statement: "Just as the poet has responded to one particular set of circumstances in a particular moment of time, so each reader will bring a unique set of circumstances to the reading of the poet's texts. Meaning evolves with each reader and reading of the texts."[36] Yet even if we acknowledge that González's complex language may lead to divergent interpretations, we might argue that the Spanish postwar environment that spawned his early poetry somehow restricted the range of his creativity or at the very least that the indirectness of his poems expresses, metaphorically speaking, a partial loss of speech. Not only the dialectic of presence and absence identified by Persin but also the indirectness of the ironic parody and the objective correlative pointed to by Villanueva are in a sense ways of speaking and of simultaneously remaining silent. If in his love poems from *Áspero mundo* González wrote fictions based on poetic models that had nothing to do with his own reality (about "cosas que no existían" [things that didn't exist], as he himself expresses it),[37] and if in his political poems he subordinated language play to either utility or to making covert subversive beliefs recognizable by initiated readers, perhaps it could be said that he suffered in both cases from an impairment or loss of his own expressive voice. Whether his voice was restrained by internalized repression, as in the case of his love poems, or held back by censorship, as with his political poems, the effect is the same: he yearns—like the speaker in "Si serenases"—for people who speak his language.

Paul Ilie's study of "inner exile" supports the notion that certain features of González's early poems were symptoms of the repressive conditions under which they were written. Arguing that exile signifies a deprivation among not only those who have left their homeland but also those left behind, Ilie quotes Francisco Ayala's reference to "'both Spains, the wandering one and the captive one,'" who "'yearn reciprocally for one another.'"[38] Even among those leftists not exiled physically from Spain, censorship and defeat led to isolation and to alienation—even from self. Eugenio de Nora's assessment of the situation in 1959 is revealing: "«Los poetas de hoy, . . . están o estamos a la defensiva. Parecen sentirse desarraigados, marginales, inútiles, con la timidez del que va a cantar "un caso"—el suyo—y siente que su caso no interesa»"[39] [The poets of today . . . they—or rather we—are on the defensive. They seem to feel rootless, marginal, useless, with the timidity of those who set out to tell a story—their own—but feel that their story is of no interest]. Ilie describes the psychologically destructive effects of censorship as follows: "Censorship inflicted invisible privations upon the community's emotional space, cutting off citizens from the creative expression that lay latent among them." Ilie's discussion of Juan Goytisolo describes the novelist's understanding of the ravages of both inner exile and actual expatriation. Ilie states:

> Goytisolo stresses not only the errors of most emigrés and clandestine groups who inhabit a 'universe of ghosts,' but also his own mistaken embrace of

unattainable ideals. The fatal mistake of social poets and impractical intellectuals, he maintains, is that each group takes "desires for realities, and works some magic substitute of the facts in the name of revolutionary subjectivism and voluntarism."[40]

The inner exile that González experienced in this early period thus affected the poet in many ways, leading him to write love poems with no real basis in his own intimate experience, to speak indirectly through shared keys and codes, and to escape his own present into either past or future.[41] Even the dialectic of presence and absence perhaps reflects the lingering effects of González's losses during the civil war, the lack of freedom to speak out, and the excision from national life of leftist ideology through expatriation or censorship. As Ilie points out, the regime's stake in establishing the worthlessness of the departed elements (and by extension of fellow leftists who stayed) contributed to the inhospitable climate. According to some criteria, the urgency of González's message may have even undermined the very moral vision he sought to serve. Many of these early poems were indeed motivated by moral purpose. But if as Susan Sontag has suggested, poetry or art is moral if it enlivens "our sensibility and consciousness," and if the aesthetic experience consists of "disinterestedness, contemplativeness, attentiveness, the awakening of the feelings" and the aesthetic object of "grace, intelligence, expressiveness, energy, sensuousness," then we must see the early works of González as stressed and diminished by the postwar environment of both *engagement* and repression of individual feelings.[42]

As time goes on, González's poetry becomes less indirect, less constrained by inner exile, as he moves first toward overtly political poems and then, as will be seen in chapter 4, toward less purposeful works of more expressive freedom. In *Grado elemental* González's political poetry continues to predominate. In this book, however, the poetic voice earlier fractured and distorted by censorship and inner exile (as seen in "Discurso a los jóvenes," "Mensaje a las estatuas," and "Entreacto") becomes richer, less abstract, less dependent on keys and codes. In such poems as "Estío en Bidonville," "Prueba" ["Proof" (DDW)] "Perla de las Antillas," "Camposanto en Colliure" [Graveyard in Collioure], and "Alocución a las veintitrés," González continues to express political values he shared with other leftist writers—the need for social change, the existentialist belief in ethical responsibility, a positive attitude toward socialist revolution in Cuba, devotion to cultural heroes like Antonio Machado, and a belief in the imminent demise of the Franco dictatorship. But his voice is frequently more direct and sure than in the preceding period just examined.

In "Estío en Bidonville" (pp. 140–41) González describes a decaying urban slum where a crippled child waits out his bleak existence while nothing happens. Although the slum is not particularized to the point of being identified specifically (it is simply "Bidonville," site of "bidones," or oil drums), González nevertheless makes his setting believable and concrete through visual and auditory imagery. He focalizes the scene through the lame boy whose only entertainment is the dirty papers blown about, a goat gnawing on a withered tree, and the sound of his caged crickets. In the closing lines González portrays the debris of Bidonville as the remains of a giant shipwreck:

> Silencio.
> La ciudad rompe contra el campo
> dejando en sus orillas amarillas,
> en el polvo de hoy que será barro
> luego,
> los miserables restos de un naufragio
> de colosales dimensiones: miles
> de hombres sobreviven. Enseres y artefactos
> —como ellos rotos, como ellos
> oxidados—
> flotan aquí y allá, o bien reposan
> igual que ellos, salvados
> hoy por hoy—¿sólo hoy?—sobre esta tierra.
>
> Mañana es un mar hondo que hay que cruzar a nado.
>
> [Silence.
> The city breaks against the countryside,
> leaving on its yellow shores,
> in today's dust that will later be
> mud,
> the wretched remains of a shipwreck
> of colossal proportions: thousands
> of men survive. Tools and utensils—
> broken like them and like them
> rusted—
> float here and there, or else lie
> like them, saved
> right now—only for now?—upon this earth.
>
> Tomorrow is a deep sea across which we must swim.]
>
> (DDW)

Many elements in this poem suggest that like "Entreacto" it could be interpreted as an allegory of Spain as a whole at the time it was written. An unclear future ("sucios cristales ante turbios cielos" ["dirty windowpanes facing muddy skies" (DDW)]), stagnation, restraints ("el niño / cojo" ["the lame / boy" (DDW)]; "los grillos . . . / en su carcel" ["the crickets . . . / in their jail" (DDW)]), and the challenge of an uncertain tomorrow suggest such a reading. But unlike in the case of "Entreacto" the two readings are complementary and somehow fused, since the social intent—the view of Spain as shipwrecked and off course—has meaning both on the particularized level of the slum and on a more generalized national scale. There is no distortion of either or both terms of comparison, as there was in "Entreacto" and "Mensaje a las estatuas," where a play takes on inordinate significance and statues are too bitterly attacked. Here the reaction to the slum is consonant with the reaction to Spain's overall situation.

González's new and more direct voice takes a more complex form in one of his most overtly political poems, "Perla de las Antillas" (pp. 147–48), where he celebrates the Cuban revolution. Through irony and a voice that shifts in perspective, González presents two points of view simultaneously. The speaker at the beginning, representing imperialistic, capitalistic interests, views the revolution as capable of spreading and of threatening "las grandes Compañías, / . . . los trusts y los cártels, / . . . los jugadores de Bolsa / y . . . los propietarios de prostíbulos" [large Companies . . . / trusts and cartels, / . . . / stock market investors / and . . . proprietors of whorehouses]. In contrast, the voice that emerges seamlessly from the first speaker's discourse depicts Cuba at the end as "pura, viva, poderosa, / fértil semilla de la libertad" [pure, alive, powerful, / fertile seed of freedom].

The opening lines read like the news report of a natural disaster, an explosion that could affect an entire continent. But instead of by noxious dust or lava, the region is menaced by the by-products of social revolution: "libertad" [liberty] and "dignidad" [dignity]. These human values are counterposed to the speaker's "valores fundamentales" [basic values; fundamental stocks and bonds] that the use of the word "cotizados" [esteemed; quoted (as stock prices)] links to bastions of capitalism like the stock market and to purely material worth. The poem's interpretation hinges on the double meaning of the word "valores," from which the two perspectives diverge. As the poem ends, the feared and damaging contagion expressed by a code of destruction ("escoria" [lava], "la quemadura" [the burn], "cenizas" [ashes], "llama" [flame]) has become instead a positive germinating force, suggested by such words as "siembran" [sow], "fertilizan" [fertilize], "frutas" [fruits], "polen" [pollen], "una simiente" [a seed], "fértil semilla de la libertad" [fertile seed of freedom]. Through the activation of these opposing codes, we see throughout the poem the seamless transformation of one speaker into another. Unlike in "Discurso a los jóvenes," in which the meaningless rhetoric of a Francoist speaker occupies the entire poem and where González's point of view emerges as much from what is not stated as from what is actually said, here a new speaker—one politically in line with González himself—takes over the actual words of the text. In the context of the idea of inner exile, the poem may be viewed as González's appropriation of the new freedom and dignity he speaks of in the poem, as well as an opening up to international perspectives. Still, the poet continues to subordinate his work to a sense of purpose, writing a topical poem in which words are at the service of such political ideals as solidarity and anti-imperialism.

En "Camposanto en Colliure" (pp. 149–50), González continues to take a political stance as a point of departure. The poem pays homage to Antonio Machado, whose poignant death in exile had made him a kind of cultural icon for González's generation.[43] The text points additionally to another exile situation, this time depicted as a type of dehumanizing capitalistic exploitation—the exportation of Spaniards as cheap labor to the rest of Western Europe during the sixties. Despite the consistency of González's leftist sentiments, the poem is significantly different from many of those seen thus far. It is more personal, having been based on a visit the poet made to Machado's tomb. González's voice is direct and unified, with no dependence on parodic irony or coded references. As Debicki significantly notes, its narrator, unlike those of many poems of *Grado elemental*, is "reliable."[44] The repetition of the expression "Aquí paz, y después gloria" [Peace in this world, and afterward, glory] gives rise to a meditation on the aftermath of war. Those who died are compared with those who survived, and Machado's "gloria"—a tomb that beside a cypress tree resembles a flag at the foot of a mast—is counterposed to the "humana mercancía" [human merchandise]—"ejército / vencido por el hambre" [an army / defeated by hunger]—that ignominiously crosses the borders in peacetime, "derrotados / — . . . sin gloria" [routed / . . . without glory]. González here has abandoned the defiance he expressed in some of the poems seen above. In the last stanza he comes close to declaring the uselessness of words and thus assuming the position on which he will base the poems of his second period:

> Quisiera,
> a veces,
> que borrase el tiempo
> los nombres y los hechos de esta historia
> como borrará un día mis palabras
> que la repiten siempre tercas, roncas.
>
> [I wish,
> sometimes,
> that time would erase
> the names and deeds of this story
> as one day it will erase my words
> that repeat it, always stubborn, hoarse.]

He is still a witness, but his words seem to will the silencing of his testimonial voice. The poem thus prefigures the disillusionment with words that began to characterize his attitude in the late sixties.

3 / The Poetry of Engagement

The poems I have discussed so far vary in the extent to which they embody political opinions, but in general they reflect González's determination to make his work socially and politically useful, with the result that he speaks to move his audience and to consolidate positions. At times, the need for his readers to recognize his allusions without his speaking directly shapes his poems, which embody stereotypes and abstractions that evoke either admiration or ridicule. The poems serve group affiliation through specific signs, emblems, allegiances, and generational rallying cries. Language is a tool that can capture and further beliefs.

The purposefulness of the poems thus far examined presupposes the poet's ability to express social and political realities successfully. As critics have shown, his language at this point is far from simple, lending itself to deconstructive analysis and to multilayered readings. Even within the framework of utility, playful elements may be discerned. The need to outwit censors gave rise to multiple strategies of indirection. As will be seen further in chapters 4 and 5, existentialist leanings led not only to the expression of ethical responsibility but also brought about a sense of the absurd, entailing a certain kind of play with logic and the defamiliarization of time and place. It is evident, however, that some of the indeterminacy of these early texts was due to the difficulties of González's situation in the postwar period. As he moved into his second period, his historical context changed, as did his views on poetry. By the time he wrote *Tratado de urbanismo*, González had begun to play with genre and to question conventional aesthetic values, as his appending a lengthy footnote to the poem "Lecciones de buen amor" (pp. 199–202) demonstrates. But by the late sixties, play in González's poetry had begun to acquire a new dimension that in certain ways would overshadow the political and social dimensions that until then had been one of his primary concerns. As chapter 4 will show, only a new level of awareness of the limitations of language as an active force will allow González—a deeply ethical and committed person—to abandon purposefulness for play.

4
The Textures of Politics and Verbal Play in González's Second Period

"[U]na segunda etapa en mi poesía" [a second stage in my poetry]: thus González terms the new and vital stage that his admitted disillusionment with the word led him to enter toward the end of the 1960s. As we saw in chapter 2, he has identified *Tratado de urbanismo* as the transitional volume separating his earlier and later poetry. Likewise, he has pointed to the poem "Preámbulo a un silencio" ["Preamble to Silence" (DDW)] as signaling his loss of the "ilusión en la capacidad activa de la palabra poética" that had sustained him until then.[1] Although he has not totally abandoned political subjects since *Tratado de urbanismo* (he has occasionally still written poems against tyranny and commemorating leftist heroes Allende and Neruda), his texts, in this second period, have often become critical explorations of language that by extension expose the inevitable limits of their own linguistic constitution.

It is important to comprehend the multiplicity of factors, beyond those mentioned in chapter 2, that led González to his avowed disillusionment. First and foremost, we must understand that his disenchantment with words and with their political significance was not unique to him. Shirley Mangini, in her valuable study *Rojos y rebeldes: La cultura de la disidencia durante el franquismo* (1987) [Reds and rebels: The culture of dissidence during the Franco regime], portrays opposition writers as almost collectively abandoning, by the early sixties, the premises of social realism in favor of new modes of expression. A host of forces—political, economic, and artistic—had conspired by that time to change how González and other writers of his generation viewed their role.

Disillusionment presupposes a prior state of enchantment—in González's case, the belief in his poetic mission, fostered in several ways by his environment during his years growing up and his early years as a poet. First of all, he and the other "niños de la guerra" [children of the war], as his generation was sometimes called, had reached adulthood aware that the world's eyes were upon Spain as the country fought its bitter civil war and emerged under Franco's rule. Then as young writers in the early fifties, they became targets of attention from Spain's Communist Party for the role they could play against the Franco regime, and practically all of them became either members or "fellow travelers."[2] When in 1953 Jorge Semprún and Ricardo Muñoz Suay took over as "agentes culturales" [cultural agents] of the party and made it one of their key goals to enlist the collaboration of these young writers in their cause, poetry—the first form that *la littérature engagée* would assume in Spain—was given special importance.[3] Semprún praised the genre in 1955 as follows: "[L]a poesía ha jugado siempre un papel importante en la vida social y cultural española, y más ahora, porque es quizá la forma de expresión más directa, y la más eficaz de las aspiraciones profundas de la intelectualidad progresiva."[4] [Poetry has always played an important role in the social and cultural life of Spain, and more so now, because it is perhaps the most direct form of expression, and the most effective way to express the profound aspirations of the progressive intelligentsia.] The absence of a free press made the poets' contribution seem especially crucial.[5] The sense of power and possibility that they themselves saw in their work is amply captured in Celaya's famous definition of poetry as "un arma cargada de futuro."

For almost all of the poets in González's group in Madrid, 1956 was "el momento epifánico de su conciencia política" [the epiphany of their political consciousness]. The years between 1957 and 1959 saw a growing expectation that Franco would fall and culminated in euphoria when Castro triumphed in Cuba. Yet 1959 brought ominous notes as well as anticipation: the Civil Guards thwarted the Communist Party's plans for a nationwide strike, Communist leader Sánchez Montero was sentenced to twenty years in jail, and the government launched its "Plan de Estabilización" [Stabilization Plan]. This Opus Dei-inspired program brought wage freezes, unemployment, and an exodus of labor to Switzerland, Holland, and Germany but nonetheless gave the Spanish economy a shot in the arm.[6]

As Spain consolidated its incorporation into the international economic community while consumerism, tourism, and American influence bloomed, opposition writers lost their faith in change, and disturbing developments within the Communist Party added to their disenchantment. As early as 1956, Juan Goytisolo, exiled in Paris, realized in frustration that French Communist intellectuals were interested in Spain only sporadically at best. He agonized as well over Soviet actions in Hungary and over Khrushchev's revelation of Stalinist purges.[7] For his part, Jorge Semprún continued for years to be deeply troubled over Khrushchev's accusations against Stalin.[8] By 1961, moreover, signs of repression had begun to appear in Cuba. In 1964, Semprún and Fernando Claudín were forced by Santiago Carrillo to abandon the Communist Party.[9]

As the concerns of the "niños de la guerra" thus expanded to include not just the Franco regime but a panoply of international economic and political developments, their role as agents of change became less simple. In the year 1959, moreover, they came face-to-face with international literary currents that ran counter to their own aesthetic. At a colloquium organized by Camilo José Cela in Formentor, the question of social utility in literature was the focus of heated debate between the Spanish novelists of González's generation and exponents of the French *nouveau roman* that included Butor and Robbe-Grillet.[10] The ascendancy of experimental techniques would become clearer as time went on. Carlos Barral, a member of González's literary generation but also an influential publisher, turned his interest increasingly toward Latin American Boom novelists. His shift in emphasis and the granting of the Spanish Biblioteca Breve Prize to the Peruvian writer Vargas Llosa in 1962 were indications that new literary winds were blowing.[11] The loosening of restrictions on the Spanish press around 1962 further undercut the notion of literature's crucial role in producing specific social and political change.[12] New writers, born after the upheaval of the civil war, were coming on the scene.

The shift González's poetry took in the mid-sixties toward "temas intranscendentes" [non-transcendent themes] and poetic games was thus neither sudden nor unmotivated. Furthermore, as Carlos Bousoño has suggested, González's radical skepticism toward the utility of words—a response to unsettling social and political realities shared with other poets of his generation—coincided with the reactions of the emerging younger poets, the *novísimos* or "poetas del 70" [poets of 1970]. For Bousoño, the main problem confronting both groups of writers at this time (to which they responded similarly, though "desde sus años" [from the perspective of their age at the time]) was a "*crisis intensísima de la razón racionalista*": a growing loss of faith in institutions, conventions, and language. As he points out, the existentialist, testimonial phase González and his contemporaries went through in the fifties and sixties had counteracted for a while the dehumanizing effects of "rationalist reason" by emphasizing the individual within a particular historical reality. But their *engagement*, as Bousoño notes, did not keep problems caused by scientific and industrial progress from worsening. Nor did the barbs and satire of poets like González weaken Franco's hold on Spain—hence their loss of faith in the word. If González's generation suffered disillusionment, the younger *novísimos* (known at times as the "generación de la marginación" [generation of marginalization]) were without illusions from the beginning, having repudiated reason, conventions, the wisdom of age, the state, and even opposition politics.[13] In Bousoño's view, they realized their powerlessness in the face of a technological and rationalistic society. And though aware that language embodies power, they recognized their lack of any effective instrument outside of it with which to criticize and combat its potency. According to Bousoño, the crisis these poets underwent was intensified by the plethora of ills besetting the globe in the late twentieth century—overpopulation, destruction of the environment, consumerism.

Bousoño attributes the *novísimos'* turn to metapoetry to their basic distrust of systems of meaning and power. Along with their consciousness of the complicity of the word in upholding power structures, he says, they recognized not only the deficiencies inherent in reason, language, and memory but the determining power of literary models as well. Thus they questioned the word as a tool of individual expression. Sensing the impossibility of rebelling from within the system of language and abandoning the attempt to capture an exterior "reality" within the poem, they turned to the theme of "*la ficción, como tal, del arte*" [the fiction, as such, of art]. In the belief that the "realidad dada en el lenguaje, sólo en él existe" [reality given in language exists only in language], they favored metapoetic play that at least could serve to expose the power structures of discourse.[14]

In tandem with his poetic juniors, then, González entered a phase of doubt toward the social and political utility of his work, ironically coinciding in many of his attitudes with the very writers he had initially criticized for their superficial and empty aestheticism. The voice contorted in his first books of poetry by indirectness, irony, and reliance on the objective correlative, and subsequently identified openly with the cause of revolutionary social and political change, was largely replaced in this second period by such poetic strategies as wordplay, metapoetry, and nonsense. Yet González's political orientation did not disappear altogether. His transitional period (as seen specifically in the book *Tratado de urbanismo*) and then his later volumes reveal the continued presence of social and political concerns, but treated in accordance with new approaches he shared with the *novísimos* and others.

Even before his transition in the mid-sixties, González frequently revealed an awareness of the limitations of language, but in the context of the failure of words to reach their potential of expressing a given content. This premise differs vastly from his later poetic practice, in which the play of discourse thwarts any type of encapsulated meaning. The ideal of exact correspondence between words and what they signify—an ideal that as we saw earlier informed Alarcos's criticism—thus still underpins these early poems. It is precisely such an ideal that González renounced in many of his later works.

"Palabra muerta, realidad perdida" [Dead word, lost reality] (pp. 108–9), from the 1961 volume *Sin esperanza con convencimiento*, explores the complicated relationship between words and what they name. In the first two stanzas, references to "latido" [pulsation], "vena" [vein], and "un solo cuerpo de luz y de belleza" [a single body of light and beauty] suggest that the poem's speaker is remembering a person. But it gradually becomes apparent that he recalls instead a word, albeit one that "uncovered" a profound reality ("descubría" "honda realidad"), one that when pronounced created sensorial experience: "Pronunciarla despacio equivalía / a ver, a amar, a acariciar un cuerpo" [Pronouncing it slowly was the same / as seeing, loving, caressing a body]. The word is thus mysteriously a vehicle and a body in its own right, and hence perhaps its treachery, chronicled in the last stanza. Here the word's magic is deflated. Its inexplicable loss of expressive power destroys the world it had created: "Cuando un nombre no nombra, y se vacía, / desvanece también, destruye, mata / la realidad que intenta su designio" [When a name doesn't name, and becomes empty, / it also dissolves, destroys, kills, / the reality it attempts to designate]. The poem shows the ability of words and verbal categories to keep experiences alive but nevertheless posits experience itself as the true origin of expression. Though words can cause frustration, the main object of the speaker's lament is the erosion of experience itself by time. Even if coincidence between words and what they evoke is not presented as absolute, such fusion is still posited as a possibility. The poem then questions the word in primarily a thematic manner, and González's own words purport to capture an experience in a way that defies time.[15]

"Penúltima nostalgia" [Next-to-the-last nostalgia] (pp. 135–39), from González's next book, *Grado elemental* (1962), is like "Palabra muerta, realidad perdida" in simultaneously questioning and affirming the word as testimony of experience. The poem depicts memory as creating through its selectivity a kind of fiction. Trivial but pleasant details from the past—the tango, the Victrola, the early motorcar—form part of collective nostalgia, but all too easily forgotten are more serious matters: the grief beneath the picturesque; the suffering behind the apparently simple existence of those forced to live off charity ("Entonces todavía todo era / sencillo: / amar, besar, comer aunque tan sólo / fuera / un pedazo de pan, / una limosna" [Then, everything still was / simple: / loving, kissing, eating, even if it were / only / a piece of bread, / a handout]); and especially wars and violence ("los cadáveres, / los campos de batalla, / el hambre de los campos, / las razones del hambre" [the corpses, / the battlefields, / the hunger in those fields, / the reasons for the hunger]). The poem must be understood as a response to what Vázquez Montalbán has called "'la vampirización del recuerdo'"[16] [the vampirization of memories] by the Franco regime. The speaker's desire to set the record straight about the past suggests González's lingering desire to be an accurate witness, and thus his continued belief in exact naming. At the same time, the poem exhibits a nascent sense of the power of discourse to distort (a power Vázquez Montalbán, referring to this poem, associates with the emergence of the mass media and the "comercialización del recuerdo" [commercializa-

4 / The Textures of Politics and Verbal Play   73

tion of memories] at the time it was written.[17] Although the poem can be read as a call to be faithful to history, "lest we forget," the text suggests as well an alternative postmodern interpretation: the poem in discrediting memory necessarily calls into question its own commemorative discourse. The speaker's words attempt to clarify the past but simultaneously remind us of the distortion inherent in all remembering and perhaps even in the act of writing or recording itself.[18]

In the short book of love poems *Palabra sobre palabra*, published in the mid-sixties, consciousness of the inadequacy of words is again prominent. In the poem "Las palabras inútiles" [Useless Words" (DDW)] (pp. 178–79), a variation on the traditional theme of ineffability, the speaker rails at his own poetic métier, which he characterizes as an impossible search for the right word to describe the person he loves:

> Aborrezco este oficio algunas veces:
> espía de palabras, busco,
> busco
> el término huidizo,
> la expresión inestable
> que signifique, exacta, lo que eres.
>
> [At times I hate this trade:
> a word spy, I hunt,
> hunt for
> the furtive term,
> the unstable expression
> that means exactly what you are.]
>
> (DDW)

He contrasts the attempt to reach his beloved with words (which keeps him "al margen de la vida" ["at the edge of life" (DDW)]) with the physical touch he would strongly prefer—"llegar a tu cuello / con mi boca" ["reach your throat / with my mouth" (DDW)]. Yet paradoxically, part of his very desire for her is the impulse to name. Thus experience is not totally independent of words but rather intimately linked to them, inadequate as they may be. Verbal categories in part create experience, rather than simply mirroring or capturing reality. And even while trying to imagine a unique, momentary experience, the poet has enmeshed himself in tradition, in words, in adapting a conventional poetic staple— the ineffability of the beloved—to his own use. Escape from the poet's task, which in any case he regards so ambivalently, is only illusory.

Though such poems as "Palabra muerta, realidad perdida," "Penúltima nostalgia," and "Las palabras inútiles" problematize language, they nevertheless, in conveying an Unamuno-like sense of struggle, embody the poet's desire to shape his discourse, to take responsibility for the poetic act as for events in the world. Like the thematic treatment of his struggle with his medium, other features of his early poetry—irony, subjectivity, the gaps produced by inner exile, the sense of absurdity with which he portrayed a world in seeming disorder—make González's shift to more open, indeterminate poetic practice less obvious.[19] But the shift is no less real for being in some senses masked. In the period of crisis that followed the time when the poems just examined were written, González contemplated actually renouncing words. His poem "Preámbulo a un silencio" (p. 212) begins as follows:

>   Porque se tiene conciencia de la inutilidad de tantas
>   cosas
>   a veces uno se sienta tranquilamente a la sombra de
>   un árbol—en verano—
>   y se calla.
>
>   [Because one is conscious of the uselessness of so many
>   things
>   at times one sits calmly in the shade of a tree—
>   in the summer
>   and is silent.]

(DDW)

His next stanza consists of a parenthetical observation sixteen lines long in which he amends line 3:

>   (¿Dije tranquilamente?: falso, falso:
>   uno se sienta inquieto haciendo extraños gestos,
>   pisoteando las hojas abatidas
>   por la furia de un otoño sombrío,
>   destrozando con los dedos el cartón inocente de una
>   caja de fósforos,
>   mordiendo injustamente las uñas de esos dedos,
>   escupiendo en los charcos invernales,
>   golpeando con el puño cerrado la piel rugosa de las
>   casas que permanecen indiferentes al paso de la
>   primavera,
>   una primavera urbana que asoma con timidez los fle-
>   cos de sus cabellos verdes allá arriba,
>   detrás del zinc oscuro de los canalones,
>   levemente arraigada a la materia efímera de las tejas a
>   punto de ser polvo.)
>
>   [(Did I say "calmly"? false, false:
>   one sits anxiously making strange faces,
>   trampling the leaves blown down

by the fury of autumn,
crumbling in his fingers the innocent cardboard of a
    matchbox,
unjustly biting the nails of those fingers,
spitting into wintry puddles,
striking with clenched fist the wrinkled skin of the houses that
    remain indifferent to the passage of spring,
a city spring that timidly reveals the fringes of her hair
    up there,
behind the dark zinc of the gutters,
lightly rooted to the ephemeral substance of the tiles about
    to be dust.)]

(DDW)

This lengthy parenthetical comment, proselike in its hyphenization of the word "flecos," on the one hand constitutes a secondary, marginal remark that exists outside the "real" text. Yet framed a different way, the section becomes a central part of another "real" text but one with different borders. The poem "proper"—that is to say the part of the poem wrapped around the parentheses—becomes marginalized, its loss of central importance seconded by its condition as a preamble to an act that is itself a renunciation. The parenthetical comment, furthermore, calls into question the accuracy of stanza 1. This comment suggests that clichéd discourse ("uno se sienta tranquilamente") distorts and must be revoked or revised. Thus the very identity of the text is called into question as contradictory versions, set side by side, lead to undecidability. The paradoxical relationship between art and life is foregrounded through the emphasis on the text's ability to distort, as well as through the contrast between words on the page and the action—in this case absence of action—that they announce. The poem fits perfectly Hassan's description of postmodern literature, which "often seeks its limits, entertains its 'exhaustion,' subverts itself in forms of articulate 'silence'."[20] In this poem, problems of language, not a social reality outside the poem, are revealed as the generating source of the discourse of the text as a whole.

In the last stanza, the poet/speaker's own name becomes a fallacious force that generates a reality founded on illusion:

Eso es cierto, tan cierto
como que tengo un nombre con alas celestiales,
arcangélico nombre que a nada corresponde:
Angel,
me dicen,
y yo me levanto
disciplinado y recto
con las alas mordidas
—quiero decir: las uñas—

> y sonrío y me callo porque, en último extremo,
> uno tiene conciencia
> de la inutilidad de todas las palabras.
>
> [That is true, as true
> as that I have a name with celestial wings,
> an archangelic name that corresponds to nothing:
> Angel,
> they call to me,
> and I stand up,
> disciplined and erect,
> with my bitten wings—
> I mean my nails—
> and I smile and am silent because sooner
>   or later
> one is conscious
> of the uselessness of all words.]
>
>   (DDW)

Named after a being that, he suggests, does not exist, he nevertheless becomes so angel-like in his discipline and rectitude that he confuses his chewed fingernails with wings. But again the word that seems to create reality is shown to lie— for the imperfection of his bitten nails contradicts his angelic discipline and perfection. The speaker/poet has reached an impasse. He recognizes that the power of words to create reality is the power to create illusions. Nevertheless, he claims to be able to shrug off the confusion words cause because he also knows them to be useless.

The tone of stanza 2 conveys enormous frustration. In the context of González's poetic project up to this point and of his comments on his work, we can reasonably attribute this reaction to his pessimistic view of Spanish society at the time. But in not making the sources of his frustration more explicit, he has already effectively carried out the promise he makes in the poem: he has silenced himself. As we saw in chapter 2, González had in some senses stifled his voice in his early works through censorship and inner exile. But at that stage, he seemed to believe in the power of the word to communicate despite gaps and the necessary covert expression. Here, on the other hand, he explicitly calls attention to how words distort and lie. Yet paradoxically his professed contempt for words does not stop him from expressing himself verbally. He still struggles to use words purposefully, even as he approaches the freedom that acceptance of verbal and personal limits will bring.

In the section of *Tratado de urbanismo* that follows the declaration of silence of "Preámbulo a un silencio," González attempted to turn away from anything that might be termed meaningful expression. Titling the section "Intermedio de canciones, sonetos y otras músicas" [Intermezzo of songs, sonnets, and other music], he seems to follow the intentions expressed in that declaration, conceiving his poems as a kind of intermission. He has said about this section: "[A]caso como resultado de la recién adquirida . . . «conciencia en la inutilidad de todas las palabras», inicio cierta apertura hacia lo imaginativo, un acercamiento a temas intrascendentes (la música ligera) y una búsqueda . . . de una expresión próxima a la canción"[21] [Perhaps as a result of the recently acquired "consciousness of the uselessness of all words," I initiate a certain rapprochement with the imagination, an approach to nontranscendent themes (light music), and a search . . . for a type of expression resembling the song]. Yet the poet's intention of avoiding serious themes altogether was thwarted, as he himself has recognized, when language, generating texts different from the ones he had intended, took a political turn. This occurred with "La paloma" [The dove] (pp. 224–25), which unexpectedly turned out to be, in the poet's words, "el poema más caracterizadamente político . . . entre los que yo escribí hasta entonces"[22] [The most distinctly political poem . . . among those that I had written up to that time]. A close look at this poem reveals a complex relationship between politics and verbal play in this transitional period for the poet.

Many features of "La paloma," reflecting González's intentions, do draw attention away from any coherent message and toward the work's surface; in particular, we notice how the poem originates not in "objective" reality but in language itself, how it combines texts, linguistic terms, and categories of discourse in a sort of poetic collage. (Collage, as Walter Redfern has said, is "antimimetic, in that it never pretends to be 'natural' or 'transparent'. It draws attention to itself, makes its presence felt, and makes the act of selecting, juxtaposing or simply plonking, palpable.")[23] The title of the composition, its epigraph, and its intermittent italicized sections are taken from the familiar Latin American popular song, "La paloma." The association between the dove and questions of war and peace generate the remainder of the poem:

LA PALOMA

(Versión libre)
"*. . . ay que vente conmigo, chinita adonde vivo yo.*"
(Popular hispanoamericana)
Se habla de la esperanza
últimamente.

. . . en donde vivo yo

Alguien la vio pasar por los suburbios
de París, allá hacia el año
mil novecientos cuarenta

y tantos. Poco después
aparecieron huellas de su vuelo
en Roma. También es cierto
que desde las Antillas voló un día
tan alta, que su sombra
cubrió pueblos enteros,
acarició los montes y los ríos,
cruzó sobre las olas,
saltó a otros continentes,
parecía . . .

. . . ay, que vente conmigo
adonde vivo yo.

Años más tarde,
un profesor ilustre
dedujo de unas plumas mancilladas,
halladas entre sangre
cerca de un arrozal, en el Sudeste
asiático, que ahí
estaba
ella:
en el sitio y la hora de la ira.

. . . en donde vivo yo

No en el lugar del pacto, no
en el de la renuncia,
jamás en el dominio
de la conformidad,
donde la vida se doblega, nunca.

. . en donde muero yo.

[THE DOVE

(Free Version)
"Oh, come with me, my dear,
come to where I live."
(Popular Spanish-American song)

They've been speaking of hope
lately.

where I live

Someone saw it pass through the outskirts
of Paris, back around the year
nineteen forty

4 / The Textures of Politics and Verbal Play

> something. Shortly afterwards
> traces of its flight appeared
> in Rome. It's also certain
> that from the Antilles it flew so high
> one day, that its shadow
> covered whole towns,
> caressed the mountains and the rivers,
> crossed the waves,
> jumped to other continents,
> seemed . . .
>
> *Oh, come with me*
> *to where I live.*
>
> Years later,
> an illustrious professor
> deduced from some stained feathers,
> found amid blood
> near a rice paddy, in Southeast
> Asia, that it
> was there:
> in the time and place of wrath.
>
> *where I live*
>
> Not in the place of agreement, not
> in that of renunciation,
> never in the domain
> of resignation,
> where life gives in, never.
>
> *where I die.*]

The poem's politics are hard-line; hope, characterized as a rare bird, is said to have been glimpsed in various corners of the world associated with resistance, revolution, and struggle. First sighted in the Paris of the forties, the creature was subsequently seen in Rome, then observed soaring triumphantly over the Antilles. Somewhat later, its bloody remains were identified by "un profesor ilustre" near a rice paddy in Southeast Asia. Submission and resignation, the last six lines tell us, are incompatible with the habitat of this bird, which ranges only through areas of resistance and strife.

"La paloma" is clearly a product of the Vietnam era during which it was written. Although the expansive imagery of lines 10–17 alludes to the Cuban revolution as an exalted period of promise and triumph, the view of the bloody struggle in Southeast Asia, in contrast, is not as hopeful. The last six lines may be interpreted as an exhortative response to the war that was in progress in Vietnam at the time of the poem's composition.

Though the closed, coherent vision of political struggle (and even the political doctrine) embodied in "La paloma" aligns the poem with González's "social" bent, its technique prefigures his increasing tendency toward open, associative, and indeterminate poetic texts, toward poetry as a playful process of exploring verbal fields rather than as a presentation of a coherent viewpoint or an emotional reaction to some aspect of social or personal reality. The poem is a collage of three basic elements, only one of them political in any way: (1) the love song "La paloma," intermittently quoted in italics throughout the poem; (2) the discourse of rare bird sightings, replete with references to flight and feathers and to the inevitable birdwatching professor; and (3) allusions to sites of global resistance and conflict. The relationship between these elements is loose and associative. The song and its text have nothing whatsoever to do with politics; its reference to a dove, as those familiar with its words will know, appears in the following phrase not quoted by González: "Si a tu ventana llega una paloma, trátala con cariño que es mi persona" [If a dove comes by your window, treat it kindly, for it is I]. The song thus echoes various traditions associated with the dove (love, spirituality, transcendence). It resembles as well countless fairy-tale transformations of people into plants, animals, or inanimate objects. Yet the song generates the rest of the poem through an entirely different symbolic association, one in particular evidence during the Vietnam era: the identification of the dove with peace. Thus unrelated elements are brought together in the poem through an extratextual association that is part of the cultural sign system. The dove of the song acquires the connotation of peace through its association with the rest of the poem; likewise, the characterization of hope as a rara avis owes its existence to antiwar symbolism. These linguistic and symbolic relationships, which call attention to the generation of the poem's imagery, compete with the apparent message of the poem for the reader's attention, and in this tension resides the technical innovation of the poem.

"La paloma," then, aptly exemplifies González's transitional period, with its conscious or unconscious ambivalence toward political poetry. On the one hand, the poem espouses political struggle, yet on the other, it portrays the dove of peace as a bloodied victim of that struggle. The poem's technique, in drawing attention to the way the work is generated, seems to subvert any political content. The song that gives rise circumstantially to the speaker's meditation, in a stream-of-consciousness fashion, may in fact serve to play off the personal and political spheres within which the individual must operate—arenas that in the discourse of political *engagement* are frequently in conflict.

"La paloma" documents the convergence, in a transitional period for the poet, not only of different aspects of his poetic personality but of con-

4 / THE TEXTURES OF POLITICS AND VERBAL PLAY 81

flicting visions of the art of poetry as well. The poem combines González's intimate and political veins and expresses his wavering between poetry as meaningful statement and poetry as intranscendent game. In this sense the dove as a symbol of communication and transcendence is bloodied, as if to reflect the poet's ambivalence, at this point, about the value of words, messages, and even poems. In the light of his avowed intention of writing a poem with no transcendent meaning, furthermore, "La paloma" is a document that reveals much about the role of the unconscious in the process of composition. In seeming to take a certain form in spite of itself, the text becomes a poem about its own composition. Its self-referentiality—in exposing the limits of reason, in revealing the power of unconsciously apprehended language systems in shaping consciousness, and in contesting the artistic will—is decidedly postmodern.

From this transitional period on, González evinces new doubts about the individual's role in shaping history. Strands from his earlier work continue to appear—criticism of excessive aestheticism in "Oda a los nuevos bardos" [Ode to the new bards] (p. 310), sympathy for the Marxist experiment of Allende's Chile in "Otra vez" [Once again] (p. 287), mild social satire in "Eruditos en campus" [Learned men on campus] (p. 371). But what in his earlier works was most frequently a critique of particular historical events and personages becomes in the later works *Muestra* and *Prosemas o menos* a critique of historical discourse itself and of human attempts to affect history. His doubts regarding the premises of humanism and his suspicion of reason align him at this point with younger poetic contemporaries.

"Divagación onírica" [Dream delirium] from *Muestra* (p. 284) offers a view skeptical of the capacity of words to correspond to reality. The poem is on the one hand a dream allegory, a wish-fulfillment vision of the reversal of historical facts, and on the other an expression of both the vanity of victory and the distortions of historical interpretation. The poem portrays a military victory celebration interrupted by the announcement that the win was all a mistake and that those celebrating had actually lost the war:

> La victoria
> había sido un error del alto mando,
>   menos
> tal vez que una ilusión
> —acaso una traición o una mentira.
>
> [The victory
> had been an error of the high command,
>   less
> perhaps than an illusion—
> maybe a betrayal or a lie.]

The essence of victory—made up in large part of perceptions and signs, verbal trappings—evaporates by decree:

> Su sueño heroico,
> sus himnos,
> su grandeza,
> su Imperio de humo y sangre,
> quedaban abolidos,
> teñidos de ignominia por decreto.
>
> [Their heroic dream,
> their hymns,
> their magnificence,
> their Empire of smoke and blood,
> were abolished,
> tinged with dishonor by decree.]

In the last stanza, some die, never realizing the "truth" (in this dream world, had they been dead all along? Were they the corpses of earlier battles?):

> Algunos
> jamás llegaron a saberlo.
> Y la borrosa duda sugerida
> por sus ojos abiertos y asombrados
> no llegó a desvirtuar esa sonrisa
> insolente, distante, dura, helada
> para siempre en sus labios
> por el rictus amargo de la muerte.
>
> [Some of them
> never even learned of it.
> And the blurry doubt suggested
> by their open, astonished eyes
> couldn't undo that smile—
> that insolent, distant, hard, icy smile—
> put on their lips for all time
> by the bitter rictus of death.]

The poem suggests the illusory nature of historical constructs, the limits and the force of human visions, and the transforming power and deceptive potential of language. History may be a myth based on lies, but nevertheless power has a way of legitimizing itself, bringing with it glory regardless of how—or how rightfully—it was won. If González's characters die living a fiction without knowing it, then that fiction has become their truth. The poem allegorizes the limited capacity of human beings to assess historical success and failure. Born of an awareness of how history creates fictions, the work not only critiques the reframing of Spanish history that accompanied Franco's dictatorship but is also relevant to the rhetoric of success, the image-creation, and the sudden reversals of fortune so common within the post-Watergate world in which it was written.

In a similar fashion, the poem "Yarg Nairod" (p. 303)—Dorian Gray spelled backward—reframes history, in this case using a literal frame to expose the distortions of official discourse. Portraying what is already a portrayal, as postmodernist works so often do,[24] the poem depicts an aging dictator who remains forever young in his official portrait. Though keyed by some to Franco, the text applies more generally to the myriad of fictions imposed by any state. The poem explores as well the problem of truth, or lack of it, in the work of art. Problematizing the separation between art and life, the poem on the one hand foregrounds the difference between the dictator and his portrait but on the other calls attention through the frame to the distinction between the poem and life. The use of a literary allusion—to Dorian Gray—further emphasizes the fictionality of the poem, as does its title that must be decoded, read backward much as the dictator's portrait must be deciphered.[25] The poem poses what Calinescu considers "the central questions of postmodernist writing":

> Can literature be other than self-referential, given the present-day radical epistemological doubt and the ways in which this doubt affects the status of representation? Can literature be said to be a "representation of reality" when reality itself turns out to be shot with fiction through and through? In what sense does the construction of reality differ from the construction of mere possibility? [26]

For González in this later period, historical illusions are not the exclusive property of repressive regimes. In "Chiloé, setiembre, 1972" [Chiloé, September, 1972], subtitled *"(Un año después, en el recuerdo)"* [*One year after, in memory*], (p. 320), the speaker/poet reflects on events in Chile between his visit to that country in 1972 and the time when the poem was written (1973, presumably after Allende's death). In 1972, he was taken back to his youthful idealism in a Chilean spring that seemed to fulfill the vanished hopes of Spain's yesterday. In retrospect, the idealism he detected seems to have been only a mirage: "¡Espejismo de rostros y de muros / iluminados con palabras / puras: *libertad, compañeros!*" [Illusion of faces and of walls / lit up with pure / words: *freedom, comrades!*]. His sympathies have not changed, but his belief in words has faltered before the reality of repetitive human violence.

González's new awareness of the incapacity of sign systems to lead us to any real truth represents his version of the postmodern rejection of "universalist conceptions" (whether based on progress, Marxism, capitalism, or other ideology) that, for Calinescu, inform modernism.[27] González's abandonment of his own Marxist metanarrative leads to a more ludic approach to political themes. In "Glosas a Heráclito" [Glosses of Heraclitus] from *Muestra* (p. 302), the poet's perennial political concerns are present in references to social injustice, violence, and radical politics. But instead of coherently interpreting history, he humorously deconstructs Heraclitus's statement that "you cannot step twice into the same river, for other waters are continually flowing in." In González's glosses, continual change is embodied in the transformations that the original maxim undergoes when placed in different contexts, its words transformed by the infusion of "other waters" that are other words. Apparent here is González's play with the Marxist concept of dialectical materialism (which, according to the dictionary, "maintains the material basis of a reality constantly changing in a dialectical process and the priority of matter over mind," emphasizing as well the process of thesis, antithesis, and synthesis).

"Glosas a Heráclito" consists of four aphorisms, linked together in a chain of transformations that, as Susan Stewart would say, threatens infinity. In the first version, "Nadie se baña dos veces en el mismo río. / Excepto los muy pobres" [No one bathes twice in the same river / Except for very poor people], González first activates Heraclitus's principle that all is in flux, then gives the saying a new context and an ironic new meaning: that anyone of means will keep seeking new playgrounds. The second transformation goes one step further: "Los más dialécticos, los multimillonarios: / nunca se bañan dos veces en el mismo / traje de baño" [The most dialectical people, the multimillionaires: / They never bathe twice in the same / bathing suit]. Here González invokes a double meaning of "bañarse en" [to bathe in], completing the phrase with an article of clothing instead of with the body of water we expect. In the third aphorism, parenthetically subtitled "*Traducción al chino*" [translation into Chinese], he states that "Nadie se mete dos veces en el mismo lío. / (Excepto los marxistas-leninistas)" [No one steps twice into the same tangle. / (Except Marxist-Leninists)]. Here he draws attention away from the notion of an idea-generated text. This version of Heraclitus is ostensibly generated by sound—a stereotypical Chinese mispronunciation of the *r* in "río." The mistaken pronunciation bears no relationship to meaning and thus creates nonsense by highlighting the "arbitrary relationship between form and content."[28] Though the second line of the poem endows the nonsensical "lío" with a seemingly commonsensical context, the initial accident of pronunciation remains in the background, raising the undecidable question of whether this "lío" simply stands for "río" or really means "lío." Finally, in the fourth section, the speaker compares history to "la morcilla de mi tierra" [the blood-sausage back home]: "se hacen las dos con sangre, se repiten" [They're both made with blood, they repeat themselves (Their taste

4 / The Textures of Politics and Verbal Play   85

keeps coming back up)]. Again, his linguistic play makes discourse suspect; only on a verbal plane are the two comparable. Yet linking them in the poem suggests that history is no more elevated or understandable than a string of blood-sausages and that meaning is highly relative. Words can create many realities; a different version of Heraclitus applies to each of the social or political groups he cites. In "Glosas a Heráclito," clearly, González in a sense presents a chain of "misunderstandings" of Heraclitus that threaten to proliferate ad infinitum, in a kind of nonsense causality described by Susan Stewart.[29] He has come far in his treatment of political themes since "Perla de las Antillas" and "Discurso a los jóvenes," though in the lament over seemingly endless cycles of human violence there remains an echo of the old González, for whom poetry should serve social utility.

The poem beginning "Cuando el hombre se extinga" [When people die out] (p. 351) offers another view of the disruption of the verbal order. A variant on the apocalyptic theme, the poem envisions a day in the not-too-distant future when human beings will disappear altogether. At that time, all myths, free of human control, will reverse themselves:

>   Cuando el hombre se extinga,
>   cuando la estirpe humana al fin se acabe,
>   todo lo que ha creado
>   comenzará a agitarse,
>   a ser de nuevo,
>   a comportarse libremente
>   —como
>   los niños que se quedan
>   solos en casa
>   cuando sus padres salen por la noche.
>
>   Héctor conseguirá humillar a Aquiles,
>   Luzbel volverá a ser lo que era antes,
>   fornicará Susana con los viejos,
>   avanzará un gran monte hacia Mahoma.
>
>   Cuando el hombre se acabe
>   —cualquier día—,
>   un crepitar de polvo y de papeles
>   proclamará al silencio
>   la frágil realidad de sus mentiras.
>
>   [When people die out,
>   when the human race at last is gone,
>   all that they have created
>   will begin to stir,
>   to be again,

to act freely
   —like
children who stay
home alone
when their parents go out at night.

Hector will succeed in humbling Achilles,
Lucifer will return to what he was before,
Susanna will fornicate with the elders,
a great mountain will go toward Mohammed.

When humans are gone
—any day now—
a crackling of dust and of papers
will proclaim to the silence
the fragile reality of their lies.]

The poem, presenting cultural order as a self-perpetuating, repressive, and limiting force, suggests that as long as human beings exist, their arbitrary cultural myths will have the legitimacy of authority. González's skepticism about change has evidently reached the point where he can paradoxically envision freedom from cultural oppression only through the disappearance of humanity itself. Verbal ordering appears in the poem as distortion that suppresses alternative truths.

Thus in his second period González has abandoned faith in human words. Because of this disillusionment his works no longer express a sense of urgency or a desire to name injustices, to rally support, and to move to a new historical plane. In keeping with trends around him and schooled by his own experiences, he has become keenly aware of the fallacies of meaning systems, both the tyranny and arbitrariness of language. But if even in his early period of greater faith in words his voice, ironically, was channeled and sometimes silenced by the need for coded communication with his peers, in this second period he is freer and at times, paradoxically, communicates more effectively. A poem that illustrates this fact is "Notas de un viajero" [Notes of a traveler] from *Muestra* (pp. 315–17). Here González's social and political interests continue to be evident, but in a much less message-oriented way than in early poems. The result of his poetic growth is a fresher vision.

In keeping with the title of the volume, which promises a sampling of narrative procedures, González draws attention to the form, to the poem as travel notes. He describes a city, the center of an empire, that is a crossroads, a crucible. The first few lines evoke both continuity ("Siempre es igual aquí el verano: / sofocante y violento" [The summer is always the same here: / stifling and violent]) and transformation ("Pero / hace muy pocos años todavía / este paisaje no era así" [But just a few years ago, / this landscape was not

4 / THE TEXTURES OF POLITICS AND VERBAL PLAY

this way]), the consistency only a surface reality that lightly masks waves of cultural change and conflict. Thus from the start, historical change is played off against repetition and identity. As the poem continues, a complex set of discursive strategies unfolds to elaborate upon this play of sameness and change. Literary and historical resonances abound. The speaker assumes a testimonial posture, but his perspective is deformed by the play of discourse, as literary models become filters through which we are asked to see. And defamiliarization recreates present experience with heightened immediacy and authenticity but confronts the reader with the need to interpret and to distinguish past from present.

>   Era
> más limpio y apacible—me cuentan—,
> más claro, más sereno.
>
> Ahora
> el Imperio contrajo sus fronteras
> y la resaca de una paz dudosa
> arrastró a la metrópoli,
> desde los más lejanos confines de la tierra,
> un tropel pintoresco y peligroso:
> aventureros, mercaderes,
> soldados de fortuna, prostitutas, esclavos
> recién manumitidos, músicos ambulantes,
> falsos profetas, adivinos, bonzos,
> mendigos y ladrones
> que practican su oficio cuando pueden.
>
> Todo el mundo amenaza a todo el mundo,
> unos por arrogancia, otros por miedo.
> Junto a las villas de los senadores,
> insolentes hogueras
> delatan la presencia de los bárbaros.
> Han llegado hasta aquí con sus tambores,
> asan carne barata al aire libre, cantan
> canciones aprendidas en sus lejanas islas.
> No conmemoran nada: rememoran,
> repiten ritmos, sueños y palabras
> que muy pronto
> perderán su sentido.
> Traidores a su pueblo,
>   desterrados
> por su traición,
> despreciados
> por quienes los acogen con disgusto
> tras haberlos usado sin provecho,
> acaso un día

sea ésta la patria de sus hijos;
nunca la de ellos.
Su patria es esa música tan sólo,
el humo y la nostalgia
que levantan su fuego y sus canciones.

Cerca del Capitolio
hay tonsurados monjes mendicantes,
embadurnados de ceniza y púrpura,
que predican y piden mansamente
atención y monedas.

                          [It was
cleaner and more placid—they tell me—,
brighter, more serene.

Now
the Empire has contracted its borders
and the undertow of a dubious peace
has dragged to the metropolis,
from the farthest confines of the earth,
a picturesque and dangerous throng:
adventurers, traders,
soldiers of fortune, prostitutes, newly freed
slaves, roving musicians,
false prophets, fortune-tellers, bonzes,
beggars and thieves
who practice their trade when they can.

Everyone threatens everyone else,
some out of arrogance, some out of fear.
Next to the senators' villas,
insolent bonfires
betray the presence of the barbarians.
They have come here with their drums,
they roast cheap meat in the open air, they sing
songs learned on their distant islands.
They don't commemorate anything; they remember,
they repeat rhythms, dreams, and words
that very soon
will lose their meaning.

Traitors to their people,
                          exiled
for their betrayal,
despised
by those who take them in with distaste
after having used them to no advantage,

4 / The Textures of Politics and Verbal Play

> maybe some day
> this will be the country of their children;
> never their own.
> Their country is only that music,
> the smoke and the nostalgia
> that their fires and their songs produce.
>
> Near the Capitol
> there are tonsured mendicant monks,
> smeared with ashes and purple dye,
> who preach and meekly beg
> for attention and coins.]

Although the city González describes is thus far unnamed and does not match any immediately identifiable locale, numerous terms evoke the Roman Empire: *paz, Imperio, metrópoli, fronteras, esclavos / recién manumitidos, villas, senadores, Capitolio.* The "bárbaros" with their open fires suggest the Gallic barbarians who camped in the Roman Forum, destroying much of Rome, in 390 B.C. As the poem continues, commemorative marbles and coins recall the pomp of Rome. That city is also evoked in the reference to decadence in lines 57–58, and by further allusions to decay, contamination, and dirt scattered throughout the poem. The city is said to have been cleaner before (l. 7), the air is filled with smoke (l. 33), monks are smeared with ashes, and black men spit at soldiers:

> Orgullosos negros,
> ayer todavía esclavos,
> miran a las muchachas de tez clara
> con sonrisa agresiva,
> y escupen cuando pasan los soldados.
> (Por mucho menos los ahorcaban antes.)
>
> Desde sus pedestales,
> los Padres de la Patria contemplan desdeñosos
> el corruptor efecto de los días
> sobre la gloria que ellos acuñaron.
> Ya no son más que piedra o bronce, efigies,
> perfiles en monedas, tiempo ido
> igual que sus vibrantes palabras, convertidas
> en letra muerta que decora
> los mármoles solemnes en su honor erigidos.
>
> [Proud blacks,
> just yesterday still slaves,
> watch with aggressive smiles
> the light-skinned girls,

and they spit when the soldiers pass.
(For much less they would hang them, before.)

From their pedestals,
the Founding Fathers contemplate disdainfully
the corrupting effect of time
on the glory that they minted.
Now they're only stone or bronze, effigies,
profiles on coins, time gone by
just like their vibrant words, turned
into a dead letter that decorates
the solemn marbles erected in their honor.]

Only in the last stanza does González situate the poem precisely in Washington, D.C. His reference to the Potomac brings us suddenly back to contemporary history, clarifying certain earlier details in the poem and requiring a reinterpretation of others:

El aire huele a humo y a magnolias.
Un calor húmedo asciende de la tierra,
y el viento se ha parado.
En la ilusoria paz del parque juegan
niños en español.
Por el río Potomac remeros perezosos
buscan la orilla en sombra de la tarde.

[The air smells of smoke and of magnolias.
A humid heat rises from the earth,
and the wind has stopped.
In the park's illusory peace
children play in Spanish.
On the Potomac River lazy rowers
seek the shaded shore of the afternoon.]

A comparison between "Notas de un viajero" and the early "Mensaje a las estatuas," analyzed in chapter 3, reveals the distance González has traveled since his early poems of commitment. The philosophical tone, the particularizing details, the specific locale, and the complexity of the speaker's perceptions, which include literary and historical references as well as details observed, all distinguish this later poem from that earlier work in which political bite was primary. Here, as in those previous texts, there is a political layer (a vision of a crumbling, exploitative, imperialistic United States, a nation of white supremacists threatened by diverse cultures), but the meditative aspect—the confrontation between history as change and history as repetition and myth—predominates.

4 / The Textures of Politics and Verbal Play 91

Through misleading codes and allusions, González thus defamiliarizes Washington. Presenting the city as remote and in a sense exotic, he undercuts the standard image of the United States as the seat of modernity and/or staid Anglo-Saxon values, at the same time drawing a comparison that suggests imperialism, decadence, and perhaps an impending decline in power. González's defamiliarization renews the reader's perspective on the American capital through requiring a process of interpretation and reinterpretation. At the same time, the speaker's perceptions are impossible to separate from his memory of historical and literary myths and models (which themselves in turn become filters through which the reader perceives). In this respect his poem comes close to illustrating the *novísimos'* belief that "la realidad dada en el lenguage, sólo en él existe," a far cry from the case of earlier poems like "Mensaje a las estatuas," whose raison d'être is the reality—outside the poem—of a distasteful regime.

By referring to the fall of Rome and by casting the poem into the conventional form of travel notes, González evokes a wealth of previous literary treatments. One similar to his in ending a portrait of decadence with reference to a river is a sonnet by Francisco de Quevedo. As in "Notas de un viajero," the baroque traveler/speaker sees in Rome only decay, the Tiber's perpetual change lending the sole sign of uneasy permanence to the scene:

> *A Roma sepultada en sus ruinas*
>
> Buscas en Roma a Roma, ¡oh, peregrino!,
> y en Roma misma a Roma no la hallas:
> cadáver son las que ostentó murallas,
> y tumba de sí proprio el Aventino.
>   Yace donde reinaba el Palatino;
> y limadas del tiempo, las medallas
> más se muestran destrozo a las batallas
> de las edades que blasón latino.
>   Sólo el Tibre quedó, cuya corriente,
> si ciudad la regó, ya sepultura
> la llora con funesto son doliente.
>   ¡Oh, Roma!, en tu grandeza, en tu hermosura,
> huyó lo que era firme, y solamente
> lo fugitivo permanece y dura.

[*To Rome buried in its ruins:* You search in Rome for Rome, oh pilgrim!, and in Rome itself you don't find Rome: a corpse is the walls which it once displayed, and a tomb for itself the Aventine. The Palatine lies where it used to reign; and the medallions, worn away by time, reveal themselves to be more the victims of the ages' battles than the glory of Latium. Only the Tiber has remained, whose current, if it once watered it as a city, now weeps over it as a tomb with funereal sound. Oh Rome!, in your grandeur, in your beauty, that which was firm has fled, and only what is fugitive remains and endures.][30]

Despite obvious differences, the similarities between González and Quevedo are striking. Though Quevedo's poem is more narrowly focused, its central conceit of absence is clearly echoed in González's version. Just as Rome is no longer Rome but its own tomb, so America's Founding Fathers are now only effigies of themselves, commemorations of themselves, and their words "convertidas / en letra muerta que decora / los mármoles solemnes en su honor eregidos" (p. 316). The paradox of the simultaneous presence and absence of things remembered and commemorated runs strongly through both poems. In González's case, the threat of becoming a "letra muerta" extends self-referentially to his own poetry as well; thus his title has a provisional ring.

Besides Quevedo's sonnet, "Notas de un viajero" recalls numerous other literary texts and conventions. The title of González's poem evokes the eighteenth-century literary tradition of the traveler as social and political critic, as in the *Cartas marruecas* [Moroccan letters] of Cadalso in Spain or the defamiliarizing *Lettres persanes* [Persian letters] by Montesquieu in France. (The latter author, moreover, coincided with González in treating the decay of imperial grandeur in his *Considérations sur les causes de la grandeur des Romains et de leur décadence* [Considerations on the causes of the greatness of the Romans and their decadence] and, interestingly, was influential among the American Founding Fathers González depicts). More recent resonances appear in the poem in the final lines, where two Spanish poets—Jorge Guillén and Federico García Lorca—who preceded González in encountering the United States are also evoked. The rowers who "buscan la orilla" recall Guillén and his poem "Primavera delgada" [Slender spring] with its boaters and its question "¿Dónde la orilla?" [Where, the shore?]; the phrase "en sombra de la tarde" reproduces one of the most arresting lines of Lorca's famous elegy, "Llanto por Ignacio Sánchez Mejías" [Lament for Ignacio Sánchez Mejías]. The quotation from Lorca evokes that poet's encounter with New York and the record he made of that experience, his *Poeta en Nueva York* [Poet in New York]. In his depiction of his own encounter with America, González's speaker, then, acknowledges Lorca's nightmarish portrait of New York and Guillén's much more affirmative New World vision.

The last stanza returns us to the images of change and permanence of the opening lines. The river of historical change is counterposed to the futile attempts to arrest time through commemoration, suggested by the marble, the glory that the Founding Fathers minted ("acuñaron"), and even by the words from Lorca's poem. Mirroring the flux of history, the flow of words—both written and spoken—becomes only a trace of what once was. The signs of immediacy—children's voices, smoke drifting in the air—are at the same time traces or echoes. These notes of immediacy only make more poignant the fact that González's own works—as his references to Lorca and Guillén underscore—are implicated in the historical process.

In maturity, then, González lets go of some of the urgency and sense of duty that informed many of the poems of his first period and that may have been intensified by the "mala conciencia" [guilty conscience] that, Mangini shows, characterized the dissident writers of the fifties and sixties. In this he can be said to follow postmodern currents that doubt the possibility of knowing, challenge totalizing schemes, and question objectivity and reason. The difference between "Perla de las Antillas" and "Notas de un viajero" parallels the shift from strong to weak thought that has sometimes been viewed as characteristic of postmodernity. (Calinescu cites this shift and describes as well the postmodernists' replacement of the need to destroy old forms with a desire to "revisit" the past.)[31] In "Notas de un viajero," González's voice acquires a new freedom and richness and a less labored sound as he gives up on controlling the linkage of words to events of the past, present, and even future and surrenders responsibility for some of those events. He himself has attributed his new freedom to a less onerous political situation in Spain. But with events worldwide more and more onerous, we might suspect instead that he is responding to personal changes within himself, as well as to an aesthetic shift toward postmodernism, which recognizes and legitimizes such a loss of control. Most importantly, González has paradoxically furthered those elements that according to Sontag make art moral. His loss of control has led to works that in being more exploratory are more expressive and disinterested, more apt to enliven "our sensibility and our consciousness."[32]

5
Play with the Logic of Time and Place

As my previous chapters suggest, in the seventies and eighties González often gave language primacy over communication and theme. Subject matter ceased to be a means for the poet to take responsibility in his world, becoming instead a point of departure for the creation of verbal play. Likewise, the poetic self evolved from witness or lyric source to a simple structuring principle that permits the categories and oppositions of language to unfurl and display themselves to readers. González developed a poetry that in many cases achieves its effect not through sensorial richness, sound patterns, or original metaphors, but through the manipulation and overturning of common sense, logical thought, and conventional organizing principles.

As preparation for considering how González plays with the premises of logic and common sense, a review of certain basic features of communication is helpful. Susan Stewart, in her book on nonsense, discusses the social processes that underpin the creation of texts and their interpretation. Like many students of discourse, such as Paul Ricoeur, she defines texts very broadly to encompass not just literature but social interactions in general. She describes social life as a series of texts, "written" as people interact and "read" as they engage in the constant process of interpretation and reinterpretation. For Stewart, all texts, whether literary works or social events, are constituted and interpreted in relation to established conventions. Each text belongs to a sphere or province of meaning that has its own rules of relevance and hierarchy. Provinces of meaning arise out of the commonsense world, based on "certain relations we hold to time, space, and causality." The consistency of such provinces is normally upheld not by some natural self-evident truths but by the interpretive process itself. And even the commonsense world is subject to constant redefinition. Stewart points out that "[r]elevance and hierarchy are not features of 'nature,' but are the result of interpretive work in social life. Relevance provides us with a procedure for separating out domains of meaning that would produce contradictions if

5 / Play with the Logic of Time and Place

combined." As she further maintains, "[t]he juxtaposition of two or more systems of sense will point to the nonsensical character of one or more of them, for such a juxtaposition undermines the suspension of doubt needed to engage in at least one of the domains of reality."[1] In depicting our sense of reality as based on a series of construals rather than on any kind of objective truth, Stewart coincides with certain postmodernist stances. Her description of nonsense resembles the "impossibility" that some thinkers deem the postmodern replacement for modernism's "hypothesis." Matei Calinescu describes how such thinkers as D. W. Fokkema conceive of this change:

> To . . . expansive "modernist hypotheses" the postmodern writers . . . oppose, according to Fokkema, their "impossibilities" and a pervasive sense of radical, unsurpassable uncertainty, a sort of epistemological nihilism, as I would call it. In the postmodernist view, there simply is no "reality" that might validate such hypotheses, even under ideal conditions. The modernist play of hypothesis and counterhypothesis . . . has lost its basis. "Reality" being nothing but a composite of construals and fictions, Fokkema argues that the postmodernists can no longer write from hypothesis; they will write, as it were, from impossibility.[2]

For his part, González, partially letting go of social intent (for reasons discussed in chapter 4), has made more and more frequent incursions into the realm of impossibility, intensifying play with logic, common sense, relevance, and hierarchy.

Although González's ludic manipulation of logic and common sense has flowered most fully in his second period, its seeds were present from *Aspero mundo* on. The poet has categorized this first book as imitative of Juan Ramón Jiménez and other writers he read during his confinement at Páramo de Sil. Still, many of its poems reveal his sensitivity to the ludic possibilities of the basic building blocks of the communicative process—logic and commonsense reasoning, on the one hand, and social, linguistic, and literary conventions, on the other. But in this early period of his first volumes, when the goals of the opposition forces in Spain had not yet begun to founder through disillusionment and when "referential realism" had not yet been deconstructed by structuralism,[3] González's manipulation of logic was still tied to a referential existentialist and testimonial ideal. Like the ludic techniques of his early political poems, which served his desire to dissent, his play with logic in this period was not entirely gratuitous but reflected a sense of the absurd rooted in philosophical and social considerations. His depiction of an absurd world (existential in such poems as "Para que yo me llame Angel González" [So that I might be called Angel González], more social in many of the poems of *Sin esperanza, con convencimiento*) obeyed the demand for responsibility that his free choice made of him even amid the absurdity of Spanish postwar society.[4]

As time went on, González continued to mine the vein of illogic and absurdity, but with a different purpose: poetic play as an end in itself. Many of the jokes and games he began to write, especially (as he has noted) after 1969, do indeed achieve their effect through violating the premises of common sense. They depart further and further from realism and from the realistic illusion of continuity between text and commonsense world.[5] Instead of targeting an absurd world *beyond* the poem, these works highlight the problematics of the making of meaning itself. These texts juxtapose different meaning systems, exposing the inconsistencies of those systems, and at times foreground semiotic qualities while undermining verisimilitude.

González overthrows the norms of relevance, hierarchy, and logic throughout his oeuvre to varying degrees and in many ways. Andrew P. Debicki has repeatedly referred to how he breaks the conventional rules of reality through which we perceive the world. Especially in his treatment of time and space, the poet often overturns rules by violating formal procedures of logic. His transgressions include the use of tautologies, the separation of wholes from their parts, and the categorizing of classes of items as members of themselves. In many cases the norms he overturns are commonsense conceptions of time, space, and causality.

The development of González's treatment of time is of particular interest for its abiding presence in his work. In some fairly traditional poems of González's early period, his temporal concerns take the form either of elegy or of testimonial commemoration. The first poem of *Aspero mundo*, for example, laments the loss of an "acariciado mundo" [cherished world], that "te me volaste de los brazos"[6] ["You have flown from my arms" (DDW)], while another poem from the work, "*Aquí, Madrid, mil novecientos*" [Here, Madrid, nineteen-hundred], bears witness to a particular time and place. Yet, as is typical of González's work, phases are not divided neatly but tend to overlap. Three poems from González's two earliest books in which he anticipates his later, more ludic, approach are "Cumpleaños" ["Birthday" (DDW)] from *Aspero mundo* and "Cumpleaños de amor" [Birthday of love] and "Ayer" ["Yesterday" (DDW)] from *Sin esperanza, con convencimiento*. The traditional elegiac strain and the testimonial bent he owes to his historical context are replaced in these poems with play upon commonsense notions of time and everyday conventions of naming and measuring it. In these poems, commonplace temporal categories are sometimes given new contexts that make them absurd; at other times their purely conventional nature is highlighted. These texts make us reflect upon the difference between time as something mysterious, beyond human comprehension and control, and time

5 / Play with the Logic of Time and Place

as something that human beings measure and name for purely practical reasons.

"Cumpleaños" (p. 15) is typical of these poems. Its primary effect is to keep its reader poised uncertainly between assent and dissent.[7] Its speaker, comparing himself to a worn-out article of clothing, is credible to his reader when he describes how time and experience have aged him:

> Yo lo noto: cómo me voy volviendo
> menos cierto, confuso,
> disolviéndome en aire
> cotidiano, burdo
> jirón de mí, deshilachado
> y roto por los puños.
>
> [I notice it: how I am slowly getting
> less certain, confused,
> melting in the daily
> air, rough
> tatter of myself, frayed
> and ragged at the cuffs.]
>
> (DDW)

But in explaining *why* he is frayed, his credibility itself wears thin. His reasoning conflicts with commonsense perceptions of what makes one feel eroded by life:

> Yo comprendo: he vivido
> un año más, y eso es muy duro.
> ¡Mover el corazón todos los días
> casi cien veces por minuto!
>
> [I understand: I have lived
> another year, and that is very hard to do.
> Moving one's heart every day
> nearly a hundred times a minute.]
>
> (DDW)

What seemed suitable as a concrete metaphor (the person as a garment that wears out) has become all too concrete and physical. Not only does the speaker overemphasize precise numbers (conferring, as does Western society generally, a special meaning on birthdays), but he attributes the complex aging process to a single facet of physical existence insufficient to explain his psychic disorientation. The involuntary beating of the heart—a basic animal level of aliveness—has little to do with the emotional wear and tear that the reader can accept and which literary tradition deems a matter worthy of poetic treatment. In attributing the stress of one more year to a single aspect of being alive, the speaker misdirects the reader and the poet questions ordinary hierarchies and relevance. Concentrating on an automatic, physical function of the human organism, the speaker violates our everyday assumptions that persons are organically integrated wholes, at the same time endowing a contextual or background condition with the import of a main event. What was first seen as a legitimate concrete metaphor for a complex physical and emotional process has come to refer to an exclusively physical phenomenon and in so doing has lost its commonsense validity. (The poem, in embodying the point of view of a speaker trapped in a meaningless world, whose life is a living death, can be understood as an expression of the absurdity of human life. Naturalized in this way, as is possible with many poems of this period, the work becomes an expression of González's existentialism.)

The speaker in "Cumpleaños de amor" (p. 92)—another birthday poem of sorts—adopts a traditional poetic stance: he promises to be faithful in love. But departing from convention, he emphasizes physical aspects of the human body that are irrelevant in a discussion of psychological and emotional realities. Like the speaker of "Cumpleaños," he thus violates the conventional commonsense notion of the human being as an integrated organism who maintains a basic identity across time. The poem opens with a logical contradiction, the conceit of the poem in nugget form:

> ¿Cómo seré yo
> cuando no sea yo?
> Cuando el tiempo
> haya modificado mi estructura,
> y mi cuerpo sea otro,
> otra mi sangre,
> otros mis ojos y otros mis cabellos.
> Pensaré en ti, tal vez.
> Seguramente,
> mis sucesivos cuerpos
> —prolongándome, vivo, hacia la muerte,
> se pasarán de mano en mano,
> de corazón a corazón,
> de carne a carne,
> el elemento misterioso
> que determina mi tristeza
> cuando te vas,
> que me impulsa a buscarte ciegamente,
> que me lleva a tu lado
> sin remedio:
> lo que la gente llama amor, en suma.
> Y los ojos
> —qué importa que no sean estos ojos—
> te seguirán a donde vayas, fieles.

5 / Play with the Logic of Time and Place

[What will I be like
when I'm no longer myself?
When time
has modified my structure
and my body is a different one,
my blood different blood,
my eyes different eyes and my hair different hair.
I'll think of you, perhaps.
Certainly,
my successive bodies
—prolonging me, alive, toward death,
will pass along from hand to hand,
from heart to heart,
the mysterious element
that causes my sadness
when you go,
that makes me blindly seek you,
that takes me to your side
irremediably:
what people call love, in short.
And my eyes
—what does it matter if they're not these eyes—
will follow you, faithfully, wherever you go.]

The changes that at first seemed merely to express metaphorically the normal aging process have become, by line 9, so literal, so focused on what is exclusively physical, that they have begun to seem absurd. A scientific commonplace indeed affirms that human cells are continuously replaced, making today's eyes materially different from those of the past. But in commonsensical practical and emotional terms, individuals tend to be viewed as maintaining a continuous identity over time.

Thus like "Cumpleaños," "Cumpleaños de amor" presents complex changes mechanistically. At the same time, it embodies an error in scale—expressing deeply felt and consciously experienced emotions in terms of microscopic cellular changes. In the light of its vision of the human body, the birthday itself seems somewhat mechanical and impertinent. The poem approaches nonsense, which, Susan Stewart says, can result from "a radical shift towards the metaphoric pole accompanied by a decontextualization of the utterance."[8] Though the poem can be read as a variant of the literary tradition of love outlasting time or as a mimetic vision of a speaker overcome by genuine feelings of attachment, decontextualization remains in the picture at some level to undermine the poem as a traditional expression of love.

In the third example from González's earliest works, "Ayer" (pp. 84–85), the poet plays with everyday, commonsense categories of time:

Ayer fue miércoles toda la mañana.
Por la tarde cambió:
se puso casi lunes,
la tristeza invadió los corazones
y hubo un claro
movimiento de pánico hacia los
tranvías
que llevan los bañistas hasta el río.

A eso de las siete cruzó el cielo
una lenta avioneta, y ni los niños
la miraron.
          Se desató
el frío,
alguien salió a la calle con sombrero,
ayer, y todo el día
fue igual,
ya veis,
qué divertido,
ayer y siempre ayer y así hasta ahora,
continuamente andando por las calles
gente desconocida,
o bien dentro de casa merendando
pan y café con leche, ¡qué
alegría!

La noche vino pronto y se encendieron
amarillos y cálidos faroles,
y nadie pudo
impedir que al final amaneciese
el día de hoy,
tan parecido
pero
¡tan diferente en luces y en aroma!
Por eso mismo,
porque es como os digo,
dejadme que os hable
de ayer, una vez más
de ayer: el día
incomparable que ya nadie nunca
volverá a ver jamás sobre la tierra.

[Yesterday was Wednesday all morning.
In the afternoon it changed:
it became almost Monday,
sadness invaded hearts
and there was a clear
movement of panic toward the

5 / PLAY WITH THE LOGIC OF TIME AND PLACE

    trolleys
    that take the swimmers down to the river.

    At about seven a small plane slowly
    crossed the sky, and not even the children
    looked at it.
                   Cold
    was unleashed,
    someone went outdoors wearing a hat,
    yesterday, and the whole day
    was like that,
    you see,
    how amusing,
    yesterday and still yesterday and so up to now,
    unknown people
    constantly walking through the streets
    or else indoors having snacks of
    bread and coffee; how
    nice!

    Night fell suddenly and they lighted
    warm yellow street-lamps,
    and nobody could
    after all hold off the dawn
    of today's day,
    so similar
    yet
    so different in lights and in fragrance!

    For that very reason,
    because it's as I tell you,
    let me talk to you
    about yesterday, once more
    about yesterday: the incomparable
    day that nobody now will ever
    see again upon the earth.]
                                                  (DDW)

    Debicki, in a concise and perceptive analysis, points out two fundamental characteristics of the poem: its disconcerting violation of the norms of everyday thought, and the irony of the clichés used to communicate the "happiness" of the people described. According to Debicki, the disparity between the subject matter of the poem and the tone used at the end makes us see "las múltiples dimensiones del tema"[9] [the multiple dimensions of the theme]. A close look at the poem's language reveals what kind of linguistic substitutions and violations of logic the poem employs: assertions in themselves literally true but impossible in the light of common sense and of the connotations of their context. The poet creates two levels that oppose and discredit each other, leading readers to distance themselves from both the mimetic subject of the poem (the previous day) and the process of communication itself.

From the first sentence of "Ayer," problems of language are apparent. The assertion that "Ayer fue miércoles toda la mañana" appears to be true; its veracity can scarcely be doubted. Yet the statement is nevertheless laughable and even mendacious, since it implies that what is by definition inevitable could somehow have been otherwise. The sentence taken by itself is tautological, because "miércoles" by definition *always* encompasses complete mornings. (The phrase recalls the somewhat tired joke response to the question "What day is today?": "Today is Monday, all day.") The grammar too is flawed, "miércoles" appearing where an adjective would seem to be called for. And *estar* rather than *ser* would seem to be required in the first line, to parallel the use of *ponerse* in line 3. These opening lines, then, overturn grammar and threaten unthinkable calendarial disorder. By postulating qualitative differences, even of an inherent or fixed nature, between one day of the week and another, they also deny the fundamental arbitrariness of conventional distinctions between days of the week.[10] On a certain level, the ungrammatical nature of these lines in the poem brings under scrutiny the entire notion of classifications, distinctions, and conventions itself, revealing as well the arbitrariness of the text in relation to the natural world.

When a few lines later the word "ayer" reappears as an adjective ("todo el día / fue igual, / . . . / ayer y siempre ayer y así hasta ahora"), the poem again turns tautological, suggesting, through an excess of information—through remarks on the unremarkable—that what by definition lasts twenty-four hours could have lasted for a shorter period of time. (Just as absurd would be baptizing a baby John, then commenting later that "he continues to be just as John as ever.") "[A]sí hasta ahora," additionally, blurs the borders between two separate and mutually exclusive time categories, ignoring the fact that the identity of "yesterday" depends on its relationship, and difference from, "today." The text thus makes us consider not only the arbitrariness of some temporal categories but also the exclusively relational nature of others.

The speaker then laments that "nadie pudo / impedir que al final amaneciese / el día de hoy." While a patent and undeniable truth, this statement is simultaneously a half-lie, its use of "pudo" suggesting a failed attempt—and thus the possibility that someone, sometime (ironically inverting the action of folktale roosters who must crow to make the sun rise) actually might have been able to prevent dawn's arrival.

The speaker, furthermore, comments with surprise on what is inevitable, obvious, and generally taken for granted. Adopting the tone of a journalist, he notes "un claro / movimiento de pánico hacia los / tranvías." Yet the trivial news he reports should be dubbed "non-news": a small plane passes overhead, but children don't even glance up; a man appears on the street wearing a hat; strangers stroll about. The speaker mishandles scale and hierarchy, confusing contextual aspects like the day of the week with events that could be viewed as action. By commenting on apparently insignificant facts, the poem offers a disorienting surplus of signification, a myriad of loose ends that impede logical interpretation. At the same time, details threaten to proliferate ad infinitum (see Stewart for a discussion of such phenomena in literature).[11]

At the end of the poem, the speaker refers to yesterday as a "día / incomparable." Again, the phrase is entirely true from a literal perspective. Each day, on a microlevel, is incomparable and unique. But given the trivial nature of its ironically "everyday" events, the uniqueness of this particular "yesterday," so touted here, doesn't compute on the broad scale of memorable and important human events.

The elevated, encomiastic tone of the poem's ending recalls funeral oratory. A rereading of the poem reveals throughout a sketch of the last day of a dying man. Stable in the morning, so endangered by afternoon that distracted children don't even notice the airplane overhead, he is commemorated in the evening with candles, the "amarillos y cálidos faroles" that herald his inevitable demise. "Ayer," it turns out, falls within the tradition of carnivalesque funerals. What the speaker laments is the colorless, insipid existence lived in the modern urban collectivity.

"Ayer," then, according to this festive and liminal reading,[12] communicates the passing of time by personifying the day as someone dying from the moment he is born. The contradictions and ambivalence that at the time accompanied the events of yesterday—panic, joy, indifference—and the absurd reality of a day that, like all of us, lives dying, disappear in the passionate praise uttered by the speaker at the close of the poem. Exposing, as in "Penúltima nostalgia,"[13] the fallacious nature and distorting potential of memory, González writes an elegy that questions, in an oblique and self-referential fashion, the elegiac tradition in literature.

The relationship of "Ayer" to Spanish postwar society is significant. The poem can be read as a critical response to certain collective illusions propagated in the country at the time—from the false image of the "España cachonda" of the early postwar[14] to the air of "autosatisfacción nacional" that ran rampant in the sixties.[15] In a study of the Spanish narrative of the period in relation to Francoist historiography, David K. Herzberger offers a perspective that can profitably be applied to "Ayer." González's poem, on the one hand, counters the Franco regime's narrow and mythical conception of Spanish history with a reversal of myth of the kind Herzberger has seen as typical of social realism: "[I]nstead of implying the ennobling continuity of an epic past, this fiction calls forth the bathos of the mock epic. Rather than ennoble the individual, the social realists esteem the virtues of the collective, and rather than deify the heroic, they celebrate the mundane and quotidian." But unlike certain other González poems ("Estío en Bidonville" is one) that follow unquestioningly the social realist premise that language copies reality, this poem has more in common with the novels of memory that question "the referential illusion of truth and wholeness."[16] Nevertheless, in comparison with later poems, the text, in its underlying message, still exhibits the "bifurcation of form and content" (the term is Perloff's)[17] that characterized González's early period.

Another poem from González's transitional period that exemplifies his use of absurdist techniques for a testimonial purpose is "Inventario de lugares propicios al amor" (p. 187) from *Tratado de urbanismo*. Its speaker considers, among the sites appropriate for love, spring, summer, and "también esas grietas que el otoño / forma al interceder con los domingos / en algunas ciudades" ["Also those crevices that Autumn / makes when it intercedes with Sundays / in some cities" (DDW)]. Finding none of these spaces adequate, he thinks of seeking a different locale: "¿A dónde huir, entonces?" ["To where does one escape to?" (DDW)]. With his practical tone and his concern over "propitious places" rather than over the many other romantic aspects of love, the speaker of "Inventario" conveys a mechanistic approach similar to the one we saw in "Cumpleaños de amor." The confusion between time and place communicates a frustrating disorder, a world out of whack. Within the context of the social criticism found in *Tratado de urbanismo*, the closing reference to "este tiempo hostil, propicio al odio" ["this hostile time, propitious for hatred" (DDW)] recalls not only a time but also a place, Spain at the time the poem was written.

Although the four poems examined so far express images of reality fairly typical of the period in which they were written, they fully demonstrate both González's sensitivity to the constraints of logical discourse and his tendency to violate those constraints. These poems distort reality and at times even suggest the fallibility of meaning systems. In his later books, González continues to develop in a similar vein, though more for ludic than for social or existential reasons. The poem "Acaso" [Perhaps] (p. 330), from *Prosemas o menos*, like "Ayer," plays with the concept of the arbitrary division of time into days of the week. Here the poet employs inappropriate contexts, bifurcation of meaning, and figurative and literal levels. As if it were a matter of transcendent importance, the speaker ponders the question of whether, as he has heard, "hoy es jueves" [today is Thursday]:

> Me dicen que hoy es jueves.
>
> La pequeña certeza
> no la confirma nada:

5 / Play with the Logic of Time and Place

> ni el sol en los cristales
> —débil y desteñido—,
> ni la brisa que mece
> borrosas ramas, lejos,
> ni la lenta pereza
> pesarosa
> con la que me dispongo a ver qué pasa.
>
> Salgo a la calle, y miro
> sin comprender.
> ¿Qué tienen esos rostros
> que no sea concebible cualquier martes?
> El perro que olisquea la acacia desvaída,
> ¿no es el perro de ayer, por desventura?
>
> Otros son los que insisten.
> Me dicen que hoy es jueves.
>
> [They tell me this is Thursday.
>
> That little certainty
> is confirmed by nothing:
> not the sun on the windows
> —weak and faded—
> nor the breeze that makes
> blurred branches sway, far away,
> nor the slow, sad
> lethargy
> with which I prepare to see what is happening.
>
> I go out on the street, and I gaze
> without understanding.
> What is there about those faces
> that wouldn't be conceivable any Tuesday?
> The dog sniffing the faded acacia bush,
> isn't that the same dog as yesterday, by mischance?
>
> Others are the ones who insist.
> They tell me this is Thursday.]

The speaker's earnest tone, and his questioning and confused demeanor as he studies what he encounters on the street, suggest a philosophical or metaphysical quandary. But the subject of his doubt—whether today is really Thursday—is a merely conventional detail that could be clarified by a glance at any newspaper. The gap between tone and subject makes the poem absurdly tragicomic.[18]

"Acaso" shares certain themes and techniques with the earlier "Ayer."

Like that poem it is a text with multiple planes. Also similarly, "Acaso" plays with the arbitrary nature of the names societies give to specific fragments of time. Additionally, the question of authority is raised by the speaker's urge to compare his own observations with what others claim to be true. Though he challenges their categories, his seriousness in doing so ironically reinforces societal emphasis on order and proper naming. Like those he cites who "insisten, . . . / . . . que hoy es jueves," he himself attributes profound, intrinsic meaning to something quite arbitrary—the linguistic signifiers assigned through convention to the seven diurnal components of our week, itself a temporal cycle of culturally determined length.[19]

The poem, so consistent and philosophical from the point of view of the speaker, yet so absurd in the light of common sense, exhibits a characteristic of nonsense texts described by Susan Stewart: misdirection. As Stewart explains this phenomenon, any text exists only physically until the reader interprets it through systems of classification, relevance, and appropriateness. She states: "Nonsense [of certain types] . . . points to the essentially undifferentiated nature of information prior to interpretation. . . . Significance is attributable through the activities of interpretation; it is interpretation that makes the arbitrary nonarbitrary."[20] Because the speaker's point of view in "Acaso" does not lend itself to becoming relevant, the poem remains nonsensical, the process of interpretation itself assuming the foreground.

The arbitrariness that persists in poems like "Acaso" is related, for Stewart, to problems of causality.[21] Normally, she explains, our interpretations make sense and are seen as nonarbitrary because of the social context out of which they arise, the situational constraints that give to language a feel of appropriateness. In "Acaso," an alienated speaker who doesn't understand why Thursday is any different from any other day (thus attributing causative power to the name "jueves") calls into question the tendency of social life, described by Stewart, to endow language with nonarbitrariness. This aspect of the poem recalls a film title from the sixties, *If It's Tuesday, This Must Be Belgium,* which by ignoring the travel agent's decisive role in preparing an itinerary suggests a cause-and-effect relationship between the day of the week and the relatively more momentous displacement from one country to another. Like tourists dazed by a superficial and hurried tour, the speaker of "Acaso" (perhaps simply because he, like his creator Angel González, is a "trasnochador impenitente" who may have arisen very late after a night on the town) feels alienated, beset by a "lenta pereza / pesarosa" that prevents him from connecting with what others affirm and take for granted.

"Acaso" belongs, finally, to an important poetic tradition that explores the relationship between things and their names. An ironic reversal of Guillén's "Los nombres" [Names], the poem reveals the arbitrariness of naming. Guillén's celebration of the wonders of normal existence, moreover, is replaced

5 / Play with the Logic of Time and Place

with a portrait of a humdrum daily reality whose most marvelous aspect is a dog that sniffs a faded acacia bush.

"Diatriba contra los muertos" [Diatribe against the dead] (p. 350), also from *Prosemas o menos*, likewise exhibits both misdirection and statements that are literally true but false in what they imply. The poem portrays completely involuntary attributes of the dead as signs of willful misbehavior. Their coldness, their silence, their need to be carried, their impassivity are all depicted as indications of selfishness and indifference:

> Los muertos son egoístas:
> hacen llorar y no les importa,
> se quedan quietos en los lugares más inconvenientes,
> se resisten a andar, hay que llevarlos
> a cuestas a la tumba
> como si fuesen niños, qué pesados.

> [The dead are selfish:
> they make people cry and don't even care,
> they stay still in the most inconvenient places,
> they refuse to walk, one has to pick them up
> and carry them to their tombs
> as if they were children, how tiresome.]

Ironically "lo peor de nuestra vida" [the worst part of our lives], the dead become a kind of ineradicable, termitelike pest, whose continuous destructive activity (illogical given their actual powerlessness to act) cannot be halted:

> Lo malo que tienen los muertos
> es que no hay forma de matarlos.
> Su constante tarea destructiva
> es por esa razón incalculable.
> Insensibles, distantes, tercos, fríos,
> con su insolencia y su silencio
> no se dan cuenta de lo que deshacen.

> [What's bad about dead people
> is that there's no way to kill them.
> Their constant labor of destruction
> is for that reason incalculable.
> Insensitive, distant, stubborn, cold,
> with their insolence and their silence
> they don't realize what they are undoing.]

As in other poems, here a literally true statement ("[N]o hay forma de matarlos") has false implications. The dead indeed are the only ones who are truly in no danger of dying, not because of their superior resistance, however, but because they are already irrevocably dead. Yet the false implications of the statement disappear on a metaphorical level; the living are unable to erase the presence and effect of loved ones who may have died but who continue to eat at and destroy them. Like the dead, whose absence changes and undoes our world, the prefix "des-" undoes the set phrase into which it is inserted.

"No tuvo ayer su día" [Yesterday didn't have its day] (p. 327), like "Acaso," forms part of a section of *Prosemas o menos* dedicated to the passing of time:

> Ya desde muy temprano,
> ayer fue tarde.
>
> Amaneció el crepúsculo, y al alba
> el cielo derramó sobre la tierra
> un gran haz de penumbra.
>
> Cerca del mediodía
> un firmamento tenue e incompleto
> —¿cifra de nuestra suerte?—
> brillaba todavía en el espacio.
>   (La luna
> no iluminaba al mundo;
> su cuerpo transparente
> nos permitía tan sólo adivinar
> la existencia más alta de otro cielo
> inclemente también, inapelable.
>
> Seguimos esperando, sin embargo.
>
> Imprecisas señales
> —un latido de pájaros, a veces;
> el eco de un relámpago;
> súbitas rachas de violento viento—
> nos mantenían alerta.
>
> A la hora del ocaso
> salió un momento el sol para ponerse
> y confirmó las sombras con ceniza.
>
> [From very early on,
> yesterday was afternoon.
>
> It dawned dusk, and at daybreak
> the sky spilled over the earth
> a great beam of shadow.

5 / Play with the Logic of Time and Place

> Around noon
> a tenuous and incomplete firmament
> —a code for our fate?—
> was still shining in space.
>   (The moon
> didn't illuminate the world;
> its transparent body
> only allowed us to guess
> at the existence, higher up, of another sky,
> just as unmerciful, brooking no appeal.
>
> We continued to wait, nevertheless.
>
> Vague signals
> —the beating of wings, at times;
> the echo of a flash of lightning;
> sudden gusts of violent wind—
> kept us alert.
>
> At the hour of sunset
> the sun came out for a moment in order to set
> and confirmed the shadows with ashes.]

 This text, like others in the same vein, defamiliarizes time through violations of logic, inappropriate substitutions, and double meanings that lead to instability of interpretation. Not only the language of the poem but also its theme—yesterday remembered—can be construed in various ways. Many logical stumbling blocks suggest a nonsensical interpretation, although a reading compatible with logic and common sense can also be achieved. Even if we opt for either of these two possibilities, the alternative reading continues to insinuate itself, undermining our choice.

 The title and the first two lines of the poem at first glance seem to embody insoluble problems of logic. The phrase "Ayer no tuvo su día"—because yesterday was in fact a day— violates the law of logic that prohibits a class from being a member of itself.[22] The opposites *temprano/tarde* [early/late] in the first two lines present another stark contradiction. The description that follows—of a day without light—leads us to reinterpret "tarde" as "atardecer" [late afternoon], but now a new opposition emerges: the idea that "desde muy de mañana, ayer fue una tarde" [from early morning, yesterday was an afternoon]. Yet once again, we can overcome the stumbling block to conclude that "día" refers to daylight (a meaning that appears in another of González's poems, "Luz llamada día trece" [Light called the thirteenth day] [p. 93]). This reinterpretation solves the logical problem of the title as well; yesterday (a twenty-four-hour day) can have darkness and sunlight; on the day in question, there was no sunlight.

Thus the "ayer" that the poem describes—like the sentences and expressions just treated—can be interpreted in different ways: on the one hand, as a day without sunshine, but on the other, as a crazy day in which everything was topsy-turvy, when dawn was a sunset and nightfall a dawning. Supporting this second reading, the lines "Amaneció el crepúsculo, y al alba / el cielo derramó sobre la tierra / un gran haz de penumbra" unite the opposites *amanecer/crepúsculo* [dawn/dusk] and substitute "haz de penumbra" [beam of shadow] for the expected "haz de luz" [beam of light]. Noon, on this yesterday, is further characterized not by Guillenian plenitude of "todo / Completo para un dios" [everything / complete for a god] but by the presence of the moon in a "firmamento tenue e incompleto," an expression that itself embodies a contradiction between "firmamento" (derived from "firme" and a word that evokes grandeur) and "tenue" (which connotes what is weak or fragile). Instead of Platonic spheres of increasing ideal harmony, the moon "nos permitía tan sólo adivinar / la existencia más alta de otro cielo / inclemente también, inapelable."

The day continues, the speaker informs us, with ominous signals that recall the black sun, the partially obscured light of day, and the lightning and thunder of the biblical Apocalypse. At the end of the poem, as at the beginning with "temprano" and "tarde," the association between two opposing terms—*sunrise* and *sunset*—awakens in the text a nonsensical, impossible meaning, that of the union of birth and death.

Alongside this apocalyptic reading of the poem, there coexists a "naturalized" version in which the "crepúsculo" is the early morning light before the actual dawn (a meaning that the dictionary accepts, though preferring for such cases the word "aurora"). According to this interpretation, the birds, the lightning, and the wind are simply meteorological phenomena and not omens, and the sudden sunlight only the appearance of the sun previously covered by clouds. "No tuvo ayer su día," then, is an unstable text: on the one hand an impossible one in which language is as topsy-turvy as the order of the cosmos, presenting itself as just as "inapelable" and as disorienting as the day described; but on the other simply a description, exaggerated and stylized, of a day without sunshine. The poem is exemplary as belonging to González's second period, both in its indeterminacy and in the absence of an existential or social intent. Douglas K. Benson has noted in *Prosemas o menos* González's turn to nature as "poetizable en sí misma"[23] [able in itself to be turned into poetry]. Though Benson may be referring specifically to such texts as González's commemoration of Albuquerque sunsets, in this poem too the poet's use of nature as a point of departure underscores the fundamental differences between his early and later periods.

Many of the poems analyzed so far make us question the traditional view of poetry as a process of naming, in some cases because they reveal the arbitrariness of the names we confer on units of time, and in others because they reveal the plurality of meanings that a poetic text may embody. Other poems, in dealing with the theme of aging or the passing of time in the individual life, violate logic and common sense by imposing mechanical or purely physiological visions on processes that are in reality much more complex. In these cases absurdity stems from an erroneous attribution of cause and effect, and at times from the confusion between different levels of significance or perceptibility. In still other poems, González defamiliarizes time by characterizing it as a place.[24]

One poem where play with units of time reaches an extreme level is "Mi vocación profunda" [My profound vocation] (p. 242), from *Breves acotaciones para una biografía*. In this text, the adjective "profundo" is taken in its literal sense, and time acquires the density of a physical object in space. The speaker, who evidently likes to delve deeply into matters, practices undersea diving through time; he affirms that "[u]na vez crucé un año debajo de los días" [I once crossed a year beneath the days]. This statement not only substitutes the physically elusive substance time for the expected body of water but also violates the most elementary logic; if days constitute years, how can the two be separated to allow passage through one without passage through the other? González here creates a world in which time—though characterized in traditional fashion as a sea or a river—permits very strange operations, including the separation of the part from the whole. The fragmentation time undergoes is matched by what happens to the speaker's body. Chopped into "dedos, / narices, ojos, penes, labios, cabellos, risas" [fingers, / noses, eyes, penises, lips, hair, laughs], he becomes an assemblage of unconnected parts rather than a harmonious and consistent organic whole.

In certain cases González's poems destabilize the notion of the human being as the center and measure of all things, including time. Texts like "Igual que si nunca" [The same as if never] (p. 328) and "El día se ha ido" [The day is gone] (p. 329) from *Prosemas o menos* expose anthropocentric fictions. The first text takes its meditative tone from literary tradition, along with the use of nightfall, wind, autumn, and smoke as signs of the passage of time and of life's transience. But its central image, "Sombría claridad / será ya en otra parte / —por un instante sólo— / madrugada" [Somber light / must somewhere else already be / —only for an instant— / a dawn], offers a less traditional perspective. Just as González's texts sometimes enclose more than one interpretation, here the light of day can mean two very different things; if from the speaker's present perspective it signifies the day's passing, for someone somewhere else it is seen as dawning. To the egocentric and subjective vision of sunlight defined in terms of an individual's perspective, the poem counterposes a more global context. Much as linguistics, following Ferdinand de Saussure, emphasizes the relational nature of signs, here the poem makes manifest the relational significance of light. The traditional image of time as divided into absolute past, present, and future (and of the universe as an entity founded by God and subordinate to God's aims) is challenged by the notion of time as relative to place. Although the poem uses the metaphor of a day that is dying (a metaphor in itself "dead"), the text also indicates that this death is at once a birth. If in other poems González makes us see the arbitrariness of names given to fragments of time, here he suggests that the order imposed on time by metaphors is only relative. The answer to the question that opens the poem ("¿Es algo más que el día lo que muere esta tarde?" [Is something else, besides the day, dying this afternoon?]) must be affirmative. What dies is the speaker's experience of the day, not the day itself.

The poem "El día se ha ido" deconstructs similarly the vision of time as something defined by the individual's point of view. Likening the pair dog/cat to the opposites night/day, the first two stanzas characterize day as a noisy but useful and welcome dog, and night as a stealthy, sinister cat:

> Ahora andará por otras tierras,
> llevando lejos luces y esperanzas,
> aventando bandadas de pájaros remotos,
> y rumores, y voces, y campanas,
> —ruidoso perro que menea la cola
> y ladra ante las puertas entornadas.
>
> (Entretanto, la noche, como un gato
> sigiloso, entró por la ventana,
> vio unos restos de luz pálida y fría,
> y se bebió la última taza.)
>
> [It's probably wandering other lands now,
> carrying lights and hopes far away,
> flushing flocks of distant birds,
> and noises, and voices, and bells,
> —a noisy dog that wags its tail
> and barks before half-open doors.
>
> (Meanwhile, night, like a stealthy
> cat, came in by the window,
> saw some leftover pale, cold light
> and drank up the last bowlful.)]

In the third stanza, the speaker consoles himself with the comforting idea that although night has arrived, day will return tomorrow; but he immediately amends this cyclical notion: "Pero no será igual. Será otro día. / Será otro perro de la misma raza" [But it won't be the same. It will be another day. / It will be another dog of the same breed]. By portraying the day as a dog that passes through, never to return, he replaces an absolutist and linear conception of time, divided by our own consciousness into past and future, with a less individualistic notion. The day, instead of dying when the sun disappears from our sight, slips mysteriously away but continues to exist somewhere else.

The elements of time and place are among the strongest anchors of González's work. From the first poem of *Aspero mundo*, "Te tuve . . . ," where he laments the loss of the "acariciado mundo" that "te me volaste de los brazos" (p. 9), to "Episodio último," the final text of *Prosemas o menos*, in which he speaks of someone's death (p. 402), he repeatedly turns to the effects of time's passing and to the expression of nostalgia and loss. Such poems as "Acoma, New Mexico, diciembre, 5:15 P.M." [Acoma, New Mexico, December, 5:15 P.M.] (p. 319) and his poems on Albuquerque sunsets (pp. 335–37) reflect a continuation throughout his work of a fairly traditional sense of the combination of specific time and place. But as we have seen, from the very first he also writes poems that challenge more traditional visions of time and place through the manipulation of reader expectation.

As with González's politically oriented poems, the poet's unconventional treatment of time and place evolves over the years. We could characterize this change as a shift from the absurd to the ludic. In the early poems, the poet utilizes a variety of techniques: misdirection; violations of logic, common sense, scale and hierarchy; mechanization; and decontextualization, to name several we have explored. Nevertheless, when these elements serve the portrayal of an absurd world—when they serve a critical vision of society—they express, as Wim Tigges has suggested, "anguish at the human predicament."[25] As works belonging to the literature of the absurd, these poems are not truly playful or nonsensical (such works seldom are, according to Tigges). Because of the worldview they serve, these works of González can be disconcerting or even seem heavy and forced.

But later works are more appropriately classed as postmodern texts, in which, Ihab Hassan suggests, irony has become radical play from which fixed meaning disappears.[26] Texts like "No tuvo ayer su día" or "Mi vocación profunda" are indeterminate, in the sense used by Marjorie H. Perloff, in that their meaning is unstable, impossible to reduce to a coherent, unified interpretation. The depiction of time in such works, as we have seen, corresponds to the cubist treatment of visual perspective, described by Christopher C. Soufas as a rejection of the model of representation based on one-point perspective, dominant in the West since the Renaissance.[27] Twentieth-century shifts in scientific thought likewise influence González's development. Silvio Gaggi provides an overview of these shifts. He summarizes Werner Heisenberg's 1962 description of the challenge modern science, physics in particular, has posed to commonsense notions of "space, time, causality, and substance." Gaggi points as well to Freud's discovery of the unconscious mind and replacement of the positive term *reason* with the word *rationalization*. He views World War I as reinforcing the skepticism about human rationality, thus introducing the contribution of history (definitely a factor in González's development) to postmodernist epistemological and ontological skepticism.[28]

As he evolves as a poet, then, González uses ludic features with varying results. Sometimes such features represent only temporary stumbling blocks faced by the reader in the process of interpretation, momentary impediments that can be "naturalized," explained away, or fitted into a global interpretive scheme. In other cases, his texts remain unstable, alternating between a commonsense and a nonsense meaning. In still other instances, the incompatibilities are not only impossible to explain away but are the raison d'être of the poem as a whole, creating undecidability as in an Escher print and inexorably calling attention to poetic surfaces. But the differences between these categories of works are in González never completely categorical. Even when overcome or naturalized, the initial contradictions or logical stumbling blocks do not disappear completely. Rather, they remain as presences in the reader's mind, as part of an alternative or shadow text that can never be totally eradicated.

González's shift away from purposefulness, furthermore, does not mean that his later work is irrelevant or meaningless. As Susan Stewart suggests, nonsense is far from gratuitous, fulfilling the important function of helping us to define sense and to move between stages in the modification of our ever-evolving domains of meaning. Organization, she states, is "always a reorganization brought about by disorganization."[29] And in the twentieth century, when social and cultural change has accelerated dramatically, such a stage of disorganization seems to be an entirely appropriate, necessary, and useful response.

6
Play with Spheres of Discourse in González's Second Period

The poems analyzed in the previous chapter present mainly problems of hierarchy and relevance and of logic and common sense, both intertextual concerns in that they rupture the expectations readers bring to the reading process in the form of social texts. Their effect is thus compatible with the belief the poet has expressed in the collaborative role of the reader in bringing to life the words he has written. Though increasing in importance and changing in significance in González's later works, such questions of logic, hierarchy, and relevance represent a vein that is present in his poetry from the beginning. In many other poems, especially those published in 1969 or after, González's poetic play grows out of his sensitivity to a variety of types of discourse: scientific, didactic, journalistic, and religious as well as literary and aesthetic. Drawing from and combining different and often incompatible spheres of discourse, these later works undermine their own message and the logic of the spheres of discourse they unite. Among their most stark contradictions are those caused by the juxtaposition of the abstract and the concrete, the literal and the figurative, and the spiritual and the material. These combinations create poetic effect through violating expectations associated with certain semantic fields or subject matter. They threaten meaning itself, which, as Susan Stewart maintains, depends on the integrity of the boundaries between distinct spheres of signification. It is these boundaries, she suggests, that normally make possible the creation of texts.

In this chapter, I will analyze examples of the disruption of boundaries between spheres of discourse in González's last three books, *Procedimientos narrativos*, *Muestra*, and *Prosemas o menos*. I begin with a poem from *Procedimientos narrativos* in which González aims his demythologizing combinations of spheres of discourse at bourgeois social customs. "Del campo o de la mar" [Of the countryside or of the sea] (pp. 249–50) reads as follows:

> Huimos con nuestros enseres y nos dispersamos por
> los campos,

buscando preferentemente las orillas del mar y de los
    ríos.
(Dejamos atrás la desolación, el sufrimiento,
la ciudad desierta y calcinada.)
No sabíamos qué hacer en las mañanas
y marisqueábamos despacio por los acantilados
o, tumbados bajo el sol,
dejábamos que el tiempo planease sobre nuestras
    cabezas
—tenaz y lento como un buitre—
nuestra futura destrucción, quizá inminente.
Thelonius Monk, Vivaldi y otros monstruos
nos roían las entrañas, percutían
en nuestras vísceras, colmaban
los cuerpos de deseo, de sed de alcohol, de angustia por
    las tardes,
y la noche nos expulsaba con violencia fuera de nuestros
    refugios.
Impulsados por algo parecido al miedo,
acudíamos entonces en busca de otros rostros,
gentes de todo el mundo compartían nuestra urgencia,
acosados por ritmos y canciones
—el *rock* igual que un látigo cruzándonos el pecho—,
donde quiera que fueras Bob Dylan te encontraba.
Estábamos seguros de que todo era inútil,
mirarse, sonreír, hablar incluso,
besar, amar, nada nos salvaría.
Nadie se salvará,
nosotros mismos
nos entregamos, dóciles:
era imposible resistir más tiempo.
El regreso fue largo y doloroso.
La carretera estaba intransitable,
había policías en los cruces,
subimos a los trenes atestados,
los niños pedían agua,
las mujeres mostraban sus muslos sin malicia,
indiferentes, fatigados, sucios
—no había donde sentarse—,
así llegamos.

Perdida la costumbre, los asombrados ojos
trataban de orientarse penetrando las ruinas.

El otoño oxidaba la ciudad y sus parques.

Definitivamente,
el veraneo había terminado.

[We fled with our possessions and spread out through
    the countryside,
seeking if possible seaside or riverbank
    locations.
(We left behind the desolation, the suffering,
the charred, deserted city.)
We didn't know what to do in the mornings
and we would slowly gather shellfish among the cliffs
or, stretched out in the sun,
we would let time soaring above our
    heads
—tenacious and slow like a vulture—
plan our future destruction, perhaps imminent.
Thelonius Monk, Vivaldi, and other monsters
would eat at our insides, they would pound
our guts, they would fill
our bodies with desire, with thirst for drink, with anguish
    in the afternoons,
and night would violently eject us from our
    hideouts.
Moved by something akin to fear,
we would then go in search of other faces,
people from all over the world shared our urgency,
besieged by rhythms and songs
—rock music lashing like a whip across our chests—
wherever you went Bob Dylan found you.
We were sure that all was useless,
looking at each other, smiling, even speaking,
kissing, loving, nothing would save us.
No one would save us,
we gave
ourselves up, docile:
it was impossible to resist any longer.
The trip back was long and painful.
The highway was impassable,
there were police at all the crossroads,
we boarded the overcrowded trains,
the children called for water,
the women showed their thighs, but innocently,
indifferent, weary, dirty
—there was no place to sit down—
that's how we arrived.

No longer accustomed to what they saw, our astonished eyes
tried to orient themselves as they penetrated the ruins.

Autumn was oxidizing the city and its parks.

Definitively,
summer vacation was over.]

Here González appropriates clichés from the discourse of epic wartime evacuations and of existential anguish to defamiliarize the bourgeois custom of summering away from the big cities. The reader first reacts to the surprise ending, then goes back to tease out the strands of discourse and to note the double function they play, as signs that on the one hand misdirect the reader tuned in to their epic connotations but on the other aptly describe the typical modern-day vacationer's activities. The poem is González's version of the social criticism that many of his contemporaries directed at themselves and their compatriots at a similar moment.[1]

A review of the poem reveals the first-person plural speakers who describe their exodus as a flight, suggesting that they are refugees hiding out from an enemy. They spread out "por / los campos" like primitive survivalists, choosing for strategic reasons to settle along rivers and coasts. (We later realize that these reasons entail the recreational possibilities of bodies of water.) The desolation and suffering of the deserted city they leave behind (ll. 5–6) seems like wartime devastation (but later turns out to be merely a typical August in Spain and the misery [and self-pity] of those unfortunate few unable to leave town for the yearly vacation). These refugees, lines 7ff. indicate, forced into idleness by their exile and threatened with destruction, turn to a certain bacchanalian depravity to ease their fears, as in wartime films we have all seen. They leave their refuges (which we initially see as safe havens, later merely as restful hotel rooms) for this purpose (which we later understand to be merely the vacationer's thirst for nocturnal amusement). The image of a world holding its breath in an international crisis ("gentes de todo el mundo compartían nuestra urgencia") turns out to be merely the pressing desire of the participants in Spain's international tourist boom—perhaps on the Costa del Sol—to make the most of their summer vacation.

In the epic context, the characters' conviction that "todo era inútil," that "nada nos salvaría," suggests that theirs was a losing cause. But as we later reinterpret this section, we realize that their defeatism and ultimate surrender ("nos entregamos, dóciles") is not a wartime admission of defeat, or even the existential anguish suggested by certain overtones in the text, but simply the inevitable end of their annual vacation escape. Within the epic mode, the train ride back to the city—with its crowded cars and primitive conditions—evokes a defeated populace facing occupation. The trip turns out to depict merely the discomforts of travel during the crowded vacation season. Though all along, some references (to Thelonius Monk and Bob Dylan, for example) warn us not to take the epic features too seriously, many

6 / PLAY WITH SPHERES OF DISCOURSE   119

other elements (such as the desire to be near water) fit perfectly into both the state of siege text and the summer vacation text, and in this overlapping resides the playfulness of the poem.

"Del campo o de la mar" as a defamiliarization of the ritual vacation pilgrimage provides pleasure through partially misleading its reader, who must first in succession, and then simultaneously, decipher the poem's two basic texts. In combining stereotypical wartime fiction with everyday social behavior, the poem reveals both the trite and ritualistic elements of the former and the equally trite and ritualistic nature of the latter. In this sense, the poem illustrates what Silvio Gaggi sees as postmodernist "eclecticism"—the tendency to "quote, paraphrase, or rework previous styles or works," including not only "fine art" traditions but vernacular ones as well and, as is the case of "Del campo o de la mar," involving a "degree of wit, whimsy, and irony." As Gaggi points out, the inclusion of such past works and traditions is never "revivalist" but is used as a point of departure for "creative reworking," with a potential for exposing through juxtaposition previously unseen qualities of the various traditions brought together.[2] González's poem, finally, illustrates the richness of collective social fictions that human beings absorb and carry around with them as a kind of mental baggage.[3]

In his book *Muestra, corregida y aumentada, de algunos procedimientos narrativos y de las actitudes sentimentales que habitualmente comportan*, González acknowledges the role of nonsense in his poetry by titling one section "Poesías sin sentido" [Poems without sense]. Among poems in this group we find the marvelously humorous "Dato biográfico" [Biographical fact] (pp. 307–8), which, like "Del campo o de la mar," weaves together social and literary texts and clichés to create an absurd vision of the speaker's existence. The poem depicts the speaker's relationship with the cockroaches inhabiting his home:

> Cuando estoy en Madrid,
> las cucarachas de mi casa protestan porque leo por las
>   noches.
> La luz no las anima a salir de sus escondrijos,
> y pierden de ese modo la oportunidad de pasearse por
>   mi dormitorio,
> lugar hacia el que
>   —por oscuras razones—
> se sienten irresistiblemente atraídas.
> Ahora hablan de presentar un escrito de queja al presidente
>   de la república,
> y yo me pregunto:
> ¿en qué país se creerán que viven?;
> estas cucarachas no leen los periódicos.

Lo que a ellas les gusta es que yo me emborrache
y baile tangos hasta la madrugada,
para así practicar sin riesgo alguno
su merodeo incesante y sin sentido, a ciegas
por las anchas baldosas de mi alcoba.

A veces las complazgo,
no porque tenga en cuenta sus deseos,
sino porque me siento irresistiblemente atraído,
por oscuras razones,
hacia ciertos lugares muy mal iluminados
en los que me demoro sin plan preconcebido
hasta que el sol naciente anuncia un nuevo día.

Ya de regreso en casa,
cuando me cruzo por el pasillo con sus pequeños cuerpos
    que se evaden
con torpeza y con miedo
hacia las grietas sombrías donde moran,
les deseo buenas noches a destiempo
—pero de corazón, sinceramente—,
reconociendo en mí su incertidumbre,
su inoportunidad,
su fotofobia,
y otras muchas tendencias y actitudes
que—lamento decirlo—
hablan poco en favor de esos ortópteros.

[When I'm in Madrid,
the cockroaches in my house protest because I read at
    night.
The light doesn't bring them to leave their hiding places,
so they miss the chance to stroll about
    my bedroom,
a place to which
        —for obscure reasons—
they feel irresistibly attracted.
Now they're talking of presenting a formal complaint to the
    president of the republic,
and I ask myself:
in what country do they think they're living?;
these cockroaches don't read the newspapers.

What they like is for me to get drunk
and to dance the tango until dawn,
so they can carry out with absolutely no risk
their incessant and senseless marauding, in the dark
on the wide tiles of my bedroom floor.

6 / PLAY WITH SPHERES OF DISCOURSE

> Sometimes I humor them,
> not because I consider their wishes,
> but because I feel irresistibly attracted,
> for obscure reasons,
> to certain very poorly lit places
> where I linger without any preconceived plan
> until the rising sun announces a new day.
>
> Then when I'm finally at home,
> when in the hallway I meet their little bodies
>   sneaking away
> clumsily and fearfully
> toward the shadowy cracks where they dwell,
> I wish them an untimely good evening
> —but from the heart, sincerely—,
> recognizing in myself their incertitude,
> their inopportuneness,
> their photophobia,
> and many other tendencies and attitudes
> which—I'm sorry to say—
> speak rather poorly for those orthopterans.

The poem's nonsensical humor derives from the confluence of two distinct and incompatible classificatory systems—that of biological categories, on the one hand, and that of social caste, on the other. First, the poem employs clichés from the discourse of master/servant relations to create a comparison between the speaker and his cockroaches and a master and his servants. The first line evokes the freedom of movement of the upper-class gentleman, who, we surmise, has more than one residence. In line 2, the cockroaches are depicted as slightly subhuman fixtures attached to the household, as persons that have become objects. Their access to the privacy of his bedroom and the suggestion of surreptitious interest in his business, in lines 4–7, recall a literary cliché—servants playing key roles through secretly acquired knowledge of their master's affairs. The pilfering conventionally associated with servants and their proverbial delight at the freedom enjoyed in their oppressor's absence are alluded to in lines 14–16, which describe the cockroaches as intimate marauders who enter his bedroom to search unrestricted for something to steal.

Throughout the poem, the speaker's tone suggests the condescension of a supercilious master referring to shiftless servants he regards as inferior. He stereotypes the roaches and ridicules their credulous intention of complaining to the president. He disparages their activities as "incessant" and "senseless." With the tightfisted largesse of Lazarillo's cleric, he states that though he sometimes indulges them by going out, he does not do so out of consideration for their wishes. The pride with which he basks in his own goodwill toward this band of inferiors underscores his self-righteous, patronizing attitude.

The speaker's pains to differentiate himself from the cockroaches are nevertheless undermined throughout the poem. He gradually creates parallels between himself and his roaches, eventually acknowledging similarities. He admits that he too avoids light, seeking refuge at night in dark places (which we interpret to mean bars and nightclubs). His lack of direction during these nocturnal forays echoes the "merodeo . . . sin sentido, a ciegas" of his six-legged tenants as they reconnoiter his room. His recognition of kinship turns a commonplace story—a *madrileño* returning in the wee hours to his roach-infested apartment after a night on the town—into a festive spoof of the "brotherhood of man" theme, extended here to include ridiculously inappropriate members of the insect kingdom.

The social discourse of "Dato biográfico," with its references to (1) an environment familiar to, even shared by, a large number of González's readers; (2) an unresponsive political system; and (3) a web of social relationships and behaviors, has the ring of realism as described by Susan Stewart. Realism, she says, "partakes of the time, space, and causality, the ideology and the rhetoric, of the everyday lifeworld" of common sense and depends upon a consensus between writer and reader who share a social context.[4] The title itself suggests documentary (like Gloria Fuertes's poem "Ficha ingreso hospital general" [Admission slip, general hospital]).[5] But the realistic context is undermined by the intrusion into social discourse of biological classificatory systems, called forth by the word "ortópteros." In the light of the *species* distinctions of biological organization, the *social* class distinctions evoked by the speaker's words are inappropriate and ridiculous. The effort the human speaker expends to distinguish himself from an animal species so far removed on the spectrum of development from his own is an example of misdirection that intensifies the poem's absurdity. The poem thus creates humor through establishing similarity between spheres thought to be different, a frequent technique in works that confuse the animal and the human worlds.[6]

The dual system of classification and meaning in "Dato biográfico" results in many cases in the simultaneous activation of more than one definition of a word or phrase. Words may suggest one meaning from the sphere of animal classification and another within the system of social categories. The phrase "merodeo incesante y sin sentido" captures the roaches' instinctive foraging and at the same time the judgmental attitude of the bourgeois speaker toward the morals of the lower classes. When the speaker asks, "[Y] yo me pregunto: / ¿en qué país se creerán que viven?," adding that "estas cucarachas no leen los periódicos," we laugh because the roaches' ignorance of human geographical and political distinctions and of the printed word is their literally true and scientifically inevitable condition—an inescapable state which the speaker's attitude of moral judgment, belonging to the discourse of master-servant relations, wrongly implies to be voluntary. On the level of social distinctions, furthermore, we recognize that the speaker is guilty of unfair stereotyping of a socially less-privileged group. But from the standpoint of real humans looking at actual cockroaches, anything *but* stereotyping would be patently absurd.

In addition to the convergence of the literal and the figurative, as just seen, other areas of confusion result from the poem's juxtaposition of incompatible meaning systems. The nonsensical topsy-turviness of the poem threatens distinctions between nature and culture, instinct and reason, and even between order and formlessness. The cockroaches' instinctive avoidance of light, viewed by science in mechanistic terms, is demechanized through the speaker's anthropomorphic vision of their wants and tastes, while his own habits are mechanized through comparison to insect behavior. The careful establishment of class distinctions in the poem implies a social order in the speaker's household, but on another level the presence of cockroaches indicates the disorder of the unwanted invasion of nature in human territory and the encroachment of filth on cleanliness. If, as Stewart states, culture is classification, these cockroaches both represent culture and threaten it, as does dirt in general, which in anthropological terms was both born of, and made taboo by, the creation of order.[7]

The emphasis on classifying, in this poem, recalls Silvio Gaggi's discussion of postmodernism in *The French Lieutenant's Woman*, a work published a few years before González's poem. John Fowles's novel, according to Gaggi, foregrounds classificatory schemes, including "four major Victorian systems": "religious morality, social class, male supremacy, and empirical science." In the novel, the wildness of a character (Sarah) represents "the ineffable and uncontrollable component of human experience and nature" and challenges "all rational, scientific, and Linnaean attempts to explain, classify, objectify, and control."[8] In "Dato biográfico," likewise, classification (including several of the same categories) is undermined by the juxtaposition of distinct and incompatible spheres of discourse.

Like "Del campo o de la mar," "Dato biográfico" can not only be read as a nonsense poem but can also be naturalized to become a lyric expression of the speaker's attitude. If the first poem could be said to be a metaphorical statement of distaste for modern urban life as a kind of oppressive state of siege, the second could be viewed as expressing the despair of one who senses companionship only across the widest of social and biological barriers, and who is aware of the absurdity of human existence and the meaninglessness of his own compulsive behavior. The speaker in some respects resembles the poet himself, who has described his inner struggle between dissolution and strict self-control and in an interview even refers to the alternatives, mentioned in the poem, of either staying home to read or going out to bars until all hours of the night.[9] Through the poem, perhaps, he uses his imagination to escape the twinges of remorse he feels—by focusing on the cockroaches, whom he pleases so, in fantasy, with his absence. The poem thus creates the romantic vision of a solitary and self-deprecating speaker, but such a vision is overshadowed by the ludic elements present. The text is fundamentally a playful construction and not a lyric statement. Any emotion it might convey is "enervated" by its nonsense, something that typically occurs, according to Wim Tigges, with nonsense texts.[10] The poem, however, does exemplify the "double coding" that Charles Jencks has suggested is characteristic of postmodernism. The poet has created a type of epiphany poem, but with the "[i]rony, playfulness, parodic and self-parodic nostalgia" typifying postmodernism.[11] The poem justifies classifying González with Fowles and John Barth, whom Gaggi designates "humanistic postmoderns."[12]

Another poem from the section of *Muestra* titled "Poesías sin sentido"—"Confesiones de un joven problemático" [Confessions of a young man with problems] (pp. 305–6)— illustrates how in his second period González goes beyond parody to the radical play and "entropy of meaning" Ihab Hassan attributes to postmodern art. Reflecting contemporary culture's obsession with psychoanalysis, the poem opens with its speaker in the throes of a long, self-indulgent, self-centered, and yet rhapsodic recollection of his early childhood and his memories of the sex life of his parents. As with "Dato biográfico," the tone and subject matter at first glance suggest a realistic discourse in which the borders between the commonsense world outside the text and the fictional one within it tend to disappear or to be as inconspicuous as possible. Yet such a realism is quickly shattered by the fact that "mis papás," as the speaker childishly calls them in line 5, are not his mother and father, as we expect, but, literally, his two fathers, which explains his statement in the last two lines that "No es complejo de Edipo lo que tengo / —dice el doctor—, sino de Cleopatra" [What I have is not an Oedipus complex / —the doctor says—, / but a Cleopatra complex] (p. 306).

The entire narrative situation of "Confesiones de un joven problemático" is generated by a pun based on the ambiguity in Spanish of the words "mis papás." According to Edmund Leach's studies of the subject, puns are humorous because they straddle two discrete categories, thus breaking a taboo that prohibits us from recognizing ambiguity in words.[13] In this case, González's pun takes us to the impossible terrain of nonsense: though the word "papás" can mean "fathers," or in the child's lexicon "parents," for all the wonders of genetic engineering it cannot mean in real life two biological fathers of one child, as its context in the poem demands. We may attempt to overcome the problematical pun by viewing "Confesiones de un joven problemático" as depicting the possible indeterminacy of paternity within a ménage à trois, or by construing the words "mis papás" to be a transparent euphemism through which the child refers to his mother's multiple sex partners. Through these readings the poem becomes an example of the "[c]amp and comic pornography" that Hassan points to as a further manifestation of postmodernism.[14] But ultimately, the anomalous nature of González's use of the word "papás" prevents the pun from being eradicated from the mind of the reader, who moves back and forth between consciousness of the linguistic surface of the poem and a vision of what it depicts mimetically. On either level, the text serves to expose indeterminacy, whether within language or within social structures.[15]

"Confesiones de un joven problemático," because of the pun at its center, is clearly nonsensical. It fits the following description of nonsense offered by Stewart:

> [I]t involves the constant rearticulation of an anomalous aspect of social life—that is, the capacity of any fiction to be simultaneously p and $-p$. Secondly, as the most radical form of metafiction, it threatens the disintegration of social interaction that would occur if the unconscious was made conscious. It is the realization of the possibility that the discourse of everyday life could become totally conscious of its own procedures: it is the dispersal of attention from a purpose at hand, a halt to the ongoing nature of social discourse, and an extreme movement away from any conception of such discourse as natural.[16]

Although the radical nonsense of "Confesiones de un joven problemático" seems at first glance to be an end in itself, it is not entirely gratuitous but rather serves to permit González to unfurl a rhapsodic and romantic language.[17] Consider the following lines:

> ¡Qué momentos tan tristes y tan largos
> fuera de su ternura y sus desvelos!
> Han pasado los años
> y, aunque sé que es locura,
> aún espero que salgan, sonrientes,
> y compartan conmigo, igual que entonces,
> la alegría final
> de los últimos brindis y los últimos besos,
> que ponía en el aire sombrío de la casa
> un irreal resplandor,
> alto e intenso
> como la luz efímera que dora los crepúsculos.
>
> [Such sad, long moments
> away from their tenderness and care!
> Years have passed

and, though I know it's crazy,
I still hope they'll appear, smiling,
and that they'll share with me, just like then,
the final joy
of the last toasts and the last kisses,
which gave the house's somber air
an unreal splendor,
high and intense
like the ephemeral light that gilds the twilight.]

González clearly revels in the full-blown language in which his punning permits him to indulge.

"Eruditos en campus" (pp. 371–72), a poem from González's next-to-last book of poetry, *Prosemas o menos*, again weaves together different spheres of meaning to produce a kind of nonsense text. Much as "Confesiones de un joven problemático" is generated by the wordplay of "mis papás," much of this poem's imagery arises from the etymological link between *campus* and *campo* [countryside], a connection that generates González's own pastoral vision of the university, one that turns professors into grazing cattle:

Son los que son.

Apacibles, pacientes, divagando
en pequeños rebaños
por el recinto ajardinado,
                    vedlos.
O mejor, escuchadlos:

mugen difusa ciencia,
comen hojas de Plinio
y de lechuga,
devoran hamburguesas,
textos griegos,
diminutos textículos en sánscrito,
                        y luego
fertilizan la tierra
con clásicos detritus:
              alma mater.

Si eructan,
un erudito dictum
perfuma el campus de sabiduría.

Si, silentes, meditan,
raudos, indescifrables silogismos,
iluminando un universo puro,
recorren sus neuronas fatigadas.

6 / PLAY WITH SPHERES OF DISCOURSE

Buscan
—la mirada perdida en el futuro—
respuesta a los enigmas
eternos:
¿*Qué salario tendré dentro de un año?*
¿*Es jueves hoy?*
               ¿*Cuánto
tardará en derretirse tanta nieve?*

[They are who they are.

Placid, patient, rambling
in little flocks
about the grounds,
               look at them.
Or rather, listen to them:

they moo a diffuse science,
they eat leaves of Pliny
and of lettuce,
they devour hamburgers,
Greek texts,
diminutive texticles in Sanskrit,
               and then
they fertilize the earth
with classic detritus:
               alma mater.

If they belch
an erudite dictum
perfumes the campus with wisdom.

If, silent, they meditate,
swift, indecipherable syllogisms,
illuminating a pure universe,
traverse their fatigued neurons.
They seek
—their gaze lost in the future—
an answer to the enigmas
of all time:
What will my salary be in a year?
Is today Thursday?
               *How long
will it take for all this snow to melt?*]

"Eruditos en campus," which we surmise to have been inspired by González's experiences on university campuses in the United States, follows the pattern, seen in "Los liliputienses" [The Lilliputians] and in other poems, of the fall from the sublime to the ridiculous. Throughout the poem, a code of elevated thought and a rarefied lexicon develop the notion of the university as a place of retirement from worldly concerns, where professors wander about in Socratic dialogue, living and breathing wisdom, classic texts, and higher knowledge. In lines 23–25, the suggestion of their lofty purpose brings this code to its culmination, when they are portrayed as absorbed in solving weighty problems, seeking answers to "los enigmas / eternos." To our surprise and amusement, however, their questions turn out to be those perennial staples of intense academic concern—next year's salary scale and the weather.

Many elements present throughout the poem lead up to the final punch lines. The vision of the university campus as a bucolic refuge from worldly interests overlaps with a view of these professors as cows or sheep. The words "[a]pacibles, pacientes," combined with "rebaños," bring to mind the verb "pacer." A code of animal functions—"mugen," "comen hojas," "fertilizan la tierra," and even the homophonic "textículos"—contrasts with the elevation of the "universo puro" they seek to illuminate. Thus coexisting in the poem and contradicting each other are two distinct levels of operation—that of the disinterested search for knowledge, above worldly concerns, and that of animal survival and material well-being. (González activates the two meanings of "ruminate" in this poem. There are also echoes of the sacred cow endowed with a certain wisdom, as seen in "¡Adiós, «Cordera»!" [Good-bye, Cordera!].)[18] These codes sometimes overlap: in the zeugma "comen hojas de Plinio / y de lechuga," the word "hojas" fits into both spheres of discourse; "futuro" combines a lofty desire to affect the fate of humanity with the more mundane question of the faculty pay scale for the coming year. The poem shows the professors to be operating on a physical, material plane instead of a mental or spiritual one, attributing a vacuousness to certain academic studies as well. Science is "difusa ciencia"; books are "diminutos textículos"; Latin phrases still in use are "detritus"—scattered hackneyed expressions such as "alma mater." The scholars' syllogisms are "indescifrables," and their wisdom is the gas they belch. Thus González demythologizes not just the professors themselves for being ordinary and uninspiring but their supposedly intellectual interests as well.[19]

In many poems of González's second period, systems of meaning are foregrounded and questioned by jarring juxtapositions or, as in "Confesiones," by revealing how a purely verbal construct—a conflation of meanings—generates a seemingly realistic, referential text. Thus González increasingly tends toward ludic expression that deflects attention from the mimetic process and undermines the lyric voice. Such poetry is well-suited to González's fundamental skepticism, as well as to his reticent and self-questioning nature, which makes him hesitant to reveal himself unequivocally. Very importantly, too, such ludic poems reveal the flowering of poetic possibilities he experienced when he allowed himself simply to play with words. But the logical absurdities and juxtapositions of incompatible spheres of discourse that he employs in his ludic poetry reflect not only personal inclinations, the unfolding of his poetic inventiveness, and his disillusionment with the efficacy of words but also the "crisis of meaning" characteristic of postmodernism.[20] Nonsense in many of these poems allows the poet to bracket his speaker's emotions, simultaneously to express them and to withhold them, and thus to indulge in the double-coding typical of postmodernism.[21]

The type of bracketing of communication in which González indulges in "Dato biográfico" and "Confesiones de un joven problemático" is characteristic of much of his later work. With titles such as *Muestra, corregida y aumentada, de algunos procedimientos narrativos y de las actitudes sentimentales que habitualmente comportan* and *Prosemas o menos*, which suggest provisional samplings and approximations rather than the "real thing," he brackets entire books. Various other poems from "Poesías sin sentido" employ joking as a means of making possible types of poetic expression that would be impermissible otherwise. In "Oda a la noche o letra para tango" [Ode to the night, or lyrics for a tango] (p. 309) González celebrates the wonder and mystery of the night sky while at the same time recognizing in the poem the impossibility of straightforward lyric expression in the 1970s.[22] The title itself presents a logical dilemma that like the poem both affirms and denies, since it brings within one framework two incompatible spheres of discourse—the classical ode (reminiscent of Fray Luis) and the popular, and sentimental, tango lyric. The "o" of the title is ambiguous, denoting both equivalence and disparity. Thus the title violates distinctions between categories of poetic discourse and creates the nonsense of disorder. The poem echoes Machado's celebration of Soria by night yet simultaneously denies the possibility of such a celebration:

>   en los tiempos que corren
>   como escuálidos galgos sobre el mundo,
>   definitivamente eres un lujo
>   que ha pasado de moda.
>
>   [in the times that course
>   like emaciated greyhounds through the world,
>   you are indeed a luxury
>   that has gone out of style.]

To celebrate the night, then, González must resort to jokes and play. In characterizing the sky as a top hat (significantly, "una chistera") that has gone out of style, he acknowledges the effect of artistic fashion on our perception of nature, thus recalling Oscar Wilde's famous dictum that nature imitates art (an observation González quotes in the prologue to his *Poemas: Edición del autor*).[23]

The last stanza of the poem is full of puns and other verbal play: when he returns at night—a visionary poet, inebriated as much by his "noche de copas" [night of drinks] as by the "noche de copa" [high-hat night] that he celebrates—he carries the night both *in* his head, in his memory of Machado and of other poetic celebrations, and *on* his head; he simultaneously tips his hat (bidding farewell to the physical night that he witnesses) and raises his glass in a toast "dedicado" [dedicated], he tells the night, "a tus brillos y a mi sombra." The latter phrase, like the title, embodies two contradictory meanings, one metaphorical ("to your splendor and my insignificance") and one literal and physical ("to your lights and my shadow or image"), the first involving a relationship of contrast, the second, one of complementarity. The poem as a whole is thus a lovely joke and a magic trick with a top hat, yet at the same time the text manages to capture beautifully the affinity and wonder one feels when contemplating the nighttime sky. Perhaps this double nature itself is its trick.

The poem "A la poesía" [To poetry] (p. 297) is another poetic joke, a kind of Möbius strip in verse, in which the speaker plays on the literal and figurative meanings of the expression "tomarle el pelo a uno" [to pull someone's leg (lit., someone's hair)], combining it with the literary convention that portrays poetry as a woman. He intends to "tomarle el pelo a la poesía" [pull poetry's leg], which he characterizes as a beautiful blonde, but ends up the victim of her joke when she gradually turns into a mocking brunette.

In the preceding examples, González's demythologizing combinations of spheres of discourse are aimed at bourgeois customs, literary and social clichés, and even at his own persona. Another type of demythologizing combination that receives special emphasis in González's recent work *Prosemas o menos* is that of the spiritual and the material. The section of *Prosemas o menos* titled "Teoelegía y moral" [Theoelegy and morals], because of the subject matter of many of its poems, offers several examples of the juxtaposition of such realms of meaning. In this portion of his work, the poet combines the human and the divine and applies mundane reasoning and earthly laws of physics to great religious mysteries. "El Cristo de Velázquez" [Velázquez's Christ] (p. 345) transforms the painter's version of Christ on the Cross into a "[b]anderillero desganado" [reluctant banderillero] who has challenged death and failed. The central Christian myth, supposedly a divinely inspired event of triumph over death, becomes instead a display of human bravado, "una aventura absurda, bella y triste, / que aún estremece a los aficionados" [an absurd, beautiful, and sad adventure, / that still thrills the aficionados] (p. 345). The depiction of Christ as a petty bullfighter and of those moved by his crucifixion as "aficionados" undermines the notion of his death and resurrection as a watershed event of unique significance. Underscoring the human scale of the event is the reference to the power of art; it is Velázquez's brush, making "la apariencia de la vida" [the appearance of life] "florecer sobre tu piel" [flower upon your skin], that resurrects Christ, if only in deceptive appearance. The "piadoso pincel" [compassionate brush] that "lavó con leves / algodones de luz tu carne herida" [washed with gentle / cotton balls of light your wounded flesh] to produce this seeming resurrection suggests, in González's recasting of the Velázquez figure, the cultural practice of embellishing dead bodies in order to rewrite history, in a sense, or at least to undo the worst of its sting.

The relationship between González's poem and Velázquez's painting is similar to the one between Velázquez's *Toilet of Venus* and a reworking of that painting by Mel Ramos in 1975. Gaggi chooses Ramos's work as an example of pop art's tendency to reproduce images, to be, in fact (as Lawrence Alloway contends), "about signs and sign-systems." Gaggi describes Ramos's Venus as a reworking of the Velázquez masterpiece in a style borrowed from soft-core pornography. Gaggi views the juxtaposition of the two versions of Venus as providing critical distance from both.[24] Likewise, González's superimposition of bullfighter over Christ creates critical distance from Velázquez's painting as well as from González's poem.

González's portrayal of Christ in this poem, moreover, violates certain unspoken norms of categorization of the human and divine, for although Christ can descend to the human level (and in fact assumes many forms in popular tradition), the placing of an ordinary human being in the supreme role of Christ seems sacrilegious. González's poem, then, both secularizes Christ and suggests that he did not elude death but lives on only in other people's memories. The poem thus portrays not only the death of Christ but also the death of God. In keeping with the section's title, "Teoelegía y moral," the text is therefore an elegy for the divine,[25] calling into question one of the "metanarratives of modernity"—the Christian story of "humanity's final redemption from the original Adamic sin."[26]

González's "El Cristo de Velázquez," finally, parallels other postmodernist works in appropriating a previous work within its borders. As Gaggi points out, George Segal in 1967 created a sculptural tableau that incorporated a real Mondrian painting within its frame, leading to questions about the ethics of one artwork permanently appropriating another. Just as "Mondrian's work will not exist as itself again,"[27] so Velázquez's painting will never be viewed in quite the same way again by those who have read González's poem. González's appropriation of Velázquez in turn affects our reading of his own poem as well as our view of the painting. In reframing Velázquez's painting, he acknowledges the possibility that his own work may be reframed and thus become part of an endless *mise en abîme.*

The poem "Dos versiones del Apocalipsis" [Two versions of the Apocalypse] (p. 347) secularizes the divine in quite a different way from that employed in "El Cristo de Velázquez." The poem consists of two prose paragraphs, each one describing, in expository or journalistic fashion, the attitudes of two groups of people who have formulated ideas about the end of the world—"los apocalípticos optimistas" [optimistic apocalyptics] and the "apocalípticos pesimistas" [pessimist apocalyptics]. Unlike "El Cristo de Velázquez," the poem is subtly humorous and nonsensical. The tone is reportorial, with such phrases as "Es más" [What's more], "en cambio" [on the other hand], and "por lo tanto" [therefore] conveying a certain logic of exposition. The careful attribution of sources is suggested by the words "según ellos" [according to them] and "en su opinión" [in their opinion] and by the use of direct quotations to back up reported attitudes. Yet the prose of the poem draws the reader into a vertiginous disquisition of idle and baroque speculation about the end of the world. The text's discourse suggests in various ways a kind of twentieth-century scholasticism in which one of the grandest and most terrifying themes of art and religion has degenerated into flippant pseudoscientific technospeak expressing shallow group thinking. The tidy categories, "apocalípticos pesimistas" and "apocalípticos optimistas," do not correspond to neat conceptual distinctions between the two groups. The pessimists *fear* an anticipated end of the world, while the optimists consider the end of world to be already in progress and are expectantly awaiting instead "*El Fin del Fin del Mundo*" [The end of the end of the world]. Thus rather than being clearly in opposition to one another, both groups view negatively what they each define as the Apocalypse, and the optimism and pessimism of each is directed toward different outcomes.

Furthermore, such expressions as "error de cálculo divino" [divine mistake in calculation] and "«Ya va siendo hora»" [It's getting to be high time] place the end of the world on a colloquial, human, technological, and practical bureaucratic plane, contradicting the Apocalypse as an intentional, awe-inspiring act of a higher being whom humans are incapable of judging. Applying contemporary language to an ancient theme in an almost nonsensical fashion, the text calls into question the naïvely confident assertions of these "apocalípticos." The text's application of commonsense discourse and logical explanations to the topic of the end of the world challenges as well the more traditional and grandiose version of apocalyptic thinking itself.

Another poem from "Teoelegía y moral" that plays with religious discourse, "Invitación de Cristo" [The invitation of Christ] (p. 349) reads as follows:

6 / Play with Spheres of Discourse   133

>   Dijo:
>   >   Comed, éste es mi cuerpo.
>   >   Bebed, ésta es mi sangre.
>
>   Y se llenó su entorno por millares
>   de hienas,
>   de vampiros.
>
>   [He said:
>   >   Eat, this is my body.
>   >   Drink, this is my blood.
>
>   And all around him filled up with thousands
>   of hyenas,
>   of vampires.]

Though the poem has been interpreted as anticlerical (the "hienas" and "vampiros" being the parasitic and predatory clergy),[28] it may also be construed simply as a literal interpretation of metaphorical discourse: when Christ offers his flesh and his blood for consumption, his prime takers, following a certain logic, turn out to be bloodsucking bats and carrion-eating hyenas.

A similar example is a fragment of "Máximas mínimas" [Minimal maxims] (p. 356), where González focuses on the purely physical aspect of levitation:

>   Nadie más impotente y ridículo que Satanás tratando
>   >   de arrastrar al Infierno a un santo que levita.
>
>   Hasta que encontró el modo: lo puso boca abajo.
>
>   [There's no one more impotent and ridiculous than Satan trying
>   >   to drag down to Hell a saint who is levitating.
>
>   Until he found the way: he turned him upside down.]

By portraying Satan as solving a problem of practical mechanics, the poem casts a ridiculous light not only on the extreme spiritualism associated with levitation but on literal interpretations of religious mysteries as well.

Still another poem, "Palabras del Anticristo" [Words of the Antichrist] (p. 346), counterposes the materialist vision of the Antichrist to the spiritual message of Christ. The poem inverts that message to present its antonymic version. According to the words of this Antichrist, self-deception and death are the realities of humanity, and Christ is a child of human fears:

>   Yo soy
>   la mentira y la muerte

(es decir, la verdad última
del hombre).

Sé que no hay esperanza,
pero te dije:
    espera,
con el único fin
de envenenar la vida
con la letal ponzoña de los sueños.

No hubo resurrección.

Una gran piedra
selló mi tumba,
    en la que sólo había
silencio y sombra.
Nada hallaron en ella, salvo sombra y silencio.

Yo soy el que no fue
ni será nunca:

en la oquedad vacía,
la turbia resonancia de tu miedo.

[I am
the falsehood and the death
(that is to say, the ultimate truth
of humanity).

I know that there is no hope,
but I told you:
    hope,
with the sole purpose
of poisoning your life
with the lethal venom of dreams.

There was no resurrection.

A great stone
sealed my tomb,
    in which there was only
silence and shadow.
They found nothing in it, save shadow and silence.

I am he who was not
nor ever shall be:

in the hollow emptiness,
the confused resonance of your fear.]

The poem's speaker seems to be Christ denying his own message. But if, as the title suggests, he is instead the Antichrist, his words, according to biblical references, are lies and are not to be trusted. The text is thus not a totally stable one but leaves us puzzling over alternatives. Is González portraying Christ as an Antichrist, or suggesting that to deny Christ is to lie? The poem embodies the notion that words always contain and evoke their opposites. By confronting us with the ultimate undecidability of his text, González here calls into question not only the truth of religious mysteries but of the poetic word itself. And just as he demythologizes God in the poems of *Teoelegía y moral*, here he demythologizes, in addition to the Word and the Word made Flesh, his own role as creator of texts.

With few exceptions, these examples treat not religious experience but religious texts. In so doing, these poems embody the appropriation of earlier texts and images that is so typical of postmodernism. As poems examined earlier in this chapter confirm, in this period within González's work, secular texts also lend themselves to the mixing of spheres and levels of discourse and to the resultant nonsensical or demystifying effects. Another example of this phenomenon in "Máximas mínimas" (p. 356) describes the nobility of spirit of Lilliputians:

> Los liliputienses, revelando una grandeza de espíritu
>   que para sí quisieran las razas más altas, no hacen
> leña del árbol caído.
>
> Hacen palillos de dientes.
>
> [The Lilliputians, revealing a largesse of spirit
>   that taller races envy
> don't make firewood out of fallen trees.
>
> They make toothpicks.]

In this joke-poem, the humor resides in the fall from the sublime to the ridiculous. From the moving image of tiny beings with largesse of spirit, the poem descends abruptly to portray them as akin to the taller races, only smaller, like the toothpicks they produce from the fallen trees. The poem's effectiveness depends on the contrast between the elevated tone and noble spirit of the Lilliputians and the humble, mundane nature of the objects they manufacture, as well as on a concise play between what is in proportion and what is not.

Our examination of these poems from González's second period reveals the fundamental role of the play with spheres of discourse within his poetry, as well as the variety of verbal text-generating mechanisms he employs. Over and over again, González both proposes a vision and tells us not to trust it.

At times his bracketing techniques allow him also to proffer and to withhold communication simultaneously or to express, but only provisionally, sentiments that are ideological or lyrical in nature. There is a measure in each of these poems that is nonsensical and that mocks and exposes the ideological or lyrical elements that, at the same time, convince and captivate us. As with the play with logic seen in chapter 5, the only way to explain these poems may be through Susan Stewart's theory that nonsense is a way of moving between commonsense meaning systems. She calls nonsense a "marginal or liminal activity," a "discourse about discoursing rather than about any 'real life' content." "To engage in nonsense," she says, "is not only to engage in a state of transition, it is also to engage in an exploration of the nature of transition."[29]

Stewart's views are compatible with various theories of postmodernism under discussion in the last few years. And González's play with spheres of discourse, as this chapter has shown, allows him to raise some of the fundamental issues associated with postmodernism—the distance between art and life, the incorporation of artworks by other artworks, questions of roles and of the identity of the self—as well as to carry out his own appropriation of cultural texts and images of the past using the ironic and playful approach characteristic of postmodernist works. The ideas of Ihab Hassan shed light on González's discourse play. Hassan views the entire postmodernist movement as a period of artistic anarchy that contrasts with the "intense, elitist, self-generated orders in times of crisis" of modernism. Hassan suggests that through this contemporary artistic disorder, we have some chance of finding language adequate for addressing our unimaginable situation.[30] González's ludic poetry clearly forces us in several ways to consider questions regarding the exact nature of poetic art. By juxtaposing incongruous types of discourse, by creating poetic puns that highlight the ambiguity of words, by constantly forcing us to waver between poetry as communication of some idea or feeling separate from the text and our awareness of how the text is generated by quirks of language and by clichés of discourse rather than by real-life situations, the poet requires his reader to reconsider the reading process and makes impossible a traditional approach to his texts. His ludic poetry is an end in itself, but it may also be part of a postmodern artistic anarchy whose purpose is to pave the way for the birth of new poetic orders in the future.

7
Literary Tradition versus Speaker Experience in the Poetry of Angel González

A significant feature of González's turn toward the ludic in his second period is his tendency to play with genres and literary traditions. As was mentioned earlier, he himself divides his work into two phases, the first based on experiences and the second on schemes.[1] This division indicates González's growing awareness of literature as a metatextual system and of the individual poem as a product of previous texts and conventions rather than of concrete objects or events in the world—an appreciation he shared with many of his contemporaries. His distinction between the schematic and the experiential reflects a fundamental issue of twentieth-century linguistic and literary theory, that of the referentiality of language: its capacity, or lack thereof, for capturing facets of reality exterior to itself.[2]

Over time, González's titles have come to embody his increasing attention to literary systems. Such headings as *Procedimientos narrativos*, "Poemas elegíacos" [Elegiac poems], and "Metapoesía" [Metapoetry] have gradually replaced those that point to direct personal experience—*Aspero mundo*, "*Aquí, Madrid, mil novecientos*," "Capital de provincia" [Provincial capital], or "La lluvia" [Rain], to name a few. González, as he himself has noted, has given new emphasis to "lo convencional y formulario" [the conventional and the formulaic] since 1969.[3] Concomitantly, his critics have begun to approach his work from the standpoint of its relationship to the literary and linguistic systems of which it is a part.[4] His poems have increasingly highlighted the role of literary tradition in their own generation. In a growing number of texts, self-reflexive emphasis on the transformation of received literary conventions challenges the illusion of a poet communicating a vision of reality he shares with his readers.

It is in *Tratado de urbanismo* that González declares "la inutilidad de todas las palabras." At this decisive point in his poetic career, he turned more and more toward jokes, verbal play, and parody. He thus intensified his incursions into what Susan Stewart identifies as the "ludic genres." In lessening his reliance on personal experiences as a source of poetic material, he increased the mimetic distance between his texts and what Stewart calls the "text of 'reality'." His poems increasingly exhibit the hallmarks of the ludic as described by Stewart. As she points out, ludic texts bear "paradoxical messages regarding their own existence." They violate commonsense interpretive procedures, "either by presenting paradoxes of framing, or by juxtaposing two or more universes of discourse and thereby erasing a commonsense context." They can be created when two incompatible provinces of meaning, each having its own set of rules for interpretation, are brought together within the same frame, as I showed in chapter 6, or when a metatextual message conflicts with a textual one. For Stewart, the procedures that create ludic texts are intertextual because they are based on systems of classification. And they "tend towards nonsense," which, according to Stewart, makes them both critical and self-critical, both change and about change, and "an aspect of and . . . about the ongoing nature of social process."[5]

Metafictional (or metapoetic) elements often play an important role in the creation of ludic texts. Stewart describes metafiction as follows:

> Metafiction traverses and manipulates not only the domain of common sense, but the domains of other kinds of fictions as well. Its violation of commonsense principles of order, its foregrounding of the cultural nature of signification, its exposure of systems of interpretation as systems, its comments upon the nature of communicative modes, give it its status as a metafiction—a fiction about fictions—a fiction necessarily about itself.

Any metafictional text, because its context is "impossible, hermetic, a place that cannot happen that is the fiction itself," has, Stewart suggests, an "intimate connection with nonsense."[6]

Although González eventually acknowledged the significance of metapoetry in his work by titling a section of *Muestra* "Metapoesía," even his earliest work includes occasional metapoetic textual play. "Me falta una palabra," from *Aspero mundo*, parodies the aestheticism, stereotypically associated with Juan Ramón Jiménez, of the poet who tries to exclude the world while seeking the word, unaware that the world has in fact given him his true subject. Because of its first-person speaker, the poem is not just González's criticism of the aesthete who shuns social concerns but is also a ludic text in which play consists of the contradiction between its speaker's statement that his utterance is not a poem and the fact that his very statement makes up a poetic text. Or as Stewart would say, a negative statement made on one level implies a contradictory metastatement on another. The speaker denies the existence of a poem, but the reader sees in the combina-

7 / Literary Tradition versus Speaker Experience

tion of speaker's voice and authorial supervoice a poem about poetry-making, a poem within a poem. "Me falta una palabra" also plays with the notion of authorial intentionality and raises questions of the reader's role. In a sense the text undermines its own anti-aestheticism by giving attention as much to aesthetic matters as to social concerns.

Though present from his first book on, metapoetical play and the conscious and purposeful adoption of literary traditions as schematic bases for his poems assumed greater importance during the sixties. Many of his early poems, it is apparent in retrospect, were unconsciously influenced by poetic conventions (he himself has called these texts "muy literarios"[7] [very literary]). But by 1965 he had explicitly begun to express tension between actual experiences and categories of discourse and to wrestle with the difficulty of overcoming conventions to express immediate reality. The five-poem collection *Palabra sobre palabra*, published in that year, shows an awareness of how the most personal emotions are shaped by names our language gives us, categories we receive from our society, and literary traditions that mold our expression. A brief examination of some of these poems is warranted.

Three of the poems from the collection include the word "palabra" [word] in their title. In "La palabra" (pp. 171–73) González's speaker considers the word "amor" [love], first pronounced thousands of years ago, then passed down through its multiple manifestations in life, art, and literature:

>Pronunciada primero,
>luego escrita,
>la palabra pasó de boca en boca,
>........................
>fue tallada en madera,
>.................
>y llegó hasta nosotros
>impresa y negra, viva
>tras un largo pasaje por los siglos
>llamados de oro,
>..............

>[First pronounced,
>then written,
>the word passed from mouth to mouth,
>................................
>it was carved in wood,
>.................
>and it reached us
>printed and black, alive
>after a long journey through the centuries
>known as golden,
>.............]

Pure sentiment, free from the mediation of language, is in the present day no longer attainable: "Retrotraerse a un sentimiento puro, / imaginar un mundo en sus pre-nombres, / es imposible ahora" [To regress to a pure sentiment, / to imagine a world in its pre-names, / is impossible now]. The speaker's dependence on a collective vocabulary is in conflict with the uniqueness of his love and his will. And his insistence on the stable significance of the terms we inherit with our language is undermined when he closes the poem with the words "porque quiero" [because I want to; because I love], whose double meaning underlines the instability of language, as puns in general tend to do.[8]

The next poem, "Palabras casi olvidadas" (pp. 174–75) [Almost-forgotten words], similarly plays the immediacy of experience against the timeworn words we must rely on to express it:

> esas viejas palabras
>   *—felicidad, misterio ... —*
> que hoy vuelven a mis manos
> ....
> y que ahora escribo
> ....
>   sin vergüenza,
> ....
>
> [those old words
>   *—happiness, mystery ... —*
> that today come back to my hands
> ....
> and that I now write
> ....
>   without shame,
> ....]

Finally, "Las palabras inútiles" (pp. 178–79), discussed in chapter 4, reworks a time-honored poetic staple, the notion of ineffability. Affirming the inadequacy of words, the speaker of the poem yearns instead for the immediacy of the kiss—yet nevertheless chooses to express himself verbally. As in "Palabras casi olvidadas," the literary dimension—"poetic" words in italics—is framed. The italicized words about the poetic search deceptively make the surrounding text seem closer to life, more like experience instead of literature. The poet thus appears to be inside the poem, not outside as we know him to be. Borders between text and experience are thus blurred.

In all three of these poems, González creates a poetic game through tension between an emotion and its linguistic expression. His portrayal of words as inadequate and stale creates by contrast the illusion that the love described is immediate and fresh. Yet in the case of "Las palabras inútiles," his poem itself belongs to the category that in the poem he disavows: verbal expressions of love. His poem thus tells us that it is not a love poem, but rather love itself, which cannot be expressed. He creates a paradoxical text that purports to do on one level what it claims it can't do on another, as well as an infinite regression of images within images within images.

In *Palabra sobre palabra*, then, González turns to the personal concerns of love, but in the context of the individual's struggle between the expression of reality and the words and traditions available to express that reality. These poems incorporate verbal play, but the ludic is here subordinated to the communication of experience.[9] The emphasis on how language shapes experience here serves the poet's own reticent nature and his spirit of solidarity—the poet is a man like all others, not a privileged aristocrat of the word. Yet it is significant that in this moment of transition for González, the word, not love, predominates in the volume's titles.[10]

In *Tratado de urbanismo*, González returned to the social criticism of *Grado elemental*. His title, instead of pointing toward the object of imitation (as did *Aspero mundo*) invites us to focus on his medium. Playing on the concepts of the urban and the urbane, and violating lyric tradition through claiming that the work is a treatise, the title calls double attention to itself. As González has stated, his turn to the urban was a reaction against what he saw as the artificial rural emphasis in some poetry of the period.[11] Thus shaping his poetry to break with lyric traditions, González in *Tratado de urbanismo* initiates his conscious "antipoesía."[12]

Several poems from *Tratado de urbanismo* may be read as both conventional and anticonventional at the same time. "Chatarra" (p. 194) evokes important literary traditions: the elegy, the ruin poem, the memento mori. But the text shocks us with its unpoetic subject matter—junked machinery in place of hand-wrought artifacts or ruins of monumental buildings. The remains described—most likely cars—are made equal by death, like human dead in a graveyard:

> yacen aquí, confusos, desvaídos,
> sumidos en idéntico desprecio,
> disueltos en orín y sal, dejados
> de la mano que un día los creara.

> [here they lie, jumbled, dulled,
> plunged into uniform disregard,
> dissolved in rust and salt, abandoned
> by the hand that one day had created them.]

Eventually fire will return them to "la inercia y la nada minerales" [mineral inertia and nothingness] from which new forms will spring in a kind of apotheosis:

> surgirán otras formas limpias, puras,
> libres acaso para siempre
> del estigma fatal de la chatarra.
>
> [there will arise other clean, pure forms,
> free perhaps forever
> from scrap iron's fatal stigma.]

Numerous religious and cultural myths and clichés associated spiritually with death acquire a material sense here when applied to these junked machines: the word "yacen," linked to funerary inscriptions; ritual purification by fire; reference to the Creator ("la mano que un día los creara"—but here human hands); and transformation into new, pure forms. González thus creates a similarity between the demise of soulless machines and the death of the human body. By personifying the metallic remains, he inevitably calls into question the higher significance we mythically attach to human corpses. Andrew P. Debicki notes something similar in another González poem, "Muerte de máquina"[13] [Death of a machine].

Other poems from *Tratado de urbanismo* likewise use literary traditions and conventions antipoetically or create metapoetry in other ways. A poem of awakening, "Los sábados, las prostitutas madrugan mucho para estar dispuestas," captures not joyous rebirth but routine and sordid debasement and physical decay. "La paloma," discussed in chapter 4 for its unconsciously produced political message, is nevertheless also a metapoetic text. The presence of the lyrics of a popular song within its closed field draws attention to the poetic surface and to the arbitrary generation of its imagery. The distinction between form and content is thus subverted, and the poem is unmasked as a fiction. Borrowing Perloff's terminology, we might declare that "La paloma" is characterized by "unmediated presentation" and by indeterminacy. Like much recent poetry, it remains, at least in part, an indecipherable enigma, its poetic surface taking precedence over its function as the communication of an epiphany or higher reality.[14]

The opening poem of González's next book, *Breves acotaciones para una biografía* (p. 237), offers a slyly introduced metapoetic paradox similar to that found in "Me falta una palabra." The speaker in "A veces" [At times] is again a poet. Comparing writing verse to sexual intercourse, he complains that poems—like orgasms—just won't come sometimes. For confirmation he quotes Vallejo, then states that Vallejo was lying:

7 / LITERARY TRADITION VERSUS SPEAKER EXPERIENCE

> Lo expresaba muy bien César Vallejo:
> «Lo digo, y no me corro».
>
> Pero él disimulaba.
>
> [César Vallejo expressed it very well:
> "I say it, and I don't ejaculate."
>
> But he was only fooling.]

Like Epimenides the Cretan, who emerged from a cave to declare that all Cretans were liars, this speaker casts doubt on his own words with his final assertion. Through suggesting that Vallejo's words are untruthful, he raises the possibility that he too may be lying. He thus leaves his reader in a state of uncomfortable suspension between belief and disbelief, something not at all unusual for his poetry. On another level, González again draws attention to the generation of his own text. If taken in context, Vallejo's words would probably be read, "I say it, and I stand firm." By using Vallejo's words in a new context as a kind of encapsulation of his own comparison of poems to orgasms, González creates a pun and highlights the complex interplay between reading and writing.

During the 1970s, when González's tendency toward metapoetry fully blossomed,[15] he created several poems that take as their subject the genres to which they supposedly belong. Such poems are ludic because they telescope form and content onto the same plane, thus blurring the distinction between a class and its members. "Elegía pura" [Pure elegy] (p. 276), from *Muestra*, as an elegy devoid of content, evokes all the traditions of its genre but violates its principle of commemoration of something beyond the poem. Similarly, "Egloga" [Eclogue] (p. 251) from *Procedimientos narrativos*, supposedly a pastoral poem, is in reality "about" the conventions of the pastoral genre.

González's intensified awareness, in the 1970s, of the role of literary tradition in shaping poems can be better understood if we apply to his texts certain theories of poetry advanced at around the same time. In particular, Michael Riffaterre's description of the reading process in *Semiotics of Poetry* (1978) strikingly resembles González's reference to experience versus schemes and provides a useful approach to these poems. For Riffaterre, reading is a dialectical process that begins when the reader attempts to discover the text's mimetic, or representational, meaning. But in Riffaterre's view, a poem will always violate the very grammar it evokes on the mimetic level. The reader perceives such "ungrammaticalities," as Riffaterre calls them, precisely because of his or her prior assimilation of linguistic and cultural conventions.

The text demands a second, "hermeneutic," reading, which takes place on the level of semiosis and through which the reader integrates the poem anew by discovering a new grammar compatible with the schematic base of the poem. As Riffaterre says, the text, read semiotically, is a "variation or modulation of one structure—thematic, symbolic, or whatever—and this sustained relation to one structure constitutes the significance" of the work.[16] A semiotic reading, then, depends on the reader's perceptions of the elements of the text, not in relation to what is commonly perceived as "reality" but in relation to each other and to elements of linguistic, cultural, and literary systems beyond the work. In such poems as "Egloga" and "Elegía pura," the text's relationship to a larger linguistic system becomes in many ways the focus. González incorporates and transforms specific literary traditions, playing on particular conventions of genre and on written and unwritten codes of lyric composition. A study of the way in which he transforms these conventions offers insight into the interplay of "experience" and "schemes," or, to use Riffaterre's almost synonymous terminology, of the mimetic and semiotic dimensions of poetry.

Before discussing how González transforms certain pastoral and elegiac genres in "Egloga" and "Elegía pura," I shall consider in relation to lyric conventions one of his titles from this period: *Muestra, corregida y aumentada, de algunos procedimientos narrativos y de las actitudes sentimentales que habitualmente comportan*. González's title seems to indicate that the book is a collection of poems based not on experience but on conventional literary categories. It points directly to semiosis, thrusting the work and itself into a relationship with works that precede and follow it, evoking as context a semiotic system and echoing theories of intertextuality, of literature as an imitation not of nature but of other literature.[17] In referring to and describing the book it heads, the title seems to play a role analogous to the name Riffaterre gave his book, *Semiotics of Poetry*. By presenting the volume as a catalog, González underplays poetry as an imitation of experience and emphasizes poetry's role in transforming literary conventions. But ironically our previous assimilation of those very conventions makes us reject this literal, straightforward interpretation. Despite its precise, scientific appearance and its seemingly referential, descriptive function, the title violates literary norms, or in Riffaterre's terminology, is ungrammatical, and therefore cannot be taken literally.

The title's ungrammaticality surfaces as soon as we consider the conventions of lyric poetry. In length alone it deviates from easily observable traditions, exemplified within twentieth-century poetry by such titles as *Soledades* [Songs of solitude], by Antonio Machado, *Ninfeas* [Water lilies], by Juan Ramón Jiménez, *Cántico* [Song of praise], by Jorge Guillén, and *Presagios* [Presages], by Pedro Salinas, to name but a few. More importantly, its objective, analytical language violates the expectation of subjectivity with which a reader approaches a book of lyric poems. Its characterization of the book as a sample and of the emotions expressed within it as "habitual," furthermore, conflicts with the conventional perception of lyricism as capturing unique momentary psychic states and experiences.[18] The adjective "narrativos" is yet another ungrammatical note in the title of a collection of lyric poems. Even more significantly, the title reduces the emotions expressed in the poem to features or extensions of traditional poetic form, thus reversing the representational convention of form at the service of content. The title implies that form determines emotional content rather than the reverse—form as mimetic vehicle for capturing or mirroring experiences or realities that preceded the creation of the text.

The ungrammaticality of the title of González's book poses a challenge to his readers. Unable to reconcile their expectations of lyricism (and their conviction that the poems, many of which are in the first person, do have subjective content) with the work's claim to be simply a catalog of conventions without personal meaning, they must try to integrate text and title on a different level. As readers, they must use their sense of poetic convention, in fact, to surpass a literal acceptance of the title's assertion that the poems are purely conventional. They must reinterpret the title, which can come to attain significance as an example of what Carlos Bousoño calls the "objetivación como disfraz del yo" [objectification as a disguise of the self], that is, as a variant of "minilocuencia" ["miniloquence"], effacement of the ego aimed at the avoidance of bombastic grandiloquence.[19] Such a reading is supported by a statement González has made regarding his use of irony in earlier volumes, in which he reveals his desire to avoid immodest displays of sentiment: "[L]a ironía facilita un tono de distanciamiento que aligera la peligrosa carga sentimental de ciertas actitudes, algo importante para una persona que, como yo, intenta escribir poesía desde sus experiencias conservando un mínimo de pudor"[20] [Irony facilitates a tone of distancing that lightens the dangerous emotional charge of certain attitudes, something important for persons like me, who try to write poetry from their experiences while maintaining a minimum of reserve]. Viewed from this perspective, the title (like all those from his second period) is evidence of understatement and of authorial modesty, as well as of the narrator's ironic detachment from his own emotions and his self-portrayal as mechanically dehumanized.[21]

The title, thus, is apprehended first one way, then another, yet our reading of it never achieves finality, a fact characteristic, for Riffaterre, of the reading process. As he stresses, ungrammaticalities that point to interpretation are never completely obliterated but remain as obstacles, leading us to waver back and forth between levels. We perform, he says, "a seesaw scanning of the text, compelled by the very duality of the signs—ungrammatical as mimesis, grammatical within the significance [semiotic] network." Significance, he states, disappears and reappears in a kind of "semiotic circularity" that characterizes "the practice of signification known as poetry" and explains the endless fascination of the poetic text.[22] We can finally only integrate González's title and his text as somehow questioning the basis of the act of poetic creation, as reflecting his distinction between "experience" and "schemes." Thus although we reject the book as simply a catalog, we never lose our awareness of the importance of literary tradition in the production of the texts it contains, and though we accept the work as being about poetry itself, we also see it as being about the poet and his emotions. The title, then, plays with the reader. Play also characterizes the poems in the book, for whether serious or frivolous, the poetic text, in *Muestra* as always, is a poetic game.

The poem "Egloga" is outwardly descriptive. Its speaker, recalling the convent where, as he says, "Me eduqué" [I was educated], refers to typical convent routines: Thursday visiting hours, Sunday bells, afternoon outings in the countryside. Many details—"las tapias" [the wall fences], "una carretera sombreada de chopos" [a road shaded by poplars], "las zarzas" [the blackberry bushes]—give consistency to what seems to be an eyewitness portrait of a particularized setting. The mimetic aspects of the poem, however, are undermined and overshadowed by a myriad of details that make sense only on a semiotic level. The mimetic, created by "variation and multiplicity," according to Riffaterre,[23] is superseded by the semiotic, the schematic, where details have meaning only in relationship to other elements of a system.

The poem's semiotic level emerges from various aspects found throughout. From the first stanza forward, ungrammaticalities undermine our acceptance of the poem as literal description, beginning with the word "inteligentes" [intelligent] in line 2. Here, as in the case of the phrase "Aquí no pasa nada" [Here nothing is happening; here nothing passes] in "Elegía pura," two different sets of clichés are evoked, activating simultaneously two opposing acceptations of the word. In the context of the opening reference to the convent as a place of learning, intelligence connotes wisdom acquired through study and transmissible to students. Such a vision, however, is incompatible with the succeeding portrayal of the nuns as children bribed or rewarded by adults with offers of coins and candy. Along with the verb "se exhibían" [they were exhibited] the rewards suggest that the nuns are clever children on exhibition, or even clever monkeys, not intelligent teachers:

> Me eduqué en una comunidad religiosa
> que contaba con monjas muy inteligentes.
> Los jueves se exhibían en los claustros.
> —*Dame la manita,*
>   les decían los visitantes

    ofreciéndoles bombones y monedas.
    Pero ellas no daban nada: al contrario,
    pedían continuamente.

    [I was educated in a religious community
    that had some very intelligent nuns.
    On Thursdays they were on view in the cloisters.
    —*Give me your little hand,*
        visitors said to them
    offering them bonbons and coins.
    But they didn't give anything: on the contrary,
    they continually begged.]

A second ungrammaticality, similar to the bifurcation of meaning of "inteligentes," occurs with the forms of the verb *dar*, which in the context of the phrase *"Dame la manita"* means "to accept," but in lines 7 and 8 signifies the opposite. The text, thus riddled with departures from linguistic logic, forces us to consider it as something other than a straightforward reflection of convent reality.

 Throughout the rest of the poem, implied comparisons between the nuns and various animals reinforce the image of the convent as housing a species apart. The words "lustrosas" and "lamiéndose los velos" [licking their veils] in stanza 2, strangely unmotivated as straight description, are recognized as belonging to a feline descriptive system when viewed in the light of stanza 3, which inescapably evokes a cat depositing its prey at the feet of its master:

    En domingo tocaban las campanas.
    Era hermoso mirarlas, tan lustrosas,
    lamiéndose los velos cuando en marzo
    el sol de mediodía presagiaba tormenta.

    Había una, sobre todo, que era muy cazadora.
    Perseguía a las niñas más allá de las tapias
    y las traía sujetas por el pelo
    hasta los breves pies de la madre abadesa.

    [On Sunday they would ring the bells.
    It was lovely to look at them, so lustrous,
    licking their veils when in March
    the noonday sun foreshadowed a storm.

    There was one, especially, who was quite a huntress.
    She would pursue the little girls beyond the walls
    and would pull them back by the hair
    to the trim feet of the Mother Superior.]

Stanza 4 continues the comparison of nuns to animals. Here the description of the sisters' vespertine walks begins naturalistically, but by the end of the stanza they have been transformed into sheep. Their voices become "un tierno balido gregoriano," and they scatter at the sound of a car's horn like a bleating flock:

> Al caer de la tarde paseaban
> por una carretera sombreada de chopos.
> Se cruzaban con carros y rebaños,
> caminaban ligeras, y el murmullo
> de sus voces
> el viento lo llevaba y lo traía
> volando por los campos
> entre esquilas y abejas,
> como un tierno balido gregoriano.
> Si oían a lo lejos la bocina de un coche,
> se dispersaban hacia las cunetas,
> ruidosas, excitadas y confusas.
>
> [When evening fell they would stroll
> down a road shaded by poplars.
> They would pass carts and flocks,
> they walked lightly, and the wind
> took the murmur of their voices
> flying back and forth
> through the fields
> amid sheep bells and bees,
> like a delicate Gregorian baa.
> If they heard in the distance an automobile horn,
> they would scatter to the side of the road,
> noisy, excited, and confused.]

In stanza 5, they become birds:

> Cuando el aire
> quedaba limpio de polvo y estrépito,
> se las podía ver, al fin tranquilas,
> picoteando moras en las zarzas.
>
> [When the air
> was clear of dust and din,
> you could see them, calm at last,
> pecking at blackberries in the bushes.]

The final stanza completes this series of images with the nuns returning to their cells like escaped birds that without prodding go miraculously back to their cages, instead of claiming the freedom within their reach:

7 / Literary Tradition versus Speaker Experience

> A la hora del ángelus,
> fatigadas y dóciles,
> ellas mismas volvían a las celdas,
> como si las llevase del rosario
> —tironeando dulce y firmemente—
> la omnipresente mano de su Dueño.
>
> [At the hour of the Angelus,
> weary and docile,
> they would return to their cells on their own,
> as if pulled by the rosary
> —that tugged sweetly and firmly—
> in the omnipresent hand of their Master.]

In this final image, the rosary becomes a leash held gently by the hand of God.

González's transformations of nuns into animals provide only part of the poem's semiotic structure. Our conception of that structure expands if we relate the zoomorphic portrayal of the convent's inhabitants to linguistic and literary systems beyond the work. The most important of these is the pastoral tradition, clearly evoked not only by the title but also by the bucolic setting and the reference to sheep, the latter constituting what Northrop Frye has termed the "central archetype of pastoral imagery."[24] A second source of the poem's imagery, also related to the portrayal of nuns as sheep, is the nucleus of religious clichés depicting God as a shepherd and the faithful as His flock.[25] A final commonplace, felt in the initial stanza of the poem, is the characterization of human beings as children in relation to God. These traditions, rather than direct observation or uniquely personal experience, clearly generate much of the poem's imagery.

Certain semantic clusters, furthermore, serve as linguistic bridges between the convent setting and the archetypal topoi just mentioned, explaining as well other images present in the poem. Of particular interest is the relationship between the pastoral and the convent. The rural setting of the particular convent depicted and the idea of the cloister as a place of retirement from the complications of civilization make the association between the two a natural one. But it is the pastoral as an example of a highly conventionalized literary tradition that relates most significantly to the notion of the convent. Both words, "convent" and "convention," derive from the Latin *convenire*, meaning "to come together," and if literary conventions signify the adherence to certain rules or to a prescribed order, convent life is established through regulation, as the allied terms *orden* [order], *regla* [rule], and *hábitos* [habits] suggest.

A further link between the pastoral tradition and the depiction of the convent in the poem concerns the question of freedom versus restriction.

Throughout the poem, beginning with the references in stanza 1 to the cloister that periodically opens and closes and in which the nuns are exhibited like animals in a zoo, suggestions of confinement alternate with glimpses of liberty, hints of natural freedom with allusions to the constraints of domestication. The students who escape beyond the walls are pursued and brought back "sujetas por el pelo," and though the nuns themselves wander afield, their voices taking flight on the wind, at nightfall they return as if on leash. Except for the docile sheep, moreover, the animals to which the nuns are compared—the cat as predator and the bird, frequent symbol of liberty—combine the wild and unfettered with evidence of domestication. The pastoral tradition evoked through the title similarly unites the notions of liberty and confinement, for if in theory the pastoral celebrates freedom from societal restrictions and favors what is wild and natural over what is civilized and restrained, in practice it has often been exceptionally convention-bound and artificial.[26] Thus "Egloga" makes use of literary and linguistic conventions but raises questions that in fact subvert them: To what extent are we prisoners of our conventions and of our beliefs, to what extent children of them? Can we really escape civilization and worldliness, or our heritage and historical circumstances? The poem offers an answer of sorts to the questions it poses. Though largely derived from clichés and from tradition rather than from any kind of fresh, unmediated vision, it nevertheless both renews our perception of convent life and attests to the essential inseparability of individual experience and schematic categories in the production of the literary text.[27] The poem acquires further richness if we consider it a metapoetic document about the poet approaching the writing process. The constant play of restriction and freedom, the wild and the tame, as well as the association between the convent, in its rural setting, and pastoral literary conventions, all suggest the poet's experience as he engages in the creative attempt to portray nature and culture. His imagination allows him to transcend conventional visions and through acrobatics of the imagination to convert an orderly convent into a zoo; yet like the nuns who can only experience illusory freedom from God's control, he is subject to the invisible leash of a larger, all-encompassing social and linguistic order.

"Elegía pura," from *Muestra*, likewise plays on literary traditions and formulas while simultaneously appearing to convey a unique, personal experience of objective reality. In this brief poem, the mimetic aspect is almost overshadowed by the semiotic dimension. Through his title, González once more directs his reader to poetic convention, to literature as part of a system of works. As an elegy, the poem is expected to commemorate referentially the loss of an aspect of reality beyond the speaker, as well as to express the latter's emotional reaction. The adjective "pura," however, deflects attention away from mimesis; instead of making clear what loss is lamented, as

7 / Literary Tradition versus Speaker Experience

do traditional elegiac titles like Jorge Manrique's *Coplas por la muerte de su padre don Rodrigo* [Verses composed at the death of his father Don Rodrigo] or García Lorca's *Llanto por Ignacio Sánchez Mejías*, this title makes us ask how this elegy differs from those that precede and follow it. In fact, the title is self-contradictory in implying that there can be commemoration without a pretext. As the reader continues beyond the title in an initial approach to the text, the search for referential meaning is stymied by obstacle after obstacle:

> Aquí no pasa nada,
> salvo el tiempo:
> irrepetible
> música que resuena,
> ya extinguida,
> en un corazón hueco, abandonado,
> que alguien toma un momento,
> escucha
> y tira.
>
> [Here nothing comes to pass,
> except time:
> unrepeatable
> music that resounds,
> now extinguished,
> in a hollow heart, abandoned,
> that someone takes for a moment,
> listens to
> and throws away.]

The first obstacle encountered in the body of the poem is the opening line itself, since its colloquial tone and its reference to lack of significant activity conflict with the intensity and elevation associated with the serious subject matter of the traditional elegy. The second problem concerns the word "pasa." Purely within the context of the first line, this verb poses no great problem (though the title carries the association of the "passing" of things), but in the context of both first and second lines the word becomes ambiguous, joined in a zeugma to two subjects that give it two different meanings. In the first line we read, "Here nothing comes to pass." The second forces a new meaning out of "pasa," that of time passing. The zeugma draws attention to the words of the text, thwarting a mimetic reading. As readers, we waver between lines and interpretation in the attempt to integrate "nada" and "tiempo," trying to find a consistency that will make referential sense, which depends on words mirroring objective reality beyond the poem. We apply the meaning of "passes" to the first line, coming up with an alternative reading of line 1: "here nothing passes (or escapes)." This new reading engenders in turn the alternative interpretation of line 2, with "salvo" as the first person of *salvar* producing the reading, "I bridge time." This meaning again refers us to the poem's claim to be an elegy, which in its commemorative function does indeed keep experience from passing away completely. Despite the consistency of this reading of the title and the first two lines, however, the earlier interpretations are not obliterated, in part because of the strength, or cliché value, of the set phrase "no pasa nada," here explicit, and its implied, underlying counterpart, "el tiempo pasa."

The third stumbling block for the reader in "Elegía pura" is the opposition between "irrepetible" and "que resuena," reinforced by the further contradiction between the emptiness of the heart portrayed and the music that sounds within it. Finally, the central image of the poem, that of a disembodied heart that may be picked up and then discarded, is itself an ungrammaticality; the heart (as etymology confirms) is traditionally the core of the body around it and the seat of a person's emotions. The image inverts these conventions, giving the reader one more compelling reason to reread the poem in an attempt to find a higher compatibility among elements.

The reader's first consideration for reinterpreting the poem is its title, which combines reference to the classic form for channeling grief with an allusion to "poesía pura," often defined as poetry from which all "nonpoetic" material, such as the anecdote, is removed.[28] Thus the poem is an elegy, but one that has undergone a certain purging: the elimination of the anecdote behind the elegiac emotion. Emptying the elegy of its referential dimension poses a problem inasmuch as the serious subject matter associated with the elegiac tradition would seem to demand that form be subordinate to content, never overshadowing the significance of death. Moreover, this elegy not only eliminates the typical elegiac sense of commemoration but also breaks with formal conventions, eschewing the ritual, formality, and stylization that in the classic elegy provide for the expression of grief. As the title suggests, the poem is an elegy devoid of both aspects of the traditional elegiac model: ritualistic form and commemorative content.

The mimetic reading of "Elegía pura" is thwarted, then, by ambiguity and contradiction, as well as by the way in which the text draws attention to itself as a maverick or deviant example of a class of poems. But despite these ungrammaticalities and stumbling blocks, the reader becomes conscious of expressive features upon rereading. The poem communicates desolation through its constant reiteration of emptiness. The titular reference to purity carries with it the connotation of absence (pure poetry being poetry emptied of anecdote). The words "nada" and "hueco" also connote absence, and "extinguida" and "abandonado" add to absence the suggestion of something previously present. In an inversion of the synecdoche of the part standing for the whole, furthermore, the heart is treated as a part in the absence of the whole, the image of an alien hand picking it up impeding, on a certain level, the metonymic reading of its standing for the whole person. Finally, in the seventh line "alguien" repeats the suggestion of loss of identity that is already abundantly exemplified elsewhere in the poem. To integrate the text on a semiotic level requires recognizing this consistent reiteration of absence.

The poem's collage of imagery can be readily reconciled with the series connoting absence, just described. In the context of "música que resuena," the heart picked up, listened to, and thrown away recalls a seashell that someone finds, puts to the ear, and then discards. This image not only entails emptiness and death where once life flourished (the shell being a dead relic of life) but also evokes the conventional elegiac equation of the sea with death. And in the context of the traditional association between a watch ticking and a heart beating,[29] the action described in the last three lines evokes someone listening for a moment for the sound of a broken watch. The heart as a musical instrument is also evoked, activating the connotation in the word "elegía" of a song or a funereal dirge. All these resonances share a suggestion of absence reinforced by the poem's rhythm, which seems at the end to extinguish itself or to ebb away like the tide.

"Elegía pura" is thus in Michael Riffaterre's terminology powerfully "overdetermined," with reiteration as a central feature. As we have seen, even the title reiterates emptiness by suggesting elegy purged of conventional elegiac characteristics. It is clear, then, that although the initial mimetic meaning is blocked, the reader ultimately succeeds in reintegrating the text on a semiotic level. But because of the pull of mimesis, this reading ultimately fails to achieve finality, a fact that further illustrates Riffaterre's description of the reading process. He suggests that readers, disturbed by ungrammaticalities that "threaten language as representation," repeatedly seek the "safe reality" that mimesis provides.[30] Here that reversion becomes possible if the poem's repetitive signs of loss express the sentiments of an experiencing subject whom we identify as the poet. In keeping with the conventional assumption that lyric poems give voice to the poet's feelings in first person,[31] such a view permits us to interpret the heart, despite its concrete presentation, as a synecdoche for the poet, who becomes the traditional elegiac speaker who has suffered abandonment. Here the speaker not only mourns his lost past but also laments pessimistically the loss of the possibility of remembering, thus reworking the traditional elegiac characteristic of commemoration and triumph over forgetfulness. His memories are subject to death, as is his experience. Finally, he laments his own expression of mourning, since his elegy is as ephemeral as his experience and his memories: all survive only briefly through the attention of a reader before being abandoned again, on the sands of time, as it were.

The reading process that this short poem can elicit is, as we have seen, a complex one, resting neither on mimetic commemoration nor on schematic repetition, since the two levels are inextricably interlocked. The consistency that reading the text as a reiteration of absence or emptiness permits does not fully explain the intuited presence of a speaker who—however negatively—commemorates the past. Yet the vision of an abandoned speaker, though seemingly encompassing all details of the poem, does not fully acknowledge the continuing presence of ungrammaticality and its threat of nonmeaning. What does emerge from this analysis of "Elegía pura" is that in the poem González manages to meld form and substance, the elegy as vehicle and its traditional commemorative content, into an inseparable whole. He explores in this brief text not only the paradoxical nature of all remembering—its peculiar combination of rupture and continuity, of something salvaged and something lost, of death and life, of presence and absence—but also the rupture and continuation of literary traditions. He brings to light the fundamentally dual nature of elegy, a tradition concerning rupture and a meditation on impermanence that according to literary canons nevertheless "finds consolation in the contemplation of some permanent principle."[32] Yet the text's deepest meaning is perhaps its unresolvable existence as a verbal game.

"Elegía pura" is, finally, an example of the postmodernist tendency to foreground literary form at the expense of content. Silvio Gaggi points out a similar tendency in González's American contemporary John Barth, whose collection of stories *Lost in the Funhouse* contains, in Gaggi's words, "narrators and narrations locked inside the 'prisonhouse of language', capable only of articulating the walls of that prison." The story "Title," which Gaggi terms "[t]he most purely self-conscious story in *Lost in the Funhouse*," is Barth's attempt to create a story that has no narrative content. In this sense the tale resembles "Elegía pura." According to Gaggi, the story laments its shortcomings as a narrative and comments on the sorry state of contemporary culture and fiction:

> On various levels, the story implies that self-consciousness has the effect of impotence and removal from engagement with life. . . . On the most literal level it is a self-conscious narration, a story about its own unfolding, and not about human beings engaged in conflict and action—thus, it is an impotent form of literature. On another level it is about the general self-conscious state of modern literature which, extremely aware of its history and development, orients itself to questions of art rather than of life, turns in on itself, and becomes criticism as much as literature.

For Gaggi, Barth's humanistic postmodernism, with roots in his early existentialism, injects poignancy into the metafictional struggle with language.

7 / Literary Tradition versus Speaker Experience

If Barth's "empty story" for Gaggi "struggles for a humanistic content," González's "Elegía pura," likewise, ultimately comments on the emptiness of contemporary life and literature.[33]

A detailed analysis of one of González's most recent poems reveals continued insistence on the creation of works that through their intertextuality tend toward nonsense. "Avanzaba de espaldas aquel río . . ." [That river went forward backward] (p. 352), wavering between reference and compositional game, is typical of what Perloff sees as an aesthetic of indeterminacy.[34] The poem presents a river's seaward advance as a quintessential romantic farewell scene, complete with nearly every cliché such scenes entail: a crepuscular autumnal setting, tender handclasps, glistening eyes that caress what they must leave behind:

> Avanzaba de espaldas aquel río.
>
> No miraba adelante, no atendía
> a su Norte—que era el Sur.
> Contemplaba los álamos
> altos, llenos de sol, reverenciosos,
> perdiéndose despacio cauce arriba.
> Se embebía en los cielos
> cambiantes
> del otoño:
>   decía adiós a su luz.
> Retenía un instante las ramas de los sauces
> en sus espumas frías,
> para dejarlas irse—o sea, quedarse—,
> mojadas y brillantes, por la orilla.
> En los remansos
> demoraba su marcha,
> absorto ante el crepúsculo.
>
> No ignoraba al mar ácido, tan próximo
> que ya en el viento su rumor se oía.
> Sin embargo,
> continuaba avanzando de espaldas aquel río,
> y se ensanchaba
> para tocar las cosas que veía:
> los juncos últimos,
> la sed de los rebaños,
> las blancas piedras por su afán pulidas.
> Si no podía alcanzarlo,
> lo acariciaba todo con sus ojos de agua.
>
> ¡Y con qué amor lo hacía!

[That river went forward backward.

He didn't look ahead, he didn't heed
his North Star—which was the South.
He viewed the tall poplars,
filled with sunshine, bowing,
slowly dissolving upstream.
He became absorbed in the shifting
skies
of autumn:
        he said good-bye to their light.
He retained the willow branches for an instant
in his cold foam,
only to let them go—or rather, stay—,
shiny and wet, along the bank.
Where the water was still
he would pause,
drinking in the twilight.

He was aware of the acid sea, so close
that its roar could already be heard on the wind.
And yet,
that river continued to go forward backward,
and he swelled
to touch the things he saw:
the farthest rushes,
the thirst of the flocks,
the white stones by his eagerness polished.
What he couldn't reach
he caressed all over with the wellsprings of his eyes.

And how lovingly he did so!

The heavy intertextual resonances of "Avanzaba de espaldas aquel río . . ." are inescapable. The poem, like "Me falta una palabra" from *Aspero mundo*, evokes a Juanramonian aesthetic. The heavy-handed personification of nature and the pathetic fallacy recall Jiménez's earliest books, as a comparison with the following passage, from "Otoñal" [Autumn song] (*Ninfeas*, 1900), reveals:

    Obscuros nublados manchaban el cielo;
    el Sol moribundo se hundía en Ocaso,
    de rojo sudario cubierto; . . .
    . . . .
    el río lanzaba rumor somnolento,
    besando la orilla al dormirse,
    con ósculos tiernos;
    . . . .

7 / LITERARY TRADITION VERSUS SPEAKER EXPERIENCE

>   ¡Qué tarde más triste! ...
> ....
> El valle y el monte y el río y el cielo
> estaban vestidos de luto, ...
> y su alma y la mía vestidas de negro ...
> ....
>   Tenía en mis manos sus manos heladas,
> mi pálida frente en su pecho; ...
> 35
>
> [Dark storm clouds stained the sky;
> the dying Sun was sinking in the West,
> by a red shroud covered; ...
> ....
> the river sent forth a somnolent murmur,
> kissing the bank as it went to sleep,
> with tender kisses;
> ....
>   What a sad afternoon!
> ....
> The valley and the mountain and the river and the sky
> were dressed in mourning, ...
> and their soul and mine wore black ...
> ....
>   I held in my hands her icy hands,
> my pale brow on her breast; ...
> ....]

In "Avanzaba de espaldas aquel río ... ," then, González picks up one of the underlying threads of his own poetry—the elegiac mode—in order to parody it. The poem recalls not only Juan Ramón but also the traditional image of human lives as rivers en route to the sea that is death. The river's depiction as a person reluctantly walking backward and caressing with his eyes all that he is leaving suggests a prolonged and heartfelt good-bye in the face of permanent separation. The poem in fact recalls "*Por aquí pasa un río*" [A river runs through here] from González's first book, *Aspero mundo*, which implicitly compares a human life to the course of a river. Yet unlike that poem and other more traditional poetry, here the elegiac text is undermined by various forms of verbal play. Metaphor becomes a personification so extreme that it oversteps the limits of what common sense can accept. The poem thus attains burlesque proportions through its exaggeration of traditional poetic techniques.

Throughout the poem, wordplay that draws attention to the surface of the text or to the literal/figurative duality consistently undermines the pathos of the river's fateful progress. The juxtaposition of literal and figurative meanings and in fact their actual contradiction of one another appear first in the opening line, where the anatomical precision of the reference to the river's "espaldas" creates dissent in the reader who, though ready to accept Manrique's conceptual comparison between smaller and larger rivers and human beings of greater and lesser importance, may find the vision of a river walking backward ridiculously concrete. And as in other instances throughout the poem, contradictory wording—here the phrase "[a]vanzaba de espaldas," in which the river that is said to be advancing forward seems more properly to be withdrawing backward[36]—draws our attention away from the referent and to the poetic surface. (The verb "avanzaba" evokes, as an underlying text, its opposite, "retrocedía.") In line 3, the phrase "su Norte—que era el Sur" likewise juxtaposes literal meaning—actual direction—with the figurative connotations of the word "Norte," continuing the suggestion of unidirectional movement overlaid with bidirectional pull. Similarly, the reference to willow branches that the river retains a moment and then releases "para dejarlas irse—o sea, quedarse," in counterposing opposites, draws the reader's attention away from the implications of farewell and toward the more literary question of literal exactness versus figurative sense.

Also undermining the romantic vision of "Avanzaba de espaldas aquel río . . ." is the presence of a series of terms that though figuratively applicable to good-bye scenes belong to a scientific semantic field that refers to water. In lines 7 and 8, where the river "Se embebía en los cielos / cambiantes / del otoño," the literal suggestion of evaporation undercuts the figurative vision of the river as gazing, transfixed, at the sky. The image, in lines 11 and 12, of the river retaining the willow branches in its water—"Retenía un instante las ramas de los sauces / en sus espumas frías"—echoes the cliché, just seen in Juan Ramón Jiménez, of the tender farewell handclasp, the word "espumas" serving here to substitute for the word "manos," though both can be read literally as well. The fact that the river slows its course at times receives intentional significance, in lines 15–17 ("En los remansos / demoraba su marcha, / absorto ante el crepúsculo"). Yet the word "absorto," like "retener" and "embeberse," forms part of a semantic field that includes such scientific vocabulary relating to the properties of water as the terms *absorption, retention,* and *saturation.* Thus the presence of "absorto" has the effect of undercutting the personification of the river. Likewise, the application of the adjectives "mojadas y brillantes," which belong to a semantic field referring to tear-filled eyes, is generated by the botanical name "sauce llorón" [weeping willow]. The willows, which weep only figuratively in real life, are here presented as literally crying; at the same time, the adjectives "mojadas" and "brillantes" are literally applicable to willow branches on the riverbank.

This literal/figurative confusion continues until the end of the poem. The verb "ensancharse," applied to the river in line 22, describes a river widening as it approaches the sea, but in the context of the reference to "las blancas piedras por su afán pulidas," in line 26, it evokes as well the figurative self-satisfaction that seems to infuse the river/person in the last line, converting the river's tragic good-bye into tragicomedy.

The river's final caress, in line 29, again plays upon the literal and the figurative planes: "lo acariciaba todo con sus ojos de agua." A triple-planed pun, the phrase "ojos de agua" evokes the tears of the personified river, expresses metaphorically the water's literal contact with the riverbank as it passes, and, on a more linguistic level, plays with the set phrase "ojo de agua," signifying "spring." This phrase, which links water and eyes, could have actually generated the entire poem, which is a river's vision of its past.

In "Avanzaba de espaldas aquel río . . ." two different models of nature—the scientific and the romantic—are set against each other. The poem, in counterposing the romantic legacy of subjective symbolism to the notion of the power of linguistic conventions, expresses a quintessentially twentieth-century dilemma. Thus its subject is not the good-bye itself but rather the literary devices that make up the elegiac tradition.

In contrast to a poem by Machado in which all elements—twilight, autumn, water, for example—"fall together" in the symbolist manner, fusing and mutually intensifying each other, in a vision that evokes some transcendent mystery,[37] González's poem falls apart as literal and figurative levels conflict. The content of the poem, natural description, coexists with elements that highlight the cultural determination of this content. Given the allusions to a Juanramonian sensibility, we might almost interpret the personification of the river as suggestive of the poet, who, keeping his eyes on past literary tradition, admires the stones, his poems, that he polishes as he passes by. It would probably be too far-fetched to interpret the reference to the river's premonition of the sea as an allusion to Juan Ramón's decisive encounter with that entity, though given González's multilayered irony, such an interpretation is not altogether impossible.

In this poem, González exhibits the postmodern tendency to "quote, paraphrase, or rework previous styles or works."[38] Yet as is typical of postmodernism,[39] he does not re-create an old style but performs a "creative reworking," writing a poem that simultaneously pays homage to the past and comments ironically on that past.

"Avanzaba de espaldas aquel río . . ." and the other poems I have examined here tend toward nonsense, not only because they confuse categories, thus calling attention to themselves as texts, but also because, as poems in some sense about poetic devices, they are paradoxical. They are clearly ludic texts, demonstrating Stewart's concept of the ludic work as both critical and self-critical; they are texts that *are* change as well as being *about* change.

González evolves toward the ludic and toward conscious metapoetic play with literary categories. But as a humanistic postmodernist he never totally replaces experience with schemes (as he himself has noted). Instead, the two elements coexist and play off one another. If in "Elegía pura" a speaker and his experiences surface in a poem apparently about genre, in "Egloga" an outwardly mimetic description masks a poem at least partially about the pastoral tradition. Literary traditions, popular visions, and social clichés all serve as backdrops out of which the poems' meanings emerge, and at times even as catalysts in the generation of the texts' imagery. My analysis confirms Frye's statement that "the new poem manifests something that was already latent in the order of words," as well as upholding the following Saussurean notion, restated by Jonathan Culler: "What my words mean is the meaning they can have in this interpersonal system from which they emerge. The system is always already in place, as the ground or condition of meaning, and to interpret signs is to read them in terms of the system."[40]

This analysis of González's poems indeed seems to ratify Saussure's belief that categories we inherit with language shape our perception (or, in Fredric Jameson's words, that "you can see only as much as your model permits you to see").[41] Not surprisingly, González himself quotes Oscar Wilde's famous dictum that nature imitates art, an intuition that has much in common with Saussure's awareness of the power of linguistic categories and models and a theory that, like González's 1980 statement of his poetics, acknowledges the interrelationship between experience and schemes. This awareness surfaces in the same statement in González's words regarding "la palabra poética":

> [L]as palabras del poema configuran con especial intensidad ideas y emociones, o a veces incluso llegan a crearlas.... [L]a poesía confirma o modifica nuestra percepción de las cosas, lo que equivale, en cierto modo, a confirmar o modificar las cosas mismas.[42]
>
> [The words of the poem give shape with special intensity to ideas and emotions, or sometimes even manage to create them.... Poetry confirms or modifies our perception of things, which is equivalent, in a certain way, to confirming or modifying things themselves.]

González's poems indeed are made of old categories and conventions, but combined in new ways that offer fresh visions and create new traditions. Reading them, we recognize the literary traditions and schemes that they incorporate, but without this something new that they provide—some unique and personal experiences or reality—they would hold little interest. Though it may be true, as Saussure has said, that "linguistic signs are unrelated to what they designate," nonetheless as we read we envision a speaker talking about his world. This illusion of referential meaning, if indeed it is an illu-

7 / LITERARY TRADITION VERSUS SPEAKER EXPERIENCE

sion, would probably be acknowledged by Saussure, much as he noted a similar phenomenon: that although the linguistic system is exclusively one of relationship between signs, "nevertheless all our distinctions, our whole terminology, all our ways of speaking about it are molded by the involuntary assumption that there is substance."[43] In Riffaterre's view, we move, as we read, back and forth between mimesis and semiosis. "The reader's manufacture of meaning" he calls "a seesaw scanning of the text, compelled by the very duality of the signs—ungrammatical as mimesis, grammatical within the significance network." "This seesawing from one sign value to another," he continues, "this alternating appearance and disappearance of significance, both in spite and because of unacceptable features on the plane of mimetic meaning, is a kind of semiotic circularity . . . characterizing the practice of signification known as poetry." González's poems, like all poetry, offer us a double face. They are both complex linguistic artifacts and, in a sense, testimonial. It is precisely this duality that makes them, like all good poems, of lasting interest to their readers, for, as Riffaterre points out, "it means a continual recommencing, an indecisiveness resolved one moment and lost the next with each reliving of revealed significance, and this it is that makes the poem endlessly rereadable and fascinating."[44]

8
Iconoclastic Images of Self and Other in *Palabra sobre palabra*

In previous chapters, I have discussed González's frequently conflictive relationship with his society and with the poetic word, and I have traced the transformation he has undergone in response to an epoch of crisis and change. As his playful side has emerged alongside the purposeful poet of commitment, he has abandoned his sense of urgent participation in society's concerns from outside its institutions in favor of a consciousness of his own enmeshment within social structures, which include systems of signification themselves. But within the parameters of evolution from purposeful poet of commitment to ludic poet, he has continued to examine how art relates to life, either by considering the interrelationship between poetry and society, or through exploring the genesis of poetry, its birth from either experience or "schemes." In this chapter, I will discuss a significant aspect of the relationship between art and life in González's poetry: his portrayal of other poets, of himself as poet, and of the act of literary creativity.

González's depictions of poets and poetry reveal his changing approach to poetry as personal history or witnessing. His initial stance—strongly critical of poetic escapism, of art divorced from life—results in a distrust of images of the kind described by W. J. T. Mitchell in his book *Iconology: Image, Text, Ideology* (1986). González in certain of his later works shifts away from poetry as history to a more postmodern approach in which, as Ihab Hassan would put it, thinking is conceived as the creation of fictions.[1] This shift in how González frames poetry and the writing of poetry has clear ideological implications. Thus my inquiry into the creative act in his poetry will lead back to some of the political questions addressed in chapters 3 and 4.

Drawing on his family background and on the formative influences of Marxism and existentialism, González in many instances has portrayed unfavorably the poetic act that attempts to evade connection to sociopolitical realities. His anti-aestheticist stance can best be understood against the backdrop of the history of aesthetics in the nineteenth and twentieth centuries. In this regard the works of W. J. T. Mitchell and Terry Eagleton provide a particularly valuable context for exploring González's reaction against modernism and its cult of imagery[2] and for understanding what Mitchell would call his "iconoclastic" desire to let life speak for itself through his poetry.

Mitchell's work *Iconology* studies the relationship between the verbal text and the visual image. Mitchell—whose intention is to show how imagery connects theories of art, language, and mind to social, cultural, and political values—develops his arguments in the context of aesthetic currents going back to the Enlightenment. He discusses such writers as Gotthold Ephraim Lessing and Joseph Addison, who considered the image potentially more beautiful and revealing than life itself. He then turns to the romantics, for whom images were part of the "imagination," a faculty that went beyond the description of the purely visible and a power that they prized more highly than the simple representation of objects. But alongside the "iconophilia" and even "idolatry" he finds in certain writers from the eighteenth century on, Mitchell detects in other creators of literature an opposing fear and dislike of visual images. Exemplifying this polarization in how images are regarded is the contrast between formalist-based aesthetic values of complexity, subtlety, economy, and elegance and a Marxist iconoclasm that challenges the bourgeois pluralism of art objects as "capitalist idols of the mind and marketplace."[3]

The Marxist tradition that Mitchell explores is highly relevant to an understanding of González's approach to the question of poetry's role. Marx, Mitchell suggests, offered an iconoclastic corrective to the reverential approach to the art object, attempting, through his critique of icons, to restore the connections between images and the society out of which they emerge. Terming consciousness "from the beginning a social product," Marx could envision no images that were above social practices. Urging "a refusal to traffic in images at all," Marx called for us to "pay attention to things themselves, things as they are, without mediation." Thus on one hand, says Mitchell, Marx's iconoclasm distrusted all representations. But on the other, Marx recognized that precisely because consciousness is always a social product, direct apprehension is impossible. His solution: a "'hermeneutics of suspicion' that distrusts the manifest, surface content of representations, but can only get to the deep, hidden meaning by working its way through this surface." Thus, concludes Mitchell, Marx advocated the "negative, interpretive science of historical and dialectical materialism."[4]

Mitchell points out, finally, that even while believing themselves free of image-worship, iconoclasts create their own images; if pressed, they point to the truth or purity of *their* images as opposed to those of the idolaters from whom they distance themselves. Suggesting that the attitudes toward representation that writers embody in their texts are manifestations of ideological underpinnings and thus of a kind of mental imagery, he calls for the practitioners of the "rhetoric of iconoclasm" to turn their eyes upon themselves to examine their own premises.

Eagleton's perspective on the rise of the symbol in English romanticism complements Mitchell's analysis. Eagleton notes that the romantics, in privileging the creative imagination, were reacting against utilitarianism and early industrial capitalism. For them, the poet's work became "non-alienated labour" and his product a "mysterious organic unity, in contrast to the fragmented individualism of the capitalist marketplace: . . . creative rather than mechanical." As a result, says Eagleton, "Art was extricated from the material practices, social relations and ideological meanings in which it is always caught up, and raised to the status of a solitary fetish."[5] These perspectives are highly relevant to understanding González's poetry about poetry.

The critique of escapist aestheticism that runs throughout González's poetry can best be understood as a manifestation of the iconoclasm described by Mitchell and as a reaction against the fetishizing of art discussed by Eagleton. In this attitude González resembles other poets who matured during the height of socialist realism in Spain, such as Gloria Fuertes and Jaime Gil de Biedma.[6] These poets reacted negatively toward the aesthetic tendencies of some of their poetic predecessors, notably the acclaimed generation of 1927, whose poetry has often been viewed as a search for poetic purity through the creation of verbal icons embodying transcendence, perfection, and universality. Poets like González and Fuertes are not just rebels against successful forebears, however, but also express a Marxist-inspired desire to bear witness to a particular social and historical reality. Thus they try to close the gap between life and art and to overcome the distortions of mediation. In keeping with the desire to merge poetry and life story, Gloria Fuertes titles one of her collections *Historia de Gloria: Amor, humor y desamor* [Gloria's story: Love, humor, and lack of love] (1981). In her many poetic autobiographies she portrays herself as immersed in the life of her society, as an artisan-poet whose poetic issue is so connected to material reality that she likens her poems to daily deposits of excrement quite unlike the elevated aesthetic object of preceding generations. González at times advocates an aesthetic object fully as earthy as that of Fuertes. Though his complex attitude toward predecessor poets such as Juan Ramón Jiménez does not exclude admiration and even imitation, he often criticizes the modernist aesthetic, advocating an impure poetry that makes room for the anonymous individual's expression of urgent concerns and admits even the visceral expressiveness of such nonverbal communication as obscene gestures and spitting. Nevertheless, his resistance to the visual image and his rejection of an aesthetic of transcendence and perfection do not prevent González from creating arresting visual images and complex verbal constructions of his own.

He expresses negative attitudes toward images of beauty as a prime value and toward artistic worth set above human concerns, but at the same time, even his poetic texts critical of aestheticism often celebrate pure creativity and poetic play as ends in themselves. This tendency has been more pronounced as he has evolved from a Sartrean sense of responsibility to a Bartheian view of consciousness as an "arena of classificatory schemes and systems," as Susan Sontag describes the latter.[7] As I will show later in this chapter, González has sometimes managed to have his cake and eat it too, by using techniques that distance him from his own image making: humor, self-mockery, or a fanciful, "let's pretend" attitude.

The questions Mitchell raises about text and image, idolatry and iconoclasm, are particularly useful as we approach González's stricter (as described in chapter 2), most iconoclastic side. González problematizes image-making through what Mitchell would term *hypericons* or images of image-making in his poems about poets, through his multiple poetic self-portraits, and through his *ars poetica* as expressed in various poems.[8] González's hypericons embody his attitudes and conflicts about the aesthetic object. He often reacts against aestheticist aims in his treatment of other poets, defining himself, through differentiation from and affiliation with others, as a socially committed "materialist" poet who seeks to reflect social realities in his poetry. His depictions of other poets, who often remain anonymous, are frequently caricatures, ridiculing the model of poetry as the creation of an aesthetic object placed above the struggles of social existence and of history. From his first book onward, these portrayals often treat not the poet's product but the act of writing itself, the poet at work. But González doesn't just explicitly attack the creator of the sublime aesthetic object. In addition, in "Para que yo me llame Angel González," he obliquely questions the very possibility of the sublime. This early poem reveals that a certain iconophobia is embodied in González's work from the very beginning.

González's challenge to the sublime in "Para que yo me llame Angel González" (p. 13) becomes obvious if we examine the poem in the light of specific cultural traditions. González violates the precepts of poetic purity in the first line, naming himself in the tradition of social poetry:[9]

>   Para que yo me llame Angel González,
>   para que mi ser pese sobre el suelo,
>   fue necesario un ancho espacio
>   y un largo tiempo:
>   hombres de todo mar y toda tierra,
>   fértiles vientres de mujer, . . .
>   . . . .
>   [Y]o no soy más que el resultado, el fruto,
>   lo que queda, podrido, entre los restos;
>   . . . .

> ... El éxito
> de todos los fracasos. ...
>
> [So that I might be called Angel González
> so that my being could weigh upon the earth,
> a wide space was necessary
> and a long time:
> men of every sea and every land,
> fertile wombs of women, ...
> ....
> I am only the result, the fruit,
> what is left, rotten, among the remains;
> ....
> ... The success
> of all the failures. ...]

González's gloomy portrait of his life in a historical context can be read simply as an inversion of the notion of the survival of the fittest. But the true impact of his vision as an attack on the sublime can be felt if we read the poem as a negatively charged materialist version of José Ortega y Gasset's "razón vital" [vital reason]. Much as Ortega speaks of "la corriente de la vida, que va de pueblo en pueblo, de generación en generación, de individuo en individuo, apoderándose de la realidad universal" [the current of life, which goes from people to people, from generation to generation, from individual to individual, taking possession of universal reality], González sees the individual as a distillation of an endless vital current. In *El tema de nuestro tiempo* [The theme of our time] (1923), Ortega reevaluates the position assigned higher culture since the eighteenth century, decrying its conversion into a fetish, its elevation above life itself, as a utopian "progresismo" [progressivism]. States Ortega: "[L]a cultura, supremo valor venerado por las dos centurias positivas, es también una entidad ultravital que ocupa en la estimación moderna exactamente el mismo puesto que antes usufructuaba la beatitud" [Culture, the supreme value venerated by the two positive centuries, is also an entity beyond life that occupies in modern estimation exactly the same place that blessedness used to enjoy]. Ortega points out, furthermore, that cultural values—truth, goodness, beauty—have been divorced from life, becoming a never-realizable ideal: "De aquí que el culturalismo sea siempre progresismo. El sentido y valor de la vida, la cual es por esencia presente actualidad, se halla siempre en un mañana mejor" [Hence it follows that culturalism is always progressivism. The meaning and worth of life, which by nature is present time, is always found in a better tomorrow]. Conscious, in the early twenties, of a world in crisis, Ortega decries the separation of life from spirit as a delusion. He attempts to unite the two by envisioning each individual as possessing a partial truth, a truth that is in a

8 / Iconoclastic Images of Self and Other

sense divine ("Dios ve las cosas a través de los hombres, . . . los hombres son los órganos visuales de la divinidad" [God sees things through humans, . . . human beings are the organs of sight of the divinity).[10]

Some thirty years after Ortega wrote this essay, González, in "Para que yo me llame Angel González," likewise responds to a world in crisis. His poem reflects the contradiction between the nineteenth-century's positivistic belief in human progress and the horrifying experiences of human history in the twentieth century. Like Ortega, he rejects positivism, but instead of envisioning each eye as seeing for God, as does the philosopher, and thus each poet as a divinelike creator, he emphasizes life as survivorship, as the ability to overcome—if barely—the destructive potential of existence.[11] González's viewpoint inverts thus the notion of the human being as created in God's image, undermining the analogy between poet and God, between human and divine creativity.[12] The related belief that each human being has a spark of the divine is present in the poem, but in a negative form: the speaker is "el éxito de todos los fracasos" [the success / of all the failures]. Instead of the "alma" [soul] or breath of life passed down through human history, he grasps at the "último suspiro de los muertos" [last breath of the dying] and represents the "enloquecida fuerza del desaliento" [crazed force of discouragement]. Even at this early stage, then, González uses systems of thought as a base for his iconoclasm. He undercuts here a multitude of conceptions of humanity, including one of the axiomatic justifications for artistic imagery: that the poet, endowed with a creativity analogous to God's, can produce sublime and superhumanly beautiful images.

Not surprisingly, the first of González's texts specifically about poets and poetry criticizes its speaker's attempt to separate art from life. "Me falta una palabra" from *Aspero mundo* (analyzed in chapter 7 as a metapoetic text) has as its speaker a poet-aesthete whose search for the perfect word to go well with the rest of his poem is continually interrupted by the clamor of hungry children, by tattered men and women, by outcasts and victims of society. The speaker insensitively likens his poetic quest to these pariahs' cravings for more basic sustenance (*"Un niño pide pan; yo pido menos"* [*"A child begs for bread; I beg for less"* (DDW)]). He asks them to search their purses and their bodies for the word he lacks. But unable to shut out human beings in their historical circumstances of need and suffering, he ends up petulantly abandoning his attempt to create. The poem implicitly criticizes the ivory tower poet oblivious to the needs of humanity. Putting poetry-making into the context of a reciprocal relationship with society, González suggests that the poet and society are both ill-served by such writers' aestheticist bents.

In another poem from *Aspero mundo*, "Soneto a algunos poetas" [Sonnet to some poets] (p. 44), González depicts poets who, perhaps through fear, avoid confronting social issues directly. These poets are reduced to unsuccessfully hawking their superfluous wares: "España es una plaza provinciana, / y en ella pregonáis la mercancía: / . . . / Nadie se para a oíros" [Spain is a provincial plaza, / and in it you hawk your wares: / . . . / No one stops to hear you].

In "Zona residencial" [Residential area] from *Tratado de urbanismo*, González criticizes much more indirectly poetry's potential for blindness toward human problems and for the complacent portrayal of false and idealized versions of society. Here González does not explicitly refer to poets or poetry but through his lexicon cites his poetic elder Jorge Guillén. He appears to parody the orderly but naïve vision that, however unjustifiably, some readers have extrapolated from "Beato sillón" [Blessed armchair] with its "well-made world." González's portrait of a manicured neighborhood and its economically privileged inhabitants evokes *Cántico* through telling references to "la perfección" [perfection], "el júbilo" [jubilation], and to "un mundo . . . perfecto" [a perfect world]. But González's allusions to a servant class and to hungry pigeons (who in tenaciously gobbling crumbs are the only evidence of poor manners on the scene) undermine the notion that this perfect bourgeois paradise represents a natural order of things, as do the suspicious descriptions of youngsters as "products," appropriately packaged for a commercialized, consumer society. Here people have become commodities; teenagers are "encuadernados / en piel de calidad insuperable" [bound / in top-quality skin] and children's laughter (are they wearing braces?) is nickel-plated like their bikes. If we accept the poem's lexicon as an allusion to Guillén and thus as evidence that González is metapoetically referring to and parodying literary imagery, then "Zona residencial" illustrates a point that Mitchell stresses: images presented as universal often represent in actuality particular ideologies, such as that of the privileged class depicted here. Points of view that Guillén may have conceived as beyond politics in reality are part and parcel of political structure. Finally, González's portrait of private wealth in this poem recalls his distinction between private and public spheres in "Todos ustedes parecen felices . . . " [You All Seem Happy . . ." (DDW)] (p. 23), where he speaks of those who "se aman / de dos en dos / para / odiar de mil / en mil. . . ."[13] ["love / in couples / and . . . / hate in / thousands" (DDW)].

Criticism of poetic evasion and caution toward the universalizing of particular experience—and toward the confusion between a socioeconomic and a cosmic well-being—continue to characterize González's work, with images of sexuality and of material objects serving to refer on the one hand to a desirable incorporation of real life into poetry and on the other to the prostitution and commercialization of poetic gifts. In "Oda a los nuevos bardos" [Ode to the new bards] (*Muestra*, pp. 310–11), he caricatures a new

8 / Iconoclastic Images of Self and Other

group of poets whom he has identified in interviews as "los novísimos." He portrays these poets as prostitutes armed with a formidable technical arsenal, who display themselves to a closed circuit of open-mouthed admirers:

> Mucho les importa la poesía.
> Hablan constantemente de la poesía,
> y se prueban metáforas como putas sostenes
> ante el oval espejo de las *oes* pulidas
> que la admiración abre en las bocas afines.
>
> [Poetry matters much to them.
> They speak constantly of poetry,
> and they try on metaphors as whores do bras
> before the oval mirror of the polished o's
> that admiration opens in kindred mouths.]

Much as the poet's word was likened to bread in "Me falta una palabra" and to tawdry wares in "Soneto a algunos poetas," here poetry is tinged with materialism that takes the form of sexuality. The poets seek sterile narcissistic *frissons*: "Aman la intimidad, sus interioridades / les producen orgasmos repentinos" [They love intimacy, their private matters / give them sudden orgasms]. Turning their backs on the drama of their own historical moment, they return in fantasy to a *modernista* past, which through images of prostitution and gambling González portrays as bankrupt and decadent:

> Otras tardes de otoño reconstruyen
> el esplendor de un tiempo desahuciado
> por deudas impagables, perdido en la ruleta
> de un lejano Casino junto a un lago
> por el que se deslizan cisnes, *cisnes
> cuyo perfil*
>   —anotan sonrientes—
>
> *susurra, intermitente, eses silentes:
> aliterada letra herida,
> casi exhalada*
>   —*puesto que surgida
> de la aterida pulcritud del ala*—
> en un S. O. S. que resbala
> y que un peligro inadvertido evoca.
> ¡Y el cisne-cero-cisne que equivoca
> al agua antes tranquila y ya alarmada
> era tan sólo nada-cisne-nada!
>
> [Other autumn afternoons they reconstruct
> the splendor of a time evicted

for unpayable debts, lost in the roulette wheel
of a distant Casino beside a lake
over which are gliding swans, *swans
whose profiles*
    —they note smiling—

*whisper, intermittent, silent, s's:
wounded, alliterated letter,
nearly exhaled*
    —*since it arises
from the stiffly cold pulchritude of the wing—
in an S.O.S. that slides
and an unnoticed danger evokes.
And the swan-zero-swan that mistakes
the water, which earlier was tranquil and is now alarmed,
was only a nothing-swan-nothing!*]

González iconoclastically suggests that the swan, emblematic of poetic escapism, is an empty and deceptive image. By describing these birds using the purely conventional international distress signal SOS (whose letters, ironically, bear iconic resemblance to a swan, a pool, and a swan's reflection), he implies that rather than a visual image of reality, the swans are a hieroglyph or index that in his mind signifies identification with the sinking ship of narcissistic aestheticism.

Three of the preceding poems—"Me falta una palabra," "Soneto a algunos poetas," and "Oda a los nuevos bardos"—put poetry into the context of an alienating economic system, turning poets into beggars, hawkers, or whores. In all these cases, the fruits of poetic labor are depicted as useless to society and the poets as alienated and marginalized. Spanning a twenty-year period in González's career, these poems express a materialist viewpoint. They ridicule and expose as sterile and unproductive those who would privilege the imagination, its play, and its visions per se, thus insulating themselves from other individuals and from their own social circumstances. González is aware of the irony that though the poets depicted disdain their historical circumstances, they are nevertheless creatures whose economic access to leisure allows them to pursue poetry as an aesthetic game.

In "Orden. (Poética a la que otros se aplican)" [Order. (Poetics to which others apply themselves)] (p. 292), from the section of *Muestra* titled "Metapoesía" [Metapoetry], González continues to describe poetry-making through sexual metaphors. Impiously appropriating one of Spain's foremost cultural icons, the familiar portrait of the Virgin as the "Purísima Concepción" [Immaculate Conception], he describes certain "prudent poets," who, "como las vírgenes" [like virgins] "no deben separar los ojos / del firmamento" [must not take their eyes off / the heavens]. Once again González merges sexual imagery and commercial exchange. The Virgin's pose of purity, though signifying the absence of sexual commerce, was clearly an image that sold, its popularity guaranteeing commercial success to those who painted it. For the other young women evoked by González's image, the secular maidens, virginity traditionally permitted them to go on the marriage market. Thus the poem's exhortation to poets to contemplate the stars—to be sublime and pure—instead of looking at humanity is undermined by the very icon chosen to represent the seemingly pure ideal:

> ¡Oh, tú, extranjero osado
> que miras a los hombres:
> contempla las estrellas!
> (El Tiempo, no la Historia.)
> Evita
> la claridad obscena.
>   (Cave canem.)
> Y edifica el misterio.
>
> [Oh, you, bold foreigner
> who looks at human beings:
> contemplate the stars!
> (Time, not History.)
> Avoid
> obscene clarity.
>   *(Cave canem.)*
> And construct mystery.]

The purity ostensibly touted in the poem is one that neither names nor illuminates, and which causes these poets' words, like seed spilled on the ground, to be wasted like their lives:

>   Sé puro:
> no nombres; no ilumines.
> Que tu palabra oscura se derrame en la noche
> sombría y sin sentido
> lo mismo que el momento de tu vida.
>
>   [Be pure:
> don't name; don't illuminate.
> Let your dark word be spilled in the night
> somber and senseless
> just like the moment of your life.]

Sexual imagery, especially in its most physical manifestations of orgasm or ejaculation, will continue to underpin González's portrayal of poetry-making. Through such imagery, he traces the familiar analogy between pen and penis, suggesting that the poet's task, when not grounded in historical consciousness, is no more fertile or productive than masturbation. His grossly physical and slightly shocking analogies demystify the act of writing, serving as a corrective to overidealizations of poetry as sublime and unworldly. His comparisons serve as reminders that poets, like everybody else, are enmeshed in a particular material reality (including their own economic class), which inevitably affects their perceptions. Thus González responds to the division between body and spirit that is one of the foundations of Western thought. His reference to the poetic act through the fusion of sexual and commercial imagery is a negative version of the often-drawn analogy between human love and the poet's creative union with the world. He suggests that creativity gone awry, like sexuality misused, can result in prostitution or in sterility. The title "Orden" underscores the political implications of the false consciousness González depicts, for as Roland Barthes has observed, "the content of the word 'Order' always indicates repression."[14]

Also a part of the section of *Muestra* titled "Metapoesía," the poem "Contra-Orden. (Poética por la que me pronuncio ciertos días.)" [Counterorder. (Poetics I advocate on certain days)] (p. 293) intensifies González's rejection of aestheticist poetics. In going against an established aesthetic order, he favors what might be called an "antipoetry," the phrase "contraorden" paralleling the familiar "anti-poesía." Poetry becomes a place where the events of people's lives—their histories—are welcome, and where the restrictions of polite society don't apply. Inclusion of base material life and topical and collective concerns—spittle, urine, garbage, anonymous scrawls—and even of antisocial acts flies in the face of an aesthetic that valorizes the individual author's role and elevates the art object to the status of a mysterious fetish:

> Esto es un poema.
>
> Aquí está permitido
> fijar carteles,
> tirar escombros, hacer aguas
> y escribir frases como:
>
> *Marica el que lo lea,*
> *Amo a Irma,*
> *Muera el . . .* (silencio),
> *Arena gratis,*
> *Asesinos,*
> etcétera.
>
> [This is a poem.
>
> Here, it's permitted
> to affix posters,

to dump debris, to relieve yourself
and to write such phrases as:

Anyone who reads this is a fag,
I love Irma,
Death to . . . (silence),
Free sand,
Murderers,
et cetera.]

González's pronouncement in this poem stands at the opposite pole from Jorge Guillén's definition of "poesía pura" as what remains when what is not poetic is eliminated.[15] Similarly, the poem's iconoclasm is far removed from Lessing's advocacy of beauty undistorted by expression. The speaker in fact urges the inclusion of real people and their lives, the presence of their expression, not their images. The poem consists largely of texts that seem to originate in specific historical reality, rather than being composed of beautiful images or of abstractions. Thus the work contrasts sharply with the poems of the "pure" poets scorned in the previous poem, whose poetics called for "El Tiempo, no la Historia" [Time, not History] (p. 292). González's incorporation of language normally found on the street rather than in books does not make him unique among social poets. Blas de Otero's "Muy lejos" [Very far away], for example, reads as follows: "Y voy mirando escaparates. *Paca / y Luz. Hijos de tal.* Medias de seda. / . . ."[16] [And I go along looking at shop windows. "Paca / and Luz." "Sons of So-and-So." Silk / stockings . . .]. But the poem "Contra-Orden," unlike Otero's poem, goes beyond merely including street language to reflecting metapoetically on its presence in a poetic text.

In caricaturing poets because of their perceived narcissism and their failure to look at their fellow human beings and at history, González expresses a Marxist-influenced materialist view of art. In his poems about poets and poetry, his main task is to call into question both poetic idols and images and the act of creating them. In a sense he proceeds dialectically in examining other poets and the relationship of their works to society. If González's critique of image-makers could be considered an act of criticism as well as creativity, such poems as "Oda a los nuevos bardos" bolster Mitchell's claim that iconophobic and iconoclastic rhetoric "pervades the discourse we call 'criticism' in Western culture":

The rhetoric of iconoclasm is . . . a rhetoric of exclusion and domination, a caricature of the other as one who is involved in irrational, obscene behavior from which (fortunately) we are exempt. The images of the idolaters are typically phallic . . . and thus they must be emasculated, feminized, have their tongues cut off by denying them the power of expression or eloquence. They must be declared "dumb," "mute," "empty," or "illusory."

But Mitchell points out a danger that can entrap the iconoclast and that does in fact affect González to a degree. Iconoclasts, says Mitchell, can fall prey to a blindness of their own if they view their values and idols as universal:

> *Our* god, by contrast—reason, science, criticism, the Logos, the spirit of human language and civilized conversation—is invisible, dynamic, and incapable of being reified in any material, spatial image.[17]

González's leftist leanings, his unsystematic approach to his oeuvre, and his self-questioning nature offer some protection from the pitfall Mitchell describes.[18] But especially in his first period, before losing faith in the utility of words, he at times creates icons of his own that reflect his acculturation. Not surprisingly, these icons are treated without the irony he directs at the idols of others.

The icons González creates reflect the political *engagement* that pervades his work to varying degrees at different moments. To begin with, his self-portrayal as witness (as in "Para que yo me llame Angel González") could itself be called iconic: the poet, immersed in concrete, individual social circumstances, is depicted as directly accessing his own reality. This icon of witnessing is a staple of social poetry. Fuertes, we recall, states in *Historia de Gloria,* "Esto no es un libro; es una mujer" [This is not a book; it's a woman] and Blas de Otero likewise appropriates as an epigraph to *Esto no es un libro* Whitman's lines, "[T]his is no book, / who touches this touches a man"— in Spanish translation, "quien toca este libro toca un hombre."[19] The figure of Antonio Machado and the Cuban revolution, portrayed respectively in "Camposanto en Colliure" and in "Perla de las Antillas," both from *Grado elemental*, represent two other poetic icons in González's poetry. Even the prostitutes depicted in "Los sábados, las prostitutas madrugan mucho para estar dispuestas" from the transitional volume *Tratado de urbanismo* might be seen as icons, as signs of the human worth of those capitalism exploits or turns into commodities. Finally, the graffiti of "Contra-Orden" can be interpreted as icons that allude metonymically to the collectivity and to its anonymous voice.[20] The unusual lack of irony with which González approaches his subjects in these poems is a telling index of his iconic approach.

Despite such scattered examples of the unselfconscious elevation of ideologically based images, González's iconoclasm constitutes a strong thread running throughout his oeuvre. Yet especially in later years, he incorporates even into iconoclastic texts contrary ludic notes that counteract moral judgments or critical closure. As I have attempted to show throughout my study, González arrives at this more ludic stage only after passing through a period of deep disillusionment. The transitional poem "Preámbulo a un silencio," discussed in chapter 4, represents a rupture with the idealism of earlier *engagement* and embodies González's new, more complex attitude toward poetic witnessing. Again referring to himself by name, here González simultaneously evokes and undermines not only poetry as sublime and ethereal but poetry as an ethical tool as well. The poem is a shout of protest, an indignant and destructive outburst that emerges from beneath an exterior of Buddha-like contemplation and calm. The poet serves as a witness but at the same time expresses frustration at the uselessness of doing so. Names—icons of testimony—are here arbitrary and without meaning, his own serving only to convert his bitten nails into clipped wings in his imagination. Thus although his name endows him with the wings associated with the spiritual soaring of the poet, his reality is one of damage and frustration rather than flight. He clearly links his poetic wings with the hands that are the manual tools of the worker/poet and that in other poems he identifies with his pen/penis as an instrument of creativity. But here his wings are damaged and he is impotent, silenced, and as the word he applies to them, "mordidas" [bitten; bribes], suggests, "amordazado" [muzzled]. His smile betrays his complicity, and his silence reveals his impotence: "sonrío y me callo porque, en último extremo, / uno tiene conciencia / de la inutilidad de todas las palabras" (p. 212).[21] Questioning the poet's possession not only of a divine spark but of social usefulness as well, González here portrays the poet as a fallen angel who has failed properly to annunciate and warn.

The disillusionment portrayed in "Preámbulo" results in the poems of González's second period in which words and their interplay become the source and the raison d'être of his poetry. The poem "A veces" (p. 237), published in *Breves acotaciones para una biografía* (1969), bridges two opposing forces in González's poetics: the contempt for gratuitous technical prowess and appreciation for play as the basis of creativity. This poem draws a more explicit analogy between pen and penis than does "Preámbulo," published two years earlier.[22] Likening poetry-writing to a sexual act, the text compares writing a poem to an orgasm and ink to semen. Though the writing process can bear fruit, at times it merely frustrates:

> Escribir un poema se parece a un orgasmo:
> mancha la tinta tanto como el semen,
> empreña también más, en ocasiones.
> Tardes hay, sin embargo,
> en las que manoseo las palabras,
> muerdo sus senos y sus piernas ágiles,
> les levanto las faldas con mis dedos,
> las miro desde abajo,
> les hago lo de siempre
> y, pese a todo, ved:
>   no pasa nada.

> [Writing a poem is like an orgasm:
> ink stains just like semen,
> it impregnates more too, on occasions.
> And yet there are afternoons
> when I feel words up,
> bite their breasts and their agile legs,
> raise their skirts with my fingers,
> look at them from below,
> do what I always do
> and, in spite of everything, you see:
>   nothing happens.]

Thus González puts writing poetry into rather crass terms that must be understood as part of his reaction against the idealized view of poetry as the creation of beautiful objects or as the expression of incorporeal, spiritual truths. Focusing as usual on the act of writing instead of on the product, and emphasizing the manual manipulation necessary to creativity ("manoseo," "mis dedos"), González gives poetry-making a very different face from the pure one he will portray others as advocating in "Orden. (Poética a la que otros se aplican)," analyzed earlier. Unlike the "pure poets" who look skyward, his speaker approaches poetry as one would a flesh-and-blood lover. His approach, however, is coldly physical and mechanical, and his lover does not always respond to the repertoire of techniques he employs. But despite the speaker's clinical attitude toward his love object (the text), his writing is nevertheless creative play, whose "foreplay," as Mary Makris appropriately calls it, does not always bring results. The poem ends with another kind of play, the incorporation of misquotation from another poet:[23]

> Lo expresaba muy bien César Vallejo:
> «Lo digo, y no me corro».
>
> Pero él disimulaba.

The poem demystifies poetic creation, not only through employing crass terminology but also in its irreverent misuse (or abuse?) of a previous poetic text. At the same time it implies that poetic play, when successful, yields creative results. González's poem, like Vallejo's words, is deceptive. The poet speaks of failure, yet he creates a successful poem.

    The poem that best exemplifies González's ludic approach to the question of aestheticist poetics is "J. R. J." from *Prosemas o menos*. Here the unresponsive textual body represented in "A veces" as a woman takes the form of a car. The efforts of the poet, who is demystified even further by being cast into the role of a "laborioso mecánico" [hardworking mechanic], become even more mechanical. As in earlier poems, González focuses on the production of the poem, examining the poetic act itself and the relationship between the worker-poet and his product. His description of Juan Ramón Jiménez tightening the screws of an epithet, greasing an adverb, and painting the artifact yellow highlights the technical and artificial aspects of writing.

Like other poems examined previously, "J. R. J." undermines the almost mystical view of art as sublime and unmasks the mystery of poetic creation. And as in "A veces," González transforms a previous text's words by giving them a new context.[24] He plays with the poetic purity of Juan Ramón's two-line text "El poema" [The poem]: "¡No le toques ya más, que así es la rosa!" [Don't touch it any more, for thus is the rose!]. In their new setting, the words he quotes acquire a humorous dimension as the reader is asked to compare a rose with a broken-down car and the creation of a poem with the speaker's fragile victory over the recalcitrance of machines. Instead of the poet/creator who hits upon beauty as surely and naturally as God creates a rose, this Juan Ramón tinkers, errs, and even swears. The poem, which for Marx can become a fetish, an object of superstition and fantasy, is exposed as a mechanical device made out of words. The disapproving portrayal of the way Juan Ramón, like "los nuevos bardos" of González's ode, deals with the tools of the trade recalls Trotsky's rejection of a narrow critical approach that counts alliterations and classifies metaphors. Trotsky states: "The effort to set art free from life, to declare it a craft self-sufficient unto itself, devitalizes and kills art."[25] On the one hand, then, "J. R. J." continues González's serious debunking of artifice in poetry. Yet at the same time González's ingenious text draws our attention to its own craftsmanship. Much as Jiménez's creative imagination paints the world yellow, González's cleverly transforms the sublime poet into a "laborioso mecánico."

Thus the thread of iconoclasm that runs through González's poetry can assume in his later books a more ludic face as he explores the complexity of the creative act and of the problematic relationships between "reality," poet, text, and reader. By emphasizing the primacy of language itself and of literary systems, as well as the force of context and convention, González challenges the notion of a natural relationship between images and the world.

In this regard a brief return to González's poem "El Cristo de Velázquez," examined in chapter 6, is warranted. The poem is made possible by Velázquez's down-to-earth portrayal of religious figures, which convey the humanity of their models. González's poem gives a familiar visual icon—Christ on the Cross, as depicted by Velázquez—a new verbal context that affects the way we see it. Through defamiliarization, González thus calls attention to the verbal contexts that stand behind all visual representations. He exposes the interdependence of images and cultural history, something that, as Mitchell points out, Mark Twain's comments on a Guido Reni painting did over a hundred years ago. (Twain noted that because of the painting's title, people stood before it and wept; if they had contemplated the painting alone, they would have viewed it as depicting a "Young Girl with Hay Fever; Young Girl with Her Head in a Bag.")[26] González, like Twain, undermines the notion of the self-sufficiency of the visual image and of the separateness of the arts and requires his reader to step in and out of the framing that extratextual ideological presuppositions provide.

Thus González shows a distrust of images, a belief that they do not stand in natural relationship to the world. As in earlier poems in which statues stood for powerful repressive political figures, he shows how artists do not simply reflect reality by creating images but project contextual ideology through them. By asking us to see artistic images or poetic words as separate from their context (Velázquez's Christ, or Vallejo's sentence) or by imaginatively transforming poets like Juan Ramón Jiménez or Stéphane Mallarmé (in "S. M. nos contempla desde un daguerrotipo" [S. M. views us from a daguerreotype], p. 370), he highlights the process of interpretation, showing how poetic commemoration can and perhaps inevitably does become ideological appropriation. Though not as explicitly, González problematizes the relationship of the poet or artist to posterity much as Luis Cernuda does in his poem "Birds in the Night," which protests a society that alienates and rejects poets in life but converts them into cultural icons after death.[27] Such poems as "El Cristo de Velázquez" and "A veces" draw González's readers into his texts, leaving spaces they must enter in order to complete the poem.[28] His readers must supply the conventional contexts for his images and relate them to González's unconventional ones.

By pitting (con)text against the images he (re-)creates, González challenges the notion of natural images—of mimesis itself—through play with what words and systems of meaning can do in combination, rather than what they can portray. Also challenging the notion of texts as portraits of reality, but this time through indeterminate, self-contradictory imagery, is the poem "A la poesía" (p. 297). The poem, first of all, falls into the tradition that includes Jiménez's "Vino primero pura" [She first came pure]. Characterizing poetry as a woman, the text evokes the two poles of artifice and simplicity through such words as "oscuras" [obscure], "simple" [simple], "transparente" [transparent], "puro" [pure], and "apasionadamente" [passionately]. The first few lines refer to a tradition of statements about poetry: "Ya se dijeron las cosas más oscuras. / También las más brillantes" [The most obscure things have already been said. / Likewise the most brilliant]. The speaker, who starts to say he wants to interact erotically with the text ("Quiero tomarte" [I want to take you]) but completes his thought several lines later with the word "el pelo," suggests, by evoking the expression "tomarle el pelo a alguien" [to pull someone's leg], that the poet's relationship to the poem is both erotic and playful. The transformation of the beloved from blonde to brunette (the two beauties recall not only Bécquer but also more generalized cultural categorization and evaluation, perhaps including poetic categories themselves) challenges mimesis. If in "Poesía eres tú" [Poetry is you] González sees a verbal system (the dictionary) as the source of the poem, here play with language and with literary tradition generates an unstable image with two different faces, a blonde who turns into a brunette. The poem reveals multiple layers of language and a complex interaction between purely linguistic relationships and images themselves. This fictional portrayal of poetry's instability, moreover, contests the fixity of all representations. Further challenging the concept of poetry as image-creation is the fact that instead of a representation, the text is an action, noteworthy for what it does, not what it depicts. Finally, the changeover from blonde to brunette captures the linguistic awareness that words always evoke and contain their opposites, a notion that itself opposes mimesis.

In González's second period, then, he moves from intense anti-aestheticism to a more complex and sometimes more playful depiction of image-making and image-makers. This change permits him to enjoy the artifice of his imaginative portrayals. In addition, he uses his own image as a recurrent focus, assuming clearly fanciful poses in a number of fictional self-portraits. Much as he transformed other poets in poems discussed earlier, he transforms and defamiliarizes himself in these texts. His self-portraits increasingly suggest the fictional nature of all history-making and witnessing. González parallels in his new attitude toward poetic testimony such poststructuralist challenges to historiography itself as that posed by Hayden White, described as follows by J. Fisher Solomon:

> White effectively textualized the criticism of historical narrative itself, arguing that even the writer of history is trapped inside his or her own governing tropes, unable to achieve unmediated contact with an objective historical referent. With no transcending master code for the writing of history, the historian became a meta-historian, a writer about writing, about the irreducibly deflecting tropes of historical narration, inherently unable to represent an immediate historical presence.[29]

Although González's self-portraits are based on his personal history, he often undercuts his poems' referential thrust by pointing to language itself as his source. "Realismo mágico" [Magical realism] (pp. 254–55) is such a case. Even its title suggests the linguistic sleight of hand the poet uses to produce a seemingly documentary text out of linguistic accident. The poem's unlucky speaker has consulted a medium, whose dire predictions have all come true:

> Ese médium marica
> (y si lo llamo
> así, no es porque fuese
> un poco afeminado—que lo era—,
> sino porque, además de otros contactos,
> tenía relación con los espíritus.
> Pero en fin, a lo nuestro:)
> ese marica y médium me predijo
> con ayuda del naipe
> las peores desgracias para agosto.
> Y realmente acertó.
>
> [That gay medium
> (and if I call him
> that, it's not because he was
> halfway queer—because he was—,
> but because, apart from other contacts,
> he had relations with spirits.
> But to get back to our subject:)
> that queer and medium predicted for me
> with the help of the cards
> the worst misfortunes for August.
> And he really hit the mark.]

The speaker, fearful of more disasters, decides to "guardar silencio" [to keep quiet], but to wear around his neck "una pequeña mano haciendo la puñeta" [a little hand gesturing obscenely], which he aims "al mundo y al trasmundo, a mí y a ustedes" [at the world and at the otherworldly, at myself and at all of you]. The speaker's language has apparently assumed a doubly anti-aesthetic function. The little fist (another incarnation of the writer's hand as his instrument and as a sexual organ, both part of traditional symbology)[30] is an obscene gesture and, as the title suggests, a bit of practical magic intended to ward off the evil that could appear at any moment from any direction—not only from the gods, but from those he addresses, or even from the speaker himself. In fleeing words in favor of an obscene gesture linking reader, poet, and gods, the poet plumbs the depths of the antisublime.

Chance, which in the poem figures as a trap, generates the figure of the "médium marica," a phrase that, as González's explanation denies but simultaneously suggests, was probably born in his imagination out of the phonetic suggestiveness of the phrase "medio marica."[31] This "médium marica," conjured out of linguistic accident, represents the trickster figure that, as Stewart declares, violates taboos and bridges gaps between male and female, sacred and profane.[32] Since the trickster's role is not only to destroy but also to establish culture, he is an appropriate guide for the speaker in protecting his potency in all respects.

It is precisely the recognition that language does not match reality, the awareness of the fictional and partially aleatory nature of all linguistic expression, that shapes González's consciously imaginary self-portraits. In 1984 he expresses, under the title "Sobre poesía y poetas," the following ludic vision of poetic self-portraiture:

> [N]ada explica o justifica a la poesía salvo el poema mismo. En cambio, el poema y la poesía suelen explicar algunas cosas; entre otras, . . . al propio poeta que, más que creador del poema, debe ser considerado su criatura: un subproducto, una excrecencia de las palabras.
> El poeta no es, en consecuencia, quien escribe el poema, sino el que queda escrito, lo que es leído; una apariencia, una aparición que sólo se materializa en la fantasía del lector.
> Su existencia es precaria; depende de los otros. . . .
> Escribir poesía es una forma de diversión, una manera de distanciarnos del que somos siempre, de salir de nosotros mismos.
> Verterse en el verso, ser otro allí: verse en el verso igual que en un espejo; el mismo y distinto; ajeno, extraño, raro: in-verso.[33]

[Nothing explains or justifies poetry except the poem itself. On the other hand, the poem and poetry usually explain some things; among others, . . . the poets themselves, who, more than the creators of the poems, should be considered their children; a subproduct, an outgrowth of the words.
The poet, therefore, is not the one who writes the poem, but the one who is written, that which is read; an appearance, an apparition that only materializes in the fantasy of the reader.
The poet's existence is precarious; it depends on others. . . .
Writing poetry is a diversion, a way of distancing ourselves from the one who we always are, of getting out of ourselves.
To pour yourself into verse, to be someone else there: to see oneself in verse just as in a mirror; the same and different; alien, strange, odd: in-verse.]

In a certain way this acceptance of personal history as fiction—which permits multiple selves instead of a faithful mirroring—leads to a reconciliation between González's rejection of the sublime and the hidden romantic impulses within him.[34] Thus many of the poses that romantic poets assumed[35] crop up in González's self-portraits. Like the romantics, he sees himself variously as misunderstood, superior or God-like, crazed, inebriated, moonstruck, impecunious, hyperaware, and rebellious.

González's romantic self-portrayals are not limited to his later poetry. He played the role of anguished, dissident outsider in the transitional "Preámbulo a un silencio," for example. But such stances do become more prevalent in later years. The section of *Muestra* titled "Poesías sin sentido" offers several examples of González's tongue-in-cheek version of himself as a romantic. In "A la poesía," he is "viejo y pobre" [old and poor], a kind of outsider who nevertheless dares to approach the beauty of poetry. In "Dato biográfico," as in other poems, he adopts lyric attitudes only to bracket them as just playful or pretended. The speaker is in part a solitary, bohemian night-wanderer searching for higher meaning, but at the same time his insights are suspect because of his class-based feeling of superiority, if only over anthropomorphized cockroaches. In "Oda a la noche o letra para tango," the poet is a solitary soul, drunk with the night's beauty, a romantic looking at stars (the very act González criticizes in "Orden. [Poetica a la que otros se aplican"]). But González's reference to the stars as "un lujo / que ha pasado de moda" refers us to poetic fashion, to the historical dimension of writing, the social determinants and poetic models out of which a poem is born. "Oda a la noche" is in a sense a battle between the poet's romantic self-image and his consciousness of his own historical constraints as a writer, and between mimetic impulses and the hegemony of poetic models. González creates a romantic poem, but he frames it with a metapoetic context that says, "I know I can't do this in this day and age, but I'll pretend I can." Under the influence of a more relativistic approach that validates multiple perspectives, González has let down his guard toward poetic icons.

In the section of *Prosemas o menos* titled "Biografía e historia" [Biography and history], González's ludic approach to witnessing takes the form of joke poems in which surprise or inversion clearly conflicts with the mimetic thrust of the text. In "Así parece" (pp. 390–91) he plays a variant of the misunderstood poet at the margins of productive society: the family black sheep. González himself emphasizes the poem's fictional nature: "Quien habla ... es un personaje, a pesar de estar vestido con mis trajes y tener parientes que se llamaban como mis propias tías"[36] [The speaker ... is a fictional character, despite being dressed in my clothes and having relatives that had the same names as my own aunts]. The speaker portrays himself as a disappointment to his relatives, who silently lament his fate. He suggests that his lack of religious orthodoxy bothers his aunts ("Ciertas tías devotas no pueden contenerse, / y lloran al mirarme" [Certain pious aunts can't contain themselves, / and they cry when they look at me]). His impractical nature disturbs his aunt Clotilde, who returns from the grave to admonish *"¡Con la belleza no se come! ¿Qué piensas que es la vida?"* [Beauty doesn't put food on the table! What do you think life is?]. His mother predicts insanity and dissipation—"manicomios, asilos, calvicie, blenorragia" [insane asylums, rest homes, baldness, gonorrhea]. But his relatives' accusation "que no tengo sentido alguno de la realidad" [that I have absolutely no sense of reality] humorously and paradoxically signals the reversal of life and death that lies at the heart of the poem. The relatives who preach a sense of reality are ghosts whose continued existence in the speaker's head is precisely what betrays his sense of unreality. Even more absurd, it is he, the living, who constitutes a "funesto espectáculo" [mournful spectacle] for his dead relatives. González's poem, with its speaker who hears voices in his head, raises questions about truth and fiction. What seems truly phantasmal on the one hand expresses on the other an undeniable fact: that family relationships affect us long after our loved ones are dead.

González's playful and artful construct that allows certain touches of romanticism to intrude distances him somewhat from the iconoclastic viewpoint of certain earlier poems. But what this text, like his comments in "Sobre poesía y poetas" [On poetry and poets], has in common with his earlier, more ideologically committed poetry is his consciousness of the interpersonal nature of identity and the inescapable bearing of the past on the present. The poem is thus not totally different from much earlier poems. "Para que yo me llame Angel González," as I showed earlier, portrays him as the product of all those who had come before. Other poems envision individuals as literally keeping each other alive through psychic awareness. In the early "Muerte en el olvido" [Death in being forgotten] his beloved can keep him alive by not forgetting him, much as his relatives live on in his mind in "Así parece". The interpersonal view of existence even allies this poem with "Contra-orden. (Poética por la que me pronuncio ciertos días)" and its anonymous graffiti. Certainly his recent love poem "De otro modo" [Otherwise] suggests an interdependence between individuals and between past, present, and future. This poem continues the play on life and death, life in death and death in life, that has always characterized his poetry, as in the early "Yo mismo" [I myself] (in which his body "marcha solo" [goes along on its own], having taken over and vanquished his real self).

These analyses show the complexity of González's attitudes toward poetry and poets, including himself. It seems clear that his point of departure, aesthetically, was an iconoclasm that distrusted ideologies and perceptions that were devoid of a dialectical self-examination or a connection to a comprehensive socioeconomic picture. Such attitudes clearly underlie his poems attacking the Franco regime, such as "Mensaje a las estatuas," which exposes ideology as embodied in artistic forms, as well as poems like "Zona residencial," examined earlier in this chapter. His second period paradoxically both intensifies and erodes his iconoclastic caution as his belief in the social utility of words lessens. An even greater distrust of the images and visions individuals project leads him to the consciousness of the fictionality of all language, which in turn leads to the unleashing of imaginative play. Thus the Angel González that in earlier poems was a witness to a particular reality becomes a series of poetic fictions in later works. An enemy of artifice in his early iconoclasm, González in his later phase, more aware of the unbridgeable gap between words and things, is more permissive.

González's changing attitudes toward poetic images reflects the impact of postmodernist trends in general. In his early poetry, he might be said to challenge aesthetic impulses that believe themselves to exist outside history and politics. As he develops as a poet, he moves from dissent based on a belief in the universalist metanarrative of social progress through Marxism (which Jean-François Lyotard would term a prescriptive legitimation of knowledge)[37] to dissent based on the renunciation of universalizing schemes. As he develops, González writes less about pure and impure poetry and the political significance of each; instead he comes to problematize in his poetry the act of writing poetry itself. Like other postmodernists he raises the issue of "language as shaping human consciousness"[38] rather than vice versa. His poetry poses as well what Matei Calinescu calls one of the main questions of postmodernist writing: "Can literature be other than self-referential, given the present-day radical epistemological doubt and the ways in which this doubt affects the status of representation?"[39] As to his own self-portrayals, they become parodic recognitions that reality is made up of multiple fictions.

An incisive critic of González's poetry, José Luis García Martín, detects continuity throughout González's oeuvre. Yet he observes that the poet's division of his work into two phases nevertheless makes sense, because "los mismos elementos, reorganizados de diferente manera, adquieren un sentido nuevo." He emphasizes the ludic thrust of González's later poems: "El componente lúdico—también presente anteriormente, pero en mucho menor medida—pasará ahora a primer plano, junto a un gusto por no «engañar», por mostrar el revés de la trama: la literatura se hace manipulando las palabras; el poeta . . . no permite que nos olvidemos de ello" [The ludic component—also present earlier, but in a much lesser measure—will now come to the fore, together with a taste for not "deceiving," for showing the underside of the weave: literature is made by manipulating words; the poet . . . doesn't let us forget that fact]. García Martín expresses as follows his belief that, despite artifice and fiction, a lyrical witness can be found even beneath González's virtuosity:

> Con tal exhibición de artificio, se corre el riesgo de dejar admirado, pero no emocionado, al lector, de dejarlo sólo con la boca abierta como ante un sorprendente juego de manos. No siempre acierta a sortear tal riesgo *Angel González*: una sonrisa y un «chapeau» es el premio que entonces recibe ante su más difícil todavía. Pero su juego es, en muchas ocasiones, el de la ruleta rusa, un juego en el que le va la vida: bajo un pudoroso envoltorio de chistes, coloquialismos y ejercicios retóricos, *Angel González* ha escrito algunos de los más sobrios, intensos y emocionados poemas de nuestra lírica contemporánea.[40]

[With such an exhibition of artifice, the risk is run of leaving readers astonished, but not moved, of leaving them only with their mouths open, as in the presence of a surprising sleight of hand. *Angel González* doesn't always elude such a danger: a smile and a tip of the hat is the prize that he receives for his "even more difficult." But his game is, many times, one of Russian roulette, a game in which he risks his life: beneath a self-effacing wrapping of jokes, colloquialisms and rhetorical exercises, *Angel González* has written some of the most sober, intense, and heartfelt poems of our contemporary lyric poetry.]

9
Conclusion

In my readings of the poetry of Angel González, I have attempted not only to show the complexity of individual texts but also to examine the development of his oeuvre within its biographical, literary, and historical context. I have postulated that González's early works, although they contain the seeds of later conceptual play, are conditioned by the intensity of his sense of responsibility and by inner exile, and that only in his second period do his circumstances permit the full flowering of his ludic gifts.

My task has been complicated, at once limited and enhanced, by a peculiar quality of his work that has been aptly defined as follows by Douglas K. Benson:

> A primera vista sus poemas parecen ser bien asequibles, tanto por su empleo del habla cotidiana al estilo de la época como por su inclusión de elementos reconocibles de la cultura popular. Sin embargo, cuando intentamos precisar una *voz* poética o un centro lógico que lo unifique todo, siguiendo los preceptos de la crítica de la primera mitad de este siglo, la superficie de sus textos se vuelve arena movediza. La obra de González es por lo tanto más difícil de caracterizar que la de sus contemporáneos, y esto ha resultado en valoraciones muy desiguales. . . .[1]

> [At first sight his poems seem to be quite accessible, as much for their use of everyday language in the style of the period as for his inclusion of recognizable elements of popular culture. Nevertheless, when we try to pinpoint a poetic *voice* or logical center that unifies everything, following the precepts of criticism during the first half of this century, the surface of his texts turns into quicksand. González's work is for this reason more difficult to characterize than that of his contemporaries, and this has resulted in very uneven appraisals. . . .]

The conceptual complexity beneath the deceptive outward accessibility of González's poems and the varied tones that characterize his work explain the cautious critical judgments his work has sometimes elicited. Although especially evident in critics like Florentino Martino who approach González's poetry armed with traditional tools and expectations,[2] this reserve regarding González's unsystematic approach to writing poetry led even the innovative *novísimo* poet Guillermo Carnero to use caution in assessing *Muestra*—a book he described at its appearance in 1976 as "un alumbramiento de muchos caminos que el poeta ha señalado sin decidirse a marchar por ninguno de ellos" [an illumination of many paths that the poet has pointed out without deciding to go down any of them]. Carnero hailed the book as signaling a renewal of poetic vitality but nevertheless implied that without further works and more decisiveness on González's part in defining his poetic route, it remained to be seen whether *Muestra*'s diversity represented poetic richness or a scattering of the poet's energy. Carnero expressed hope that in González's subsequent work a pattern would emerge to reveal the coherence of the poet's development.[3]

Despite occasional hesitancy on the part of critics, scholarly interest in González's work has only increased and remains high.[4] My readings of his poetry—and the openness of his texts, noted by Andrew P. Debicki, Margaret H. Persin, and Mary Makris—suggest to me that his poetry's challenge to his reader is precisely the source of its appeal. As the poet has affirmed along with his critics, his readers must complete his texts by supplying much of the context on which his ludic transformations are based. If, as this need for completion by readers suggests, his poetry can be said to encompass its readings, the many intriguing critical refractions his poems have inspired make his work very rich indeed.

González's poetry holds special attractions for those interested in exploring how the grounds of the acts of writing and reading have changed since the late 1960s. The ludic poems of *Palabra sobre palabra* are frequently conceptual art that appeals to those concerned with postmodern trends in literature and theory. Debicki, long keenly interested in González's poetry, has accorded the Asturian a prominent position within Spanish postmodernism, citing as features that align him with postmodern tendencies the openness of his texts, his emphasis on process, and the metapoetic aspects of his poetry.[5] The very lack of system and unity that disturbed Carnero may in fact be indicative of González's assimilation of a pluralistic postmodern sensibility that rejects the purist, universalist, and utopian leanings of modernism and exhibits a "sense of multiple and partial participations and investments."[6] In questioning reason, objectivity, and language's power to coincide with something outside itself, the postmodern cast of González's work reflects the legacy of early twentieth-century science and linguistics, both influential in the development of postmodernist art. In playing with literary systems, with linguistic patterns, with commonsense notions of time, space, and causality, and with the process of poetry-writing itself, González shares with other postmodernists a debt to this early twentieth-century linguistic and logical skepticism.[7]

A few final glances at the theories and definitions of postmodernism put forth by such thinkers as Matei Calinescu, Ihab Hassan, and Jean-François Lyotard help round out the picture painted in the preceding chapters of González's ludic poetry. Hassan posits indeterminacy, derived from Nietzsche's thought, as a basic feature of postmodernism. He describes this indeterminacy as embracing many features that the preceding chapters have shown to be fundamental to González's poetry: the "demystification of reason," the rejection of the human being as the measure of all value; the portrayal of the subject as a fiction; and the recognition of "facts" as perspectives or interpretations.[8] The self-referentiality typical of postmodernist works, which Calinescu attributes to the consciousness of indeterminacy and to epistemological skepticism, is also clearly evident in González's works.[9]

The fragmentation that has resulted from the postmodernist rejection of totalizing schemes assumes a multitude of forms in González's poetry.[10] The disjunctive presentation of his *ars poetica* in the section of *Muestra* subtitled "Metapoesía," the fracturing of time in poems like "Ayer," and the breaking of the body into separate parts in "Mi vocación profunda" are typical examples of this postmodernist phenomenon. The most striking feature of González's ludic work is in fact the sense of rupture it conveys. His poetic self-portraits, as has been shown, involve mutations between animal and human realms, bodily fragmentation, breaks in the boundaries separating life and death and past and future, and the overt separation of literary form from literary content. His texts themselves sometimes break in two when his images invoke two mutually exclusive visions, as in "A la poesía." He flouts propriety and either violates literary traditions outright or stretches them to the breaking point, as in "Avanzaba de espaldas aquel río."

The quicksand that González's work represents results not only from fragmentation but also from the related postmodernist leaning toward "strange alliances and unholy couplings," from its tendency to "assume that all languages, whether natural or artistic, can only re-present already uttered discourses, in a patchwork or mosaic of references, allusions, and quotations."[11] As has been shown, González mixes high and low culture—Velázquez and bullfighting—and parodies numerous kinds of social and literary discourse.

The "self-less-ness" Hassan points to as another key feature of postmodernism, which can take the form of "self-multiplication," the suppression or dispersal and even the attempt to recover "the 'deep' romantic ego," characterizes González's fictional self-portraits, discussed in chapter 8. Hassan enumerates other tendencies that appear in many of González's poems: loss of belief in representation, decanonization, irony, hybridization, and carnivalization. For Hassan, "what Bakhtin calls novel or carnival—that is, antisystem—might stand for postmodernism itself, or at least for its ludic and subversive elements that promise renewal." González has clearly reaped the invigorating benefits of carnival, discovering what Bakhtin has termed "the peculiar logic of the 'inside out' . . . , of numerous parodies and travesties, humiliations, profanations, comic crownings and uncrownings," even of himself.[12] Carnivalization, like the disjunctive quality of González's work, is clearly related to the poet's iconoclasm, which I have also considered at length in chapter 8.

But I believe that González's poetry is compelling for readers and critics not only because of its ludic value or its postmodern cast. His development is also of interest because of his personal history, his particular response over time to the Sartrean question of what literature should be. His evolution from sociopolitical *engagement* to a more playful attitude is symptomatic of what Lyotard has described as the generalized delegitimation of the grand narratives of society after World War II due to the effects of technological development. González's disillusionment with the power of words reflects his loss of faith in Marxism, a political metanarrative that for Lyotard sometimes represents the kind of grand narrative that seeks to liberate humanity.[13]

González's rejection of totalizing schemes, related to deconstruction's exposure of the Transcendental Signified behind humanistic inquiry, has led González to concentrate in his second period on the aleatory quality of the creative as well as the interpretive act.[14] His statement on irony in his work reveals the self-subversion inherent in his messages: "La ironía como distancia está, creo, en la base de todo lo que escribo. La ironía para expresar la complejidad de la realidad, un sí y un no a la vez"[15] [Irony as distance is, I believe, at the base of everything I write. Irony to express the complexity of reality, a yes and a no at the same time]. Thus after his midcareer disillusionment with words, González challenges his readers through juxtapositions and defamiliarization that expose the limitations and pitfalls of logocentric discourse. He distances and even alienates readers but through the parataxis or negative capability that Hassan points to as another hallmark of postmodernism, promotes caution toward ways of knowing and encourages awareness that knowledge is not "a copy or image of reality imprinted on the mind" but "is better understood as a matter of social practices, disputes, and agreements, and not as the property of some particular mode of natural or unmediated representation."[16] He commemorates but shows how commemoration is determined by elegiac traditions. He expresses the romantic sublime but brackets such overblown expression as one possibility, not a totalizing transcendence. González depicts himself and his subjectivity in a romantic fashion but exposes the fictional nature of our self-constructs. His speaker becomes a "personaje de ficción, que trata vanamente de imitarme."[17] In a play-of-mirrors reversal, he thus overturns mimesis; instead of the author struggling to find the words to imitate his own reality, the character tries in vain to mimic the author. Thus González's poetry does what indeterminate art tends to do, according to Hassan: "delay closures, frustrate expectations, promote abstractions, sustain a playful plurality of perspectives, and generally shift the grounds of meaning on [its] audiences."[18]

It may be that González's ludic poetry expresses a moment Hassan describes as follows: "We have killed our gods—in spite or lucidity, I hardly know—yet we remain ourselves creatures of will, desire, hope, belief. And now we have nothing—nothing that is not partial, provisional, self-created—upon which to found our discourse."[19] Or perhaps, in line with Susan Stewart's view of nonsense as a way of learning about learning, González's ludic poetry is a manifestation of a moment in history when social consensus has been challenged and new ways of learning are desperately needed.

Notes

Chronology

1. All translations are mine, unless otherwise indicated. For the titles of González's books of poetry, I use Donald Walsh's translations for the volumes from *Aspero mundo* through *Procedimientos narrativos* and my own translations for subsequent ones. The translations of certain titles of poems and of certain poems themselves are also Donald Walsh's, in which case they are identified by the abbreviation DDW. See González, *"Harsh World" and Other Poems,* translated by Donald D. Walsh (Princeton: Princeton University Press, 1977).

2. It is difficult to do justice to González's title in a translation. The invented word "prosemas" contains both "poema" [poem] and "prosa" [prose]. The word could also be divided into "pro" [pro] and "semas," a possible Spanish version of "semes," or signs. Finally, the ending "-más" combines with "o menos" to form the Spanish phrase "más o menos" [more or less].

3. Again, González's title is not easily translated. I have taken "en fantasma" as a word play on "en persona" [in person]. My translation embodies a similar play on the English term "personified."

Chapter 1. Introduction

1. Andrew P. Debicki, *Poetry of Discovery: The Spanish Generation of 1956–1971* (Lexington: University Press of Kentucky, 1982), p. 59.

2. Debicki has noted in González's poetry of the eighties a renewed lyricism that includes many traditional elements. See Debicki, *Angel González* (Madrid: Júcar, 1989), pp. 86, 104.

3. Angel González, *Poemas: Edición del autor* (Madrid: Cátedra, 1980), p. 19.

4. Ibid.

5. González, "Angel González o la desesperanza," interview by Federico Campbell, in *Infame turba,* ed. Federico Campbell (Barcelona: Lumen, 1971), pp. 371–79.

6. Debicki, *Poetry of Discovery,* pp. 59–80; Douglas K. Benson, "Linguistic Parody and Reader Response in the Worlds of Angel González," *Anales de la Literatura Española Contemporánea* 7, no. 1 (1982): 11–30.

7. González's comments are found in *Poemas,* pp. 21–22.
8. Ibid., p. 21.
9. George Steiner, *Language and Silence: Essays on Language, Literature, and the Inhuman* (New York: Atheneum, 1967), p. 53.
10. González, *Poemas,* p. 22.
11. Silvio Gaggi, *Modern/Postmodern: A Study in Twentieth-Century Arts and Ideas* (Philadelphia: University of Pennsylvania Press, 1989), pp. 21, 109.
12. Matei Calinescu, *Five Faces of Modernity: Modernism, Avant-Garde, Decadence, Kitsch, Postmodernism* (Durham, N.C.: Duke University Press, 1987), p. 306.
13. Marjorie Perloff, *The Poetics of Indeterminacy: Rimbaud to Cage* (Princeton: Princeton University Press, 1981), pp. 37, 301. Perloff borrows the term *unmediated presentation* from Jerome Rothenberg.
14. Gaggi, *Modern/Postmodern,* pp. 20–21, 102.
15. Angel González, "Entrevista a Angel González," interview by Sharon Keefe Ugalde, in *En homenaje a Angel González: Ensayos, entrevista y poemas,* ed. Andrew P. Debicki and Sharon Keefe Ugalde (Boulder, Colo.: Society of Spanish and Spanish-American Studies, 1991), p. 122.
16. Fredric Jameson, *The Prison-House of Language: A Critical Account of Structuralism and Russian Formalism* (1972; reprint, Princeton: Princeton University Press, 1974), p. 173.
17. Fanny Rubio and José Luis Falcó, "Estudio preliminar," *Poesía española contemporánea: Historia y antología (1939–1980),* 2d ed. (Madrid: Alfaguara, 1982), pp. 76, 80–82.
18. Angel González, "Poesía española contemporánea," *Los Cuadernos del Norte* 1, no. 3 (August-September 1980): 4–7; reprinted in *Angel González: Verso a verso* (Oviedo, Spain: Caja de Ahorros de Asturias, 1987), p. 161.
19. Carlos Bousoño, "La poesía de Guillermo Carnero," introduction to *Ensayo de una teoría de la visión: Poesía 1966–1977,* by Guillermo Carnero (Madrid: Hiperión, 1979), p. 13.
20. Gaggi, *Modern/Postmodern,* p. 130.
21. Patrick Josef LeCertúa, "Angel González: Poetry as Craft and the 'Word upon Word' Experience" (Ph.D. diss., University of Kentucky, 1982), p. 129.
22. Biruté Ciplijauskaité, "Purificación y esencialidad en la más joven poesía," in *After the War: Essays on Recent Spanish Poetry,* ed. Salvador Jiménez Fajardo and John C. Wilcox (Boulder, Colo.: Society of Spanish and Spanish-American Studies, 1988), p. 113.
23. González, "Entrevista" (Ugalde interview), 125.
24. González, "Palabras pronunciadas en el acto de entrega de los premios Príncipe de Asturias 1985," in *Angel González: Verso a verso,* p. 213.
25. Both Debicki and Persin stress the role of the reader in connection with González's poetry. Persin notes the deceptive simplicity of González's poetry in "Presence versus Absence in the Early Poetry of Angel González," in *Recent Spanish Poetry and the Role of the Reader* (Lewisburg, Pa.: Bucknell University Press, 1987), pp. 98–99. Debicki repeatedly underlines the fact that González's reader is often invited to continue the creative process begun in the text (*Angel González,* pp. 87, 106).
26. Douglas K. Benson, "Las voces de Angel González," in Debicki and Ugalde,

En homenaje a Angel González: Ensayos, entrevista y poemas (Boulder, Colo.: Society of Spanish and Spanish-American Studies, 1991), p. 7.

27. Paul Ilie, *Literature and Inner Exile: Authoritarian Spain, 1939–1975* (Baltimore: Johns Hopkins University Press, 1980).
28. Bousoño, "Poesía de Guillermo Carnero," p. 22.
29. Gaggi, *Modern/Postmodern,* p. 50.

Chapter 2. Roots and Connections: The Genesis of *Palabra sobre Palabra*

1. González, "Poesía y compromiso," in *Poesía última,* ed. Francisco Ribes (Madrid: Taurus, 1963), pp. 58–59.
2. González speaks of his grandfather having left a legacy of "dos rasgos indelebles: el ovetensismo y la relación con del mundo de la enseñanza" [two indelible traits: identification with Oviedo and connection with the world of education]. See interview by Miguel Somovilla, "Breves acotaciones para una biografía: Angel González verso a verso," in *Angel González: Verso a verso,* p. 100.
3. Ibid., p. 101.
4. Ibid., p. 102.
5. Juan García Hortelano, "Prólogo," in *El grupo poético de los años 50 (Una antología)* (Madrid: Taurus, 1978), p. 10.
6. González, "Breve acotaciones" (Somovilla interview), pp. 101–2.
7. Ibid., p. 101.
8. Ibid., pp. 108, 126.
9. González, "Angel González o la desesperanza" (Campbell interview), p. 371.
10. González, "Breves acotaciones" (Somovilla interview), p. 105.
11. Ibid.
12. Ibid., pp. 106–9.
13. González, "Angel González o la desesperanza" (Campbell interview), pp. 371–75.
14. González's and Somovilla's comments are from González, "Breves acotaciones" (Somovilla interview), pp. 100, 126, 128.
15. Angel González, "Angel González, poeta: Con esperanza, sin convencimiento," interview by Víctor Claudín and Alfonso González-Calero, *Ozono* 4, no. 36 (September 1978): 51.
16. González, *Poemas,* pp. 15–16.
17. González, "Breves acotaciones" (Somovilla interview), pp. 116–18.
18. Ibid., p. 117.
19. Ibid.
20. Ibid., pp. 116–17.
21. Antonio Hernández, *Una promoción desheredada: La poética del 50* (Madrid: Zero, 1978), p. 309; reprinted in Pedro Provencio, *Poéticas españolas contemporáneas: La generación del 50* (Madrid: Hiperión), p. 32. Joaquín González Muela provides a good overview of *Aspero mundo:* "Hay un poema-prólogo, escrito sin duda a posteriori, en el que se expresa la contradicción entre el 'acariciado mundo' (que formará la última parte del libro)—un mundo que es una mujer,

'realidad casi nube'—y un 'áspero mundo' que ha venido después, más real tal vez. . . . Poemas del desengaño: por un amor perdido, 'áspero mundo'. . . ." [There is a poem-prologue, no doubt written a posteriori, in which the contradiction is expressed between the "cherished world" (which will form the last part of the book)—a world that is a woman, "a reality that is almost a cloud"—and a "harsh world" that came afterward, perhaps more real. . . . Poems of disillusionment: because of a lost love, a "harsh world." . . .]. See "La poesía de Angel González en su primer período," in *Homenaje a Casalduero: crítica y poesía,* ed. R. Pincus Sigele and Gonzalo Sobejano (Madrid: Gredos, 1972), p. 32.

22. González, "Angel González o la desesperanza" (Campell interview), p. 372.

23. González, *Poemas,* p. 20.

24. See González Muela, "La poesía de Angel González en su primer período," for a description of *Sin esperanza, con convencimiento.*

25. González, "Breve acotaciones" (Somovilla interview), p. 119.

26. González, "Poesía y compromiso," pp. 58–59.

27. González, "Angel González: el asturiano disimula con la ironía su sentimentalismo," interview by Ignacio Gracia Noriega, *La Nueva España,* 5 October 1985.

28. Angel González, "Poética: Defensa de la poesía social," in *Antología de la nueva poesía española,* 2d ed., ed. Leopoldo de Luis (Madrid: Alfaguara, 1969), p. 266.

29. Angel González, "Cuestionario," in *Antología de la nueva poesía española,* ed. José Batlló (Madrid: El Bardo, 1968), pp. 342–44.

30. González's observations are from his *Poemas,* pp. 18–20.

31. Francisco Ribes, "Nota preliminar," in *Poesía última* (Madrid: Taurus, 1963), p. 12.

32. González, "Breves acotaciones" (Somovilla interview), p. 127.

33. González, *Poemas,* p. 20.

34. Ibid., p. 21.

35. González, "Palabras pronunciadas," p. 213.

36. González, "Poesía y compromiso," pp. 57–59.

37. In Hernández, *Poética del 50,* p. 309.

38. Emilio Alarcos Llorach, *Angel González, poeta (Variaciones críticas)* (Oviedo, Spain: Universidad de Oviedo, 1969). Alarcos's observations are from pp. 10–27, 58–62, 126, 132.

39. Angel González, *Palabra sobre palabra,* 4th ed. (Barcelona: Seix Barral, 1986), pp. 201–2. Subsequent references to the poetry from this collection will be given in the text. Later editions were published by Seix Barral in 1992 and 1994.

40. Alarcos Llorach, *Angel González, poeta,* p. 110.

41. LeCertúa, "Poetry as Craft," p. 99.

42. González, *Poemas,* p. 21.

43. Guillermo Carnero, "El último libro de Angel González: Alumbramiento de muchos caminos," *Informaciones de las Artes y las Letras,* 16 December 1976, p. 5.

44. Angel González, "Antología temática," in *Guía para un encuentro con Angel González,* Luna de Abajo Cuaderno de Poesía no. 3 (La Felguera, Langreo, Spain: Luna de Abajo, 1985), p. 74.

45. Ibid., p. 85.
46. José Antonio Sotelo and Andrés Barba, *Literatura española contemporánea* (Madrid: Dossat, 1986), p. 297.
47. García Martín, "La poesía última de Angel González," in *Guía para un encuentro con Angel González,* Luna de Abajo Cuaderno de Poesía no. 3 (La Felguera, Langreo, Spain: Luna de Abajo, 1985), p. 60.
48. Rubio and Falcó, *Poesía española contemporánea,* pp. 72, 76.
49. González, "Angel González o la desesperanza" (Campbell interview), pp. 377–78.
50. González, "Angel González, poeta" (Claudín and González-Calero interview), p. 52.
51. González, *Poemas,* p. 21.
52. Northrop Frye, *Anatomy of Criticism: Four Essays,* 1st paperback ed. (Princeton: Princeton University Press, 1971), p. 97.
53. Hazard Adams, introduction to *Critical Theory Since 1965,* ed. Hazard Adams and Leroy Searle (Tallahassee: Florida State University Press, 1986), p. 1.
54. González, "Angel González o la desesperanza" (Campbell interview), pp. 367–70.
55. Ibid., pp. 371–75.
56. Daniel Sueiro, "Angel más poeta," in *Guía para un encuentro con Angel González,* p. 40.
57. Ana María Moix, "Veinticuatro horas de la vida de . . . Angel González," *Tele-eXprés,* 4 November 1972, 25.
58. Ibid.
59. Angel González, "Conversación con Angel González," interview by Faustino F. Alvarez, in Angel González, *Una antología,* 2d ed. (Oviedo, Spain: Automóviles Luarca, S. A., 1985), p. 12.
60. González, "Breves acotaciones" (Somovilla interview), p. 134.
61. Ibid., pp. 134–35.
62. Ibid., p. 131.
63. González, "Angel González" (Gracia Noriega interview).
64. Angel González, *Antonio Machado* (Madrid: Júcar, 1986), p. 8.
65. Carnero, "Alumbramiento de muchos caminos," p. 5.
66. Jaime Gil de Biedma, "Angel," in *Guía para un encuentro con Angel González,* Luna de Abajo Cuaderno de Poesía no. 3 (La Felguera, Langreo, Spain: Luna de Abajo, 1985), p. 27.
67. González, "Breves acotaciones" (Somovilla interview), pp. 123, 126.
68. Gaggi, *Modern/Postmodern,* p. 21.
69. Ibid., p. 153.

Chapter 3. The Poetry of *Engagement:* From Inner Exile to Expressive Freedom

1. For a discussion of literariness, see Victor Erlich, "Russian Formalism," in the *Princeton Encyclopedia of Poetry and Poetics,* enlarged ed., ed. Alex Preminger (Princeton: Princeton University Press, 1974), p. 727. Riffaterre made the distinction I have noted at a special session of the 1990 MLA convention.

2. Fredric Jameson, *The Political Unconscious: Narrative as a Socially Symbolic Act* (Ithaca: Cornell University Press, 1981), p. 282.

3. Susan Stewart, *Nonsense: Aspects of Intertextuality in Folklore and Literature*, 1st paperback ed. (Baltimore: Johns Hopkins University Press, 1989), pp. 44–45 n. 91.

4. Guillermo Carnero, "Precedentes de la poesía social de la posguerra española en la anteguerra y guerra civil," *Boletín de la Fundación Juan March*, 1973, 10.

5. Not coincidentally, Machado's ideological background resembles in some ways that of González's father. In *Antonio Machado*, his introduction to Machado's life and works, González describes Machado's family and ideas in terms resembling those he has applied to his own family. His tone of admiration for Machado's mother recalls González's devotion to his own mother. And as in commenting on his own life, he makes much of Machado's upbringing in a home "regido y sostenido por mujeres" [ruled and maintained by women], speculating on the intense sense of responsibility this must have produced in Machado (pp. 22–23). González's references to Machado's grandfather as an "insobornable liberal" [uncorruptible liberal] (p. 15) and to Machado himself as "un sutil negador de Dios, radicalmente escéptico" [a subtle denier of God, radically skeptical] parallel González's portrait of his own family's liberal tradition and his father's outspoken agnosticism. His sympathy with these attitudes is obvious.

6. The quotation from González's poetry is from "Contra-orden (Poética por la que me pronuncio ciertos días)," in *Palabra sobre palabra*, p. 293. The examples of prewar rhetoric applied to pure and impure poetry are from Carnero's "Precedentes de la poesía social," pp. 14–17, as are his further observations. González's choice of critical subjects—he wrote one book on Machado and one on Jiménez—is revealing regarding his perspective on the poles of this debate. González wrote another critical study of Bécquer, a poet whom Machado also favored.

7. González, "Poesía española contemporánea," p. 162.

8. Jean-Paul Sartre, "Commitment," in *Existentialism and Humanism*, trans. Philip Mairet (London: Philosophical Library, 1947); reprinted in *The Modern Tradition: Backgrounds of Modern Literature*, ed. Richard Ellmann and Charles Fiedelson, Jr. (New York: Oxford University Press, 1965), pp. 853–54.

9. Fredric Jameson traces the evolution of individual enmeshment in larger systems, apparent in many areas of critical theory and exemplified by "Marx's ever-scandalous discovery that 'it is not the consciousness of men that determines their existence, but on the contrary their social existence determines their consciousness.'" See Jameson, *Prison-House of Language*, p. 184.

10. Tino Villanueva, *Tres poetas de posguerra: Celaya, González, y Caballero Bonald (Estudio y entrevistas)* (London: Tamesis, 1988), p. 336.

11. González, "Entrevista" (Ugalde interview), p. 122.

12. Debicki, *Poetry of Discovery*, p. 58.

13. Villanueva, "Censura y creación: Dos poemas subversivos de Angel González," *Hispanic Journal* 5, no. 1 (Fall, 1983): 54.

14. See Villanueva, "Censura y creación," for a description of this phenomenon.

15. Shirley Mangini, *Rojos y rebeldes: La cultura de la disidencia durante el franquismo* (Madrid: Anthropos, 1987), p. 62.

16. Carnero, "Precedentes de la poesía social," p. 5.

17. Bousoño, "Poesía de Guillermo Carnero."
18. González himself has noted that starting with *Breves acotaciones para una biografía* in 1971, "escribo con mayor libertad, una mayor libertad expresiva" [I write with greater freedom, with a greater expressive freedom]. He attributes this fact to a temporary disillusionment with the "valor de la palabra poética" [value of the poetic word]. Alarcos Llorach and Angel González, "El poeta y el crítico," in *Angel González: Verso a verso*, p. 52.
19. Villanueva, *Tres poetas de posguerra*, p. 342.
20. These interpretations are found in ibid., pp. 166–85.
21. Ibid., p. 125 n. 18.
22. Benson, "Linguistic Parody," pp. 17, 27 n. 2.
23. Persin, *Recent Spanish Poetry*, pp. 98–99.
24. Villanueva, *Tres poetas de posguerra*, pp. 135–38.
25. Benson, "Linguistic Parody," 19–20.
26. Persin, *Recent Spanish Poetry*, pp. 100–103.
27. Ilie, *Literature and Inner Exile*, p. 81.
28. See Jonathan Culler, *The Pursuit of Signs: Semiotics, Literature, Deconstruction* (Ithaca: Cornell University Press, Cornell Paperbacks, 1988), pp. 135–54. Two of González's critics, Margaret H. Persin and Philip W. Silver, have noted the significance of his use of apostrophe and have applied Culler's remarks on the subject to González. See Persin, *Recent Spanish Poetry*, pp. 105–7, and Silver, "What Are Poets For?: Reference, Unamuno, Social Reality, Angel González," in *Simposio-Homenaje a Angel González*, ed. Susana Rivera and Tomás Ruiz Fábrega (Madrid: José Esteban, 1987), 90–93. My analysis of this poem confirms Persin's perception of the importance of the dialectic of presence versus absence in González's poetry of this period.
29. Culler, *Pursuit of Signs*, p. 146.
30. Ibid., p. 135.
31. González has himself noted that in "Campo de batalla" and "Entreacto" he is not alluding to a concrete battlefield or theatrical performance. See Alarcos Llorach and González, "El poeta y el crítico," pp. 62–63.
32. Ibid.
33. González has stated that his "torvo jardinero" was inspired by Camus's play *Le malentendu*. See González, "Entrevista" (Ugalde interview), p. 119.
34. Alarcos Llorach and González, "El poeta y el crítico," p. 63.
35. Julian Palley, "Angel González and the Anxiety of Influence," *Anales de la Literatura Española Contemporánea* 9, nos. 1–3 (1984): 94.
36. Persin, *Recent Spanish Poetry*, p. 99.
37. Alarcos Llorach, *Angel González, poeta*, pp. 15–16.
38. Ilie, *Literature and Inner Exile*, p. 12.
39. Quoted by Mangini in *Rojos y rebeldes*, p. 59.
40. Ilie, *Literature and Inner Exile*, pp. 14, 116. Ilie quotes from Juan Goytisolo's "Examen de conciencia," in *El furgón de cola* (Paris: Ruedo Ibérico, 1967).
41. Villanueva speaks of González's tendency to "esquivar su realidad histórica" [to evade his historic reality] in *Tres poetas de posguerra*, p. 123. LeCertúa views *Sin esperanza, con convencimiento* as having "opened social poetry to wider perspectives" and having "established González as one of the most articulate voices of social protest in Spain." See LeCertúa, "Poetry as Craft," p. 197. But LeCertúa has

also perceived in the "[r]hetorical strategies" of *Grado elemental* the qualities of "dissimulation, ambiguous diction, and tentativeness" that "obscure the intentions of indictment and censure" (p. 47).

42. Susan Sontag, *Against Interpretation and Other Essays* (New York: Dell, 1978), p. 25. Her comments are from her essay "On Style," written two years after *Sin esperanza, con convencimiento* was published. Sontag argues here against the separation of content and style and against the notion that art can serve any particular morality. "All great art," she says, "induces contemplation, a dynamic contemplation. However much the reader or listener or spectator is aroused by a provisional identification of what is in the work of art with real life, his ultimate reaction—so far as he is reacting to the work as a work of art—must be detached, restful, contemplative, emotionally free, beyond indignation and approval" (p. 27). For Sontag, "[o]nly when works of art are reduced to statements which propose a specific content, and when morality is identified with a particular morality (and any particular morality has its dross, those elements which are no more than a defense of limited social interests and class values)—only then can a work of art be thought to undermine morality" (p. 25).

43. Max Aub stresses the importance of the deaths of Antonio Machado, García Lorca, and Hernández in their attaining the status of cultural heroes. See *Poesía española contemporánea* (Mexico: Era, 1969), p. 200. On the twentieth anniversary of Machado's death, a large group of dissident writers gathered in Collioure to pay their respects. For Mangini, this event consolidated the goals of the "generación del 50." See Mangini, *Rojos y rebeldes*, p. 107.

44. Debicki, *Angel González*, p. 33.

Chapter 4. The Textures of Politics and Verbal Play in González's Second Period

1. González's remarks are from *Poemas*, p. 21.
2. Mangini, *Rojos y rebeldes*, p. 100.
3. Ibid., pp. 59, 85.
4. Ibid., pp. 85–86.
5. Ibid., p. 97.
6. Ibid., pp. 104, 92, 93. Mangini refers to the Opus Dei as an "organización religioso-tecnócrata," p. 92.
7. Juan Goytisolo, *En los reinos de Taifa* (Barcelona: Seix Barral, 1986), pp. 5–7.
8. Mangini, *Rojos y rebeldes*, p. 145.
9. Ibid.
10. Ibid., p. 110.
11. Ibid., p. 151.
12. Ibid., p. 171.
13. Bousoño, "Poesía de Guillermo Carnero," pp. 13, 22–24.
14. Ibid., pp. 26–27.
15. Debicki makes a similar point about "Las palabras inútiles" [Useless words] from *Palabra sobre palabra* in *Angel González*, pp. 58–59. He states that the speaker of that poem "[p]resenta su tema de la limitación de la palabra en relación con su

«cuento» de amor" [presents his theme of the limitation of the word in relation to his love "story"]. A few years later, in *Breves acotaciones para una biografía,* the emotions and experiences of the speaker are secondary: "el hablante sólo importa como creador de una imagen chocante" [the speaker only matters as the creator of a shocking image]. For Debicki, González at this point was emphasizing technique, not anecdote.

16. Mangini, *Rojos y rebeldes,* p. 25.

17. Manuel Vásquez Montalbán, *Crónica sentimental de España* (Madrid: Espasa Calpe, 1986), p. 197.

18. The speaker's complex attitude regarding memories, pointed out by Debicki in *Angel González* (p. 32), may be due in part to the phenomenon of survivor's guilt. Mangini views González's generation as prey to "la mala conciencia" [a guilty conscience]. See *Rojos y rebeldes,* p. 113. Debicki links the ambiguity he finds in González's early poems to the tensions between the poet's relatively happy adolescence and the tragic memories of the period. González has continued to explore the question of memory. In "Empleo de la nostalgia" [The use of nostalgia] *(Procedimientos narrativos),* as Debicki indicates, González again conveys the "irresolución de los recuerdos" [irresolution of memories] (p. 69).

19. As Mangini has pointed out, the work of González and other poets of his generation, because of the irony and subjectivity that had always been present in their poems, does not seem to break as sharply with social realism as did the writings of novelists like Juan Goytisolo and Juan Marsé. See Mangini, *Rojos y rebeldes,* pp. 154–55.

20. Ihab Hassan, *The Postmodern Turn: Essays in Postmodern Theory and Culture* (Columbus: Ohio State University Press, 1987), p. 169.

21. González, *Poemas,* p. 21.

22. Ibid.

23. Walter Redfern, *Clichés and Coinages* (Oxford and Cambridge, Mass.: Basil Blackwell, 1989), p. 149.

24. Gaggi, *Modern/Postmodern,* p. 20.

25. The complex relationship between art and politics, so striking in "La paloma" and "Yarg Nairod," can be said to be a constant in González's work. "Mensaje a las estatuas" and "Entreacto" are among earlier works that merge politics with the depiction of an artistic work. Douglas K. Benson and Mary Makris offer readings of "Yarg Nairod." See Benson, "Angel González y *Muestra* (1977): Las perspectivas múltiples de una sensibilidad irónica," *Revista Hispánica Moderna* 40 (1978–79): 57–58; and Makris, *Under the Influence: Intertextual Strategies in the Poetry of Angel González* (Ann Arbor, Mich.: University Microfilms International, 1990), pp. 146–47. Interestingly, in "Yarg Nairod," González alludes to Oscar Wilde, proponent of art for art's sake, an aesthetic philosophy that González clearly "reverses" in this poem.

26. Calinescu, *Five Faces,* p. 299.

27. Ibid., pp. 274–75.

28. Stewart, *Nonsense,* p. 171.

29. Ibid., pp. 138–43.

30. *Renaissance and Baroque Poetry of Spain,* ed. Elias Rivers (New York: Dell, 1966), p. 278. The English prose translation is by Rivers.

31. Calinescu cites Gianni Vattimo as the source of the terms *strong* and *weak*

thought. As described by Calinescu, postmodern "weak thought" has roots in Heideggerian philosophy. It replaces the homogenizing and universalizing force of "strong thought" with "attentiveness and compliance to the inner demands of the object of interpretation." For a full discussion of this subject and of Calinescu's concept of revisiting the past, see Calinescu, *Five Faces*, pp. 272–76.

32. Sontag, *Against Interpretation*, p. 25.

Chapter 5. Play with the Logic of Time and Place

1. Stewart, *Nonsense*, pp. 14, 17.
2. Calinescu, *Five Faces*, p. 305.
3. J. Fisher Solomon, *Discourse and Reference in the Nuclear Age* (Norman: University of Oklahoma Press, 1988), p. 12.
4. Although other ludic features (e.g., incompatible spheres of discourse) are more typical of González's second period, as will be shown in chapter 6, poems that depend on violations of common sense and logic are present from the very first—not surprising if one considers both the weight of existentialist notions prevalent during this period and the fact that at the time, González and many others experienced the world of the Spanish postwar as absurd. This attitude has been pointed out by Mangini in *Rojos y rebeldes*, p. 63.
5. Stewart, *Nonsense*, p. 172.
6. González appropriates at times traditional elegiac images, such as smoke and shadows. Pere Rovira has pointed out similar use of the river and nightfall. See Rovira, "Los *prosemas* de Angel González," *Insula*, no. 469 (December 1985): 10.
7. Many critics have discussed the need for readers to complete González's poetry and the ambiguity his texts sometimes create. See the works of Persin, Benson, and Debicki.
8. Stewart, *Nonsense*, p. 35.
9. Debicki, *Angel González*, pp. 24–25.
10. For a different reading, which takes into account the significance of Mondays and Wednesdays in relation to the work week, see ibid., p. 24.
11. Stewart, *Nonsense*, pp. 88–100.
12. For a discussion of liminality and its relation to the carnivalesque, see Gustavo Pérez Firmat, *Literature and Liminality: Festive Readings in the Hispanic Tradition* (Durham, N.C.: Duke University Press, 1986), pp. xiii–xxi, 1–15. According to Pérez Firmat, the carnivalesque inverts hierarchies, while the liminal threatens distinctions between the central and the marginal.
13. The speaker in "Penúltima nostalgia," after evoking the styles of a certain epoch, addresses past time to lament the selectivity of memory, which permits us to forget the great tragedies of history but to remember trivial details.
14. Mangini, *Rojos y rebeldes*, pp. 25–26.
15. Vázquez Montalbán, *Crónica sentimental*, p. 185.
16. David K. Herzberger, "Narrating the Past: History and the Novel of Memory in Postwar Spain," *PMLA* 106, no. 1 (January 1991): 36, 43. The poem has something in common with Juan Benet's portrayal of postwar Spain as what Herzberger terms a diseased body that is "the foundation of stasis" (p. 37). Herzberger quotes Benet's reference to "aquel cuerpo enfermo y mutilado por la guerra" [that body

sick and mutilated by the war] and to "el conjunto de numerosas, horrendas y paralizantes medicinas que le fueron suministradas en la paz que siguió" [the collection of numerous horrendous and paralyzing medicines that were administered to it in the peace that followed].

17. Marjorie Perloff, *Poetic License: Essays on Modernist and Postmodernist Lyric* (Evanston, Ill.: Northwestern University Press, 1990), p. 226.

18. The jarring dissonance between the question of whether today is Thursday and the tone of the poem recalls another text in which the same question appears. See González, "Eruditos en campus," pp. 371–72. I discuss this poem in chapter 6.

19. Different methods of organizing time in other societies—such as the Mayan, with its years of twenty-eight weeks of thirteen days each—underscore the conventional nature of some of our temporal cycles.

20. Stewart, *Nonsense,* p. 96.
21. Ibid.
22. Ibid., p. 29.
23. Benson, "Voces," p. 7.
24. Sara Martin points to this technique in her analysis of "Inventario." See Martin, *The Poetry of Angel González: Standing with the Reader* (Ann Arbor, Mich.: University Microfilms International, 1987), pp. 125–30. See also her commentary on "Cumpleaños," pp. 39–40, and on the use of defamiliarization in general in González's poetry, pp. 82–92. See also Stacey L. Parker, "Desfamiliarización en la poesía de Angel González," *Inti* 21 (Spring 1985): 75–82.

25. Wim Tigges, *An Anatomy of Literary Nonsense* (Amsterdam: Rodopi, 1988), p. 135.

26. Ihab Hassan, *Paracriticisms: Seven Speculations of the Times* (Urbana: University of Illinois Press, 1975), p. 55.

27. C. Christopher Soufas, *Conflict of Light and Wind: The Spanish Generation of 1927 and the Ideology of Poetic Form* (Middletown, Conn.: Wesleyan University Press, 1989), p. 26.

28. Gaggi, *Modern/Postmodern,* pp. 50–51.
29. Stewart, *Nonsense,* p. vii.

Chapter 6. Play with Spheres of Discourse in González's Second Period

1. Juan Goytisolo and Jaime Gil de Biedma are among those who turn a critical eye on bourgeois attitudes.

2. Gaggi, *Modern/Postmodern,* pp. 21, 65.

3. The poem has a novelistic parallel in Juan Goytisolo's *La isla* (Barcelona: Seix Barral, 1961). This narrative chronicles the experiences of a group of privileged vacationers on the Costa del Sol and the vacuous desperation of their lives. The difference between the novel and the poem reflects aesthetic shifts between 1961 and 1972. González's poem induces the reader to focus on systems of meaning rather than on society per se.

4. Stewart, *Nonsense,* p. 19.

5. Gloria Fuertes, *Obras incompletas: Edición de la autora,* 7th ed. (Madrid: Cátedra, 1981), p. 135.

6. Stewart, *Nonsense*, p. 38.
7. Ibid., p. 61.
8. Gaggi, *Modern/Postmodern*, p. 118.
9. Moix, "Veinticuatro horas," p. 25.
10. Tigges, *Anatomy of Literary Nonsense*, pp. 52–53. For Tigges, the personification of cockroaches found in this poem would be typical of the nonsense technique of mirroring, or what Stewart terms "reversals and inversions," which includes the inversion of classes, as in treating animals as persons.
11. The reference to Jencks and the characterization of postmodernism are from Calinescu, *Five Faces*, pp. 277, 283.
12. Gaggi, *Modern/Postmodern*, p. 153.
13. Christopher P. Wilson, *Jokes: Form, Content, Use, and Function* (London: Academic Press, 1979), p. 13.
14. Hassan, *Paracriticisms*, p. 57.
15. The poem might be compared with Jorge Guillén's "La hermosa y los excéntricos" [The beauty and the eccentrics], in *Aire Nuestro: Cántico, Clamor, Homenaje* (Milan: All'Insegna del Pesce d'Oro, 1968), pp. 670–87. In this poem, Guillén counterposes what he sees as the disorder of sexual indeterminacy with the order of male-female love. He chooses a political structure (that of the monarchy) to embody this order. Postmodernist González, in contrast, manifests his loss of faith in institutions and language by creating indeterminate texts like this one.
16. Stewart, *Nonsense*, p. 88.
17. At a symposium at the University of New Mexico in February 1985, González stated that he sometimes parodies poetic styles for which he feels an affinity in order to avoid simply repeating them.
18. In an essay first published in 1981, González refers to such an interpretation of the cow, used in a poem by Ramón Pérez de Ayala, as a "compendio de teosofía" [a compendium of theosophy]. González mentions Pérez de Ayala's appropriation of Clarín's view of the cow—and of that of Buddhism. He declares Pérez de Ayala's vision colored by a "costra literaria y cultural" [literary and cultural crust]. In his own poem, González clearly takes advantage of a similar cultural overlay. González's essay, titled "Ramón Pérez de Ayala: Verbalización del paisaje y credo estético" [Ramón Pérez de Ayala: Verbalization of language and aesthetic creed], is reprinted in *Angel González: Verso a verso*, pp. 167–73.
19. For a discussion of this poem, see Makris, *Under the Influence*, pp. 25–31.
20. Hassan, *Postmodern Turn*, p. 191.
21. González's avoidance of emotion through nonsense and humor may be related to postmodern trends in art that cast doubt on the possibility of "meaningful communication." Interpreting the humor of such poems as "Dato biográfico" as a form of avoidance of direct expression is compatible with Freud's belief that jokes are frequently vehicles for indirect communication rather than simply entertainment and is supported as well by sociological studies showing that joking can make possible the simultaneous proffering and withholding of a given message, as when sexual jokes are made to broach the possibility of involvement with an interlocutor in an ambiguous, inexplicit, and therefore riskless way. For an explanation of these theories, see Wilson, *Jokes*, pp. 174–75.
22. This poem may also be González's response to his own rejection of "ethereal" poetry. In another poem, he seems to chastise those who look heavenward for

inspiration. See "Orden. (Poética a la que otros se aplican)," p. 292. Here, however, he breaks his own rule and comments obliquely on the restrictions of poetic fashion.

23. González, *Poemas*, p. 23.
24. Gaggi, *Modern/Postmodern*, pp. 59, 65.
25. In portraying art as a skillful lie, González's text undermines its own credibility. In this sense it is a metapoetic text that deconstructs its own message and gives rise to an infinite regression. At the same time, in offering a kind of misreading of Velázquez, the poem comments upon the process of reading as (mis)interpretation. For an excellent discussion of the ekphrastic and intertextual dimensions of this poem (its relation to Velázquez's painting and to Unamuno's poem on that painting), see Mary Makris, "Intertextualidad, discurso y ékfrasis en 'El Cristo de Velázquez' de Angel González," in Debicki and Ugalde, *Homenaje a Angel González,* pp. 73–83.
26. Calinescu, *Five Faces*, p. 274. See also Jean-François Lyotard, *The Postmodern Condition: A Report on Knowledge,* trans. Geoff Bennington and Brian Massumi (Minneapolis: University of Minnesota Press, 1979), for a discussion of the concept of metanarratives.
27. Gaggi, *Modern/Postmodern*, p. 78.
28. José Luis García Martín, review of *Prosemas o menos,* in *El Ciervo: Revista Mensual de Pensamiento y Cultura* 34, nos. 415–16 (September-October 1985): 53.
29. Stewart, *Nonsense*, p. 88.
30. Hassan, *Postmodern Turn*, p. 45.

Chapter 7. Literary Tradition versus Speaker Experience in the Poetry of Angel González

1. González, *Poemas*, p. 21.
2. González's shift from experience to schemes is in a sense a reenactment of the linguistic revolution that started with Ferdinand de Saussure. Jonathan Culler states that for Saussure language is "form, not substance," a system of signs that have meaning only in relation to each other, that is, to the linguistic system of which they are a part. See Culler, *Ferdinand de Saussure* (1976; New York: Penguin, 1977), p. 42. For a discussion of Saussure's view of the autonomy of the system and its existence parallel but never coincident with reality or things, see Jameson, *Prison-House of Language*, pp. 13, 32. González's personal "linguistic revolution" seems to have been precipitated by frustration with language and doubts about its efficacy and relationship to reality, in much the same way as frustration (and often retreat into silence) accompanied the period of transition in the early twentieth century from "a substantive way of thinking to a relational one." See Jameson, *Prison-House of Language,* pp. 10–15.
3. González, *Poemas*, p. 22.
4. Benson, for example, has illuminated in "Linguistic Parody" González's reliance on linguistic parody to create complex poems out of political and social clichés. Debicki emphasizes how González modifies "previous views, conventions, texts, and perceptions." See Debicki, *Poetry of Discovery,* p. 60.

5. Stewart's comments are from *Nonsense*, pp. 39, 47, 200.
6. Stewart's comments on metafiction are from ibid., p. 21.
7. González, *Poemas*, p. 16.
8. Redfern, *Clichés and Coinages*, p. 14.
9. Debicki's reading of "Las palabras inútiles" confirms my opinion that the anecdotal is primary here. See Debicki, *Angel González*, p. 58.
10. LeCertúa suggests that González "associates the creative act of poetry with the concept of love," thus fusing the word and experience. See LeCertúa, "Poetry as Craft," p. 45. It is noteworthy that González chose the title of this short book of love poetry as the title of his complete works. As Debicki points out, the title signals the poet's "creciente preocupación . . . con el quehacer poético" [growing preoccupation . . . with the task of poetry]. See Debicki, *Angel González*, p. 53.
11. González, *Poemas*, p. 20.
12. LeCertúa locates the beginning of González's "antipoesía" slightly later, in *Breves acotaciones*.
13. Debicki, *Angel González*, p. 34.
14. Perloff, *Poetics of Indeterminacy*, pp. 28–29 n. 15, quotes Roger Cardinal's essay "Enigma," *Twentieth-Century Studies* 12 (1974): 42–62. Perloff also discusses the term *unmediated presentation*, which she attributes to Jerome Rothenberg (p. 37).
15. See Margaret H. Persin, Andrew P. Debicki, Nancy Mandlove, and Robert Spires, "Metaliterature and Recent Spanish Literature," *Revista Canadiense de Estudios Hispánicos* 7, no. 2 (Winter 1983): 297–309. Note particularly Mandlove's fine analysis of "Calambur" from *Muestra*, which she terms "a metapoetic pun—full of intertextual echoes and revitalized conventions" (p. 304). Also see Rubio and Falcó's discussion of metapoetry during this period in the works of such younger poets as Gimferrer, Carnero, and Talens, in *Poesía española contemporánea*, pp. 86–88.
16. Michael Riffaterre, *Semiotics of Poetry* (Bloomington: Indiana University Press, 1978), p. 6.
17. Frye, *Anatomy of Criticism*, pp. 95–97.
18. According to Elizabeth Drew, the poet reveals human beings to themselves but not "by the direct means of logical analysis." See Drew, *Poetry: A Modern Guide to its Understanding and Enjoyment* (New York: Dell, 1969), p. 32. James W. Johnson speaks of the following qualities as commonly attributed to lyric poetry: "brevity, metrical coherence, subjectivity, passion, sensuality, and particularity of image." See his article on lyric in Preminger, *Princeton Encyclopedia of Poetry and Poetics*, p. 461. German Bleiberg states that "el sentido es un elemento secundario, en una composición lírica: ésta no se somete a normas gramaticales ni lógicas. . . . La lírica es consecuencia de una eclosión emocional, producida por sentimientos elementales y comunes a todos los hombres y a todos los tiempos; su temática puede reducirse a dos sentimientos básicos: el amor y la muerte" [The sense is a secondary element, in a lyric composition: the latter is not subject to norms of grammar or logic. . . . Lyric poetry is the consequence of an emotional outburst, produced by elemental feelings common to all people and to all times; its range of themes can be reduced to two basic sentiments: love and death]. See Bleiberg and Julián Marías, *Diccionario de literatura española*, 4th ed. (Madrid: Revista de Occidente, 1972), p. 528.

19. Carlos Bousoño, *Teoría de la expresión poética,* 4th ed., enlarged (Madrid: Gredos, 1966), pp. 546–47.
20. González, *Poemas,* p. 19.
21. Debicki makes a somewhat similar point regarding the dual nature of González's poetry. He states that the poem "Meriendo algunas tardes" [I eat some afternoons] "ilustra cómo un énfasis en recursos verbales sirve para crear una experiencia imaginativa por une parte y comunicar las limitaciones de tiempo y palabras por otra" [illustrates how an emphasis on verbal techniques serves to create an imaginative experience on the one hand and to communicate the limitations of time and words on the other]. See Debicki, *Angel González,* p. 61.
22. Riffaterre, *Semiotics of Poetry,* p. 166.
23. Ibid., p. 2.
24. Frye, *Anatomy of Criticism,* p. 143.
25. Ibid., p. 142.
26. M. H. Abrams has in fact termed the pastoral elegy "the most convention-bound of literary forms." See Abrams, *A Glossary of Literary Terms,* based on the original version by Dan S. Norton and Peters Rushton (New York: Holt, Rinehart and Winston, 1960), p. 19.
27. For a different view of this poem, see Sandra Schumm, "El aspecto alusivo de la poesía de Angel González," *Hispanic Journal* 12, no. 1 (Spring 1991): 133–45.
28. The definition is Jorge Guillén's. See Bleiberg and Marías, *Diccionario de literatura española,* p. 422.
29. This association is activated, for example, in the nineteenth-century American popular song "My Grandfather's Clock," by Henry Clay Work. The link also forms the basis of some of the imagery in Edgar Allen Poe's "Tell-tale Heart."
30. Riffaterre, *Semiotics of Poetry,* pp. 21, 165.
31. According to Bleiberg, "El poeta lírico casi siempre se expresa en presente, y desde el punto de vista de su proprio yo" [Lyric poets almost always express themselves in the present, and from the point of view of their own I's]. See Bleiberg and Marías, *Diccionario de la literatura española,* p. 528.
32. Preminger, *Princeton Encyclopedia of Poetry and Poetics,* p. 215.
33. Gaggi's comments are from *Modern/Postmodern,* pp. 129, 136, 137.
34. Perloff, *Poetics of Indeterminacy,* p. 34.
35. Juan Ramón Jiménez, *Primeros libros de poesía,* 3d ed. (Madrid: Aguilar, 1967), pp. 1499–1501. I am indebted to John Wilcox for pointing out the similarity between González's poem and the poems of the early Juan Ramón Jiménez.
36. Terry Eagleton points out that in Western culture we view ourselves as moving forward into the future. In at least one other culture, humans are considered to move backward into the future. See Eagleton, *Literary Theory: An Introduction* (Minneapolis: University of Minnesota Press, 1983), p. 15.
37. Bousoño has analyzed Machado in this way in his *Teoría de la expresión poética,* 4th ed. (Madrid: Gredos, 1966), pp. 139–50. For a discussion of the integration that characterizes symbolism and modernism versus the disintegration of poetry of indeterminacy, see Perloff, *Poetics of Indeterminacy,* pp. 29–30. The characterization of modernism as a "falling together" is James McFarlane's. See Bradbury and McFarlane, "The Mind of Modernism," in *Modernism 1840–1930,* Pelican Guides to English Literature (New York: Penguin Books, 1976), p. 92.

38. Gaggi, *Modern/Postmodern*, p. 21.
39. Ibid.
40. Frye, *Anatomy of Criticism*, p. 97; Culler, *Saussure*, p. 124.
41. Jameson, *Prison-House of Language*, p. 14.
42. González, *Poemas*, p. 23.
43. The quotations from Saussure are from Culler, *Saussure*, p. 49.
44. Riffaterre, *Semiotics of Poetry*, p. 166.

Chapter 8. Iconoclastic Images of Self and Other in *Palabra sobre palabra*

1. Hassan, *Postmodern Turn*, p. 49.
2. I use the term *modernism* to refer to the international movement and the term *modernismo* to refer to the turn-of-the-century Spanish movement known by that name. Jorge Guillén says of the cult of the image as an international phenomenon during the twenties, "Este cultivo de la imagen es el más común entre los muy diversos caracteres que juntan y separan a los poetas de aquellos años, y no sólo a los españoles. . . . El cultivo se convierte en un culto supersticioso" [This cultivation of the image is the most common of the very diverse qualities that unite and separate the poets of those years, and not only the Spanish ones. . . . The cultivation becomes a superstitious cult]. See Guillén, *Lenguaje y poesía: Algunos casos españoles* (Madrid: Alianza Editorial, 1972), p. 188. First published in English under the title *Language and Poetry* (Cambridge: Harvard University Press, 1961); first published in Spanish in Madrid by Revista de Occidente, 1972.
3. W. J. T. Mitchell, *Iconology: Image, Text, Ideology* (Chicago: University of Chicago Press, 1986), pp. 2, 153, 206.
4. Ibid., pp. 167, 172–74.
5. Eagleton, *Literary Theory*, pp. 19–21.
6. This period falls between 1956 and 1962, according to Mangini.
7. Susan Sontag, preface to Roland Barthes, *Writing Degree Zero*, trans. Annette Lavers and Colin Smith (New York: Hill and Wang, 1968), p. xix.
8. González's poems on the art of poetry (some included under the rubric "Metapoesía") have attracted considerable critical attention, not surprising given current interest in literary theory in general and metapoetry and metafiction in particular. See Debicki, *Angel González*, pp. 53–83; Makris, *Under the Influence*, pp. 200–215; Maria Nowakowska Stycos, "Intertextuality in Selected Spanish Poets Since 1939: Intertext/Poetics/Reader," in *After the War: Essays on Recent Spanish Poetry*, ed. Salvador Jiménez-Fajardo and John C. Wilcox (Boulder, Colo.: Society of Spanish and Spanish-American Studies, 1988), pp. 47–54; and Douglass Rogers, "Posturas del poeta ante su palabra en la España de posguerra," also in *After the War*, pp. 55–65. Stycos relates González's perspective to that of José Angel Valente, Francisco Brines, and Gloria Fuertes.
9. Aub discusses this tradition in *Poesía española contemporánea*, pp. 198–99.
10. Ortega y Gasset, *El tema de nuestro tiempo* (1923; Madrid: Espasa Calpe, 1968), pp. 65–66, 89–90.
11. Rosario Castellanos, born in the same year as González (and trained in philosophy), wrote a similar poem. In "Mala fe" [Bad faith], she undermines the

notion of progress by imagining herself—the end product of evolution—as "la cereza / puesta sobre la punta del helado" [the cherry / put on top of the ice cream]. See Castellanos, *Poesía no eres tú: Obra poética, 1948–1971* (Mexico: Fondo de Cultura Económica, 1972), p. 295.

12. "El Cristo de Velázquez" also undercuts this notion by emphasizing the reversibility of images of God and his human creation and by suggesting a God created "in man's image."

13. It should be noted that in this poem González is not necessarily responding directly to Guillén's poetry but to one of the questions raised by the critical community with respect to that poetry. González has stated that appreciation of Guillén's work came late to him. In "Glosas en homenaje a J. G." (Glosses in homage to J. G.], from *Prosemas o menos*, González renders graceful homage to the predecessor poet, although he suggests that the light of Guillén's vision is a particular, not universal, one: "De quien madruga a verla, / y no del sol, / procede / —aunque él no se lo crea— / la luz / que ordena y fija el mundo / en sus formas más bellas: / *Damas altas, calandrias* . . . / . . ." [From the one who gets up early to see it, / and not from the sun, / comes / —although he may not believe it— / the light / that gives order and stability to the world / in its most beautiful forms: / *High ladies, larks* . . . / . . .] (p. 375).

14. Barthes, *Writing Degree Zero*, p. 26.

15. For a different reading of this poem, see Makris, *Under the Influence*, p. 211. She views the poem as a "protest against how literature . . . can be used as a propaganda tool," a reading not supported by González's comments about the poem in "Angel fieramente humano," interview by Gracia Rodríguez, *Quimera* 35 (January 1984): 25. Guillén's famous comments were made in his letter to Fernando Vela. Apropos of González's reaction against an exclusive standard of what is poetic, he speaks as follows of his poetry's resemblance to the "antipoemas" of Nicanor Parra: "Los antipoemas de Parra coinciden con mi intención de hacer poemas con materiales, con léxicos, muy poco poéticos. . . . [N]o quiero que parezca un poema; que lo sea, pero que no lo parezca. No podría explicarlo mejor, pero este tipo de poemas sería como eructar en el banquete" [The antipoems of Parra coincide with my intention of making poems with materials, with vocabulary, that are not very poetic at all. . . . I don't want it to seem to be a poem; it should be one, but shouldn't seem to be. I wouldn't be able to explain it any better, but this type of poem would be like belching at a banquet]. See "Angel González o la desesperanza" (Campbell interview), p. 371.

16. The poem is from *En castellano* (Barcelona: Lumen, 1977). It is included in Blas de Otero, *Expresión y reunión: A modo de antología*, introduction and notes by Sabina de la Cruz (Madrid: Alianza Editorial, 1981), pp. 117–18.

17. Mitchell, *Iconology*, pp. 112–13.

18. Christopher Soufas perceived that the leftist-influenced members of the so-called Generation of 1927 were aware of "larger historical forces that shape individual existence" and of history as a "guiding force" that determines them "but that cannot be contained within a single personality." The insight could apply as well to González, explaining his tendency to be aware of his own and others' biases. See Soufas, *Conflict of Light and Wind*, p. 30. Mitchell's book makes clear that self-criticism has been an ideal of Marxism. See Mitchell, *Iconology*, p. 206.

19. Fuertes, *Historia de Gloria: Amor, humor y desamor*, 3d ed., ed. Pablo

González Rodas (Madrid: Cátedra, 1981), p. 57; and Walt Whitman, *Complete Poetry and Selected Prose,* ed. James E. Miller, Jr. (Boston: Houghton Mifflin, 1959), p. 349.

20. The fact that González included this poem in a "montage" of different statements of his poetics shows that by this time he was not presenting the icon of popular expression totally without irony. See Makris, *Under the Influence,* p. 202. However, Makris's observation that bigotry could be part of the people's voice suggests to me that González did not fully examine the "self-evident" nature of the positive valuation of the collectivity that he expressed in this poem.

21. For Martin, the smile connotes the speaker's amusement at his situation. See Martin, *Poetry of Angel González,* pp. 148–49.

22. See Makris's reading of this poem in *Under the Influence,* pp. 200–202.

23. For an explanation of this quotation, see ibid., pp. 200–201.

24. This procedure is similar to the joke technique of creating incongruity by putting words into different contexts that give them new meaning. Compare with the parody of John Masefield, quoted as follows by Wilson, in *Jokes,* p. 29: "I must down to the seas again, / to the lonely sea and the sky. / I left my vest and pants there, / I wonder if they're dry."

25. Leon Trotsky, "The Limitations of Formalism," from *Literature and Revolution,* trans. Rose Strunsky (New York: International Publishers, 1925), pp. 168–83, 234–36; reprinted in *The Modern Tradition: Backgrounds of Modern Literature,* ed. Richard Ellmann and Charles Fiedelson, Jr. (New York: Oxford University Press, 1965), p. 346.

26. Mitchell, *Iconology,* pp. 40–42. Mitchell quotes from Twain, *Life on the Mississippi,* chap. 44.

27. For a discussion of Cernuda's poem, see my essay, "Society, History, and the Fate of the Poetic Word in *La realidad y el deseo,*" in *The Word and the Mirror: Critical Essays on the Poetry of Luis Cernuda,* ed. Salvador Jiménez-Fajardo (Madison, N.J.: Fairleigh Dickinson University Press, 1989), pp. 166–80.

28. Debicki, Makris, and Persin have emphasized the open nature of González's texts, the space left in them for the reader to complete the text. See Debicki, *Angel González;* Makris, *Under the Influence;* and Persin, *Recent Spanish Poetry.*

29. Solomon, *Discourse and Reference,* p. 14.

30. For a discussion of the hand as both the symbol of male authority and the instrument of expression of inner states, see J. E. Cirlot, *A Dictionary of Symbols,* 2d ed., trans. Jack Sage (New York: Philosophical Library, 1971), p. 137. For a discussion of writing implements and hands as male sexual symbols, see Sigmund Freud, *A General Introduction to Psychoanalysis* (1924), trans. Joan Riviere (New York: Permabooks, 1953), pp. 162–63.

31. A similar phenomenon may have given rise to the poem "Monólogo interior" [Interior monologue], also inspired by a term from literary criticism. The purely phonetic similarity between the word "monólogo" and the name Manolo (very possibly intensified by interference in pronunciation from the English word *monologue* among González's American students) gives rise to the "ocurrencia"— the clearly fictional text.

32. Stewart, *Nonsense,* pp. 61–62.

33. González, "Sobre poesía y poetas," *Peña Labra: Pliegos de poesía* 82 (1982): 4.

34. José Méndez aptly refers to González's "romanticismo coloquial" [colloquial romanticism]. See Méndez, "La poesía en la ciudad," *Prólogo* 6 (January-February 1990): 22. Hassan views the creation of multiple selves, and even the yearning after the romantic ego, to be aspects of postmodernism. See Hassan, *Postmodern Turn*, p. 169.
35. Biruté Ciplijauskaité, *El poeta y la poesía* (Madrid: Insula, 1966), pp. 11–42.
36. Alarcos Llorach and González, "El poeta y el crítico," p. 57.
37. See Lyotard, *Postmodern Condition*, pp. 36–37.
38. Gaggi, *Modern/Postmodern*, p. 96.
39. Calinescu, *Five Faces*, p. 299.
40. García Martín, "Poesía última," p. 67.

Chapter 9. Conclusion

1. Benson, "Voces," p. 7.
2. Florentino Martino, "La poesía de Angel González," *Papeles de Son Armadans* 57 (1970): 229–31.
3. Carnero, "El último libro," p. 5.
4. Interest has also been high among Hispanists in the United States. Indications of continued attention to González's works here include the homage volume published by the Society of Spanish and Spanish-American Studies in 1991; Makris's 1990 dissertation at Rutgers University; two more dissertations, Peter E. Browne's at the University of Nebraska and Helena Antolin Cochrane's at the University of Pennsylvania, listed as completed in *Hispania* 75, no. 2 (May 1992): 370; and one further dissertation in progress (by Diane René Fisher at Ohio State University), according to the same listing. In 1993, a volume of English translations of González's poetry, by Steven Ford Brown and Gutierrez Revuelta, was published by Milkweed editions. González's presence in the United States over many years has undoubtedly furthered his reputation in this country, but the fact that his work dovetails with the emphasis on critical theory within Hispanic Studies in the United States may have contributed more significantly to critical interest in his work.
5. Debicki, "Poesía española de la postmodernidad," *Anales de Literatura Española* 6 (1988): 165–80.
6. The words are John Johnston's, from "Ideology, Representation, Schizophrenia: Toward a Theory of the Postmodern Subject," in *After the Future: Postmodern Times and Places,* ed. Gary Shapiro (Albany: State University of New York Press, 1990), p. 91. For a discussion of postmodernism's pluralistic tendencies, see Calinescu, *Five Faces*, pp. 280–83.
7. Gaggi stresses the contribution to postmodernism of the awareness of the limitations of reason, citing the challenge that early-twentieth-century science, especially modern physics, posed to previous ways of making sense of the world. The awareness of the limits of commonsense categories of "space, time, causality, and substance" that Gaggi attributes to developments in science are clearly relevant to González's manipulation of such categories. See Gaggi, *Modern/Postmodern*, pp. 49–51.
8. Hassan derives these characteristics from Nietzsche. See Hassan, *Postmodern Turn*, pp. 47–54.

9. Calinescu, *Five Faces*, p. 299.
10. For a description of this fragmentation, see Hassan, *Postmodern Turn*, p. 168.
11. Johnston, "Postmodern Subject," p. 92.
12. Hassan quotes from Mikhail M. Bakhtin's *Rabelais and His World*, trans. Helena Iswolsky (Cambridge: Harvard University Press, 1968), pp. 10–11. For Hassan's discussion of the fundamental characteristics of postmodernism, see his *Postmodern Turn*, pp. 169–71.
13. Lyotard's comments are from *Postmodern Condition*, pp. 31–37. Calinescu sheds light on Lyotard's theories. For Lyotard, he explains, "the Marxist story of man's emancipation from exploitation through the revolutionary struggle of the proletariat" was one of the "great ideological fairy tales" that gave rise to the modern project. See Calinescu, *Five Faces*, pp. 274–75. But perhaps the Marxist tradition with which González has been affiliated politically carries the seeds of the poet's ludic critique of master narratives. In this regard, the words of Elías Díaz regarding Manuel Ballestero's book *Marx o la crítica como fundamento*, published in Madrid in 1967, are enlightening. For Díaz, the book's main idea is that "la negatividad, la no-aceptación de lo dado, aparece como base real de la dialéctica; la negatividad sería el motor del devenir, del cambio, del proceso dialéctico" [negativism, the refusal to accept the given, seems to be the real basis of dialectics; negativism would be the moving force behind becoming, behind change, behind the dialectical process]. González obeys, though certainly not in a systematic way, this Marxist principle of "la crítica como fundamento" [criticism as a foundation], as well as exemplifying, as was shown in chapter 8, Marx's distrust of ideology and his awareness of the danger of falling into what W. J. T. Mitchell has termed "distorted representations of the world." See Elías Díaz, *Pensamiento español en la era de Franco, 1939–1975* (Madrid: Tecnos, 1983), p. 151; and Mitchell, *Iconology*, p. 167.
14. For a discussion of deconstruction as a critique of humanistic disinterestedness, see William V. Spanos, *Repetitions: The Postmodern Occasion in Literature and Culture* (Baton Rouge: Louisiana State University Press, 1987), pp. 278ff.
15. Angel González, "Angel fieramente humano" (Gracia Rodríguez interview), p. 27. Along these lines, Diane R. Fisher has recently proposed that in certain poems, González writes ironic texts that are both logocentric and decentered, which affirm the possibility of language expressing reality but at the same time deny such a possibility. See Fisher, "The Voices of Logocentrism and Decentering in Two Poems by Angel González," *Revista Canadiense de Estudios Hispánicos* 16, no. 1 (Fall 1991): 45–59.
16. Mitchell, *Iconology*, p. 30.
17. González, "Antología temática," p. 74.
18. Hassan, *Postmodern Turn*, p. 73.
19. Ibid., p. 180.

Works Cited

Abrams, M. H. *A Glossary of Literary Terms* [based on the original version by Dan S. Norton and Peters Rushton]. New York: Holt, Rinehart and Winston, 1960.
Adams, Hazard. Introduction to *Critical Theory Since 1965*, edited by Hazard Adams and Leroy Searle. Tallahassee: Florida State University Press, 1986.
Alarcos Llorach, Emilio. *Angel González, poeta (variaciones críticas)*. Oviedo, Spain: Universidad de Oviedo, 1969.
——— and Angel González. "El poeta y el crítico." In *Angel González: Verso a verso*. Oviedo, Spain: Caja de Ahorros de Asturias, 1987.
Alas, Leopoldo (Clarin). *"¡Adios, «Cordera»!" y otros cuentos*. 5th ed. Madrid: Espasa-Calpe, 1975.
Aub, Max. *Poesía española contemporánea*. Mexico: Era, 1969.
Barth, John. *Lost in the Funhouse, Fiction to Print, Tape, Live Voice*. Garden City, N.Y.: Doubleday, 1968.
Barthes, Roland. *Writing Degree Zero*. Translated by Annette Lavers and Colin Smith. New York: Hill and Wang, 1968.
Batlló, José, ed. *Antología de la nueva poesía española*. Madrid: El Bardo, 1968.
———. *Poetas españoles postcontemporáneos*. Barcelona: El Bardo, 1974.
Benson, Douglas K. "Angel González y *Muestra* (1977): Las perspectivas múltiples de una sensibilidad irónica." *Revista Hispánica Moderna* 40 (1978–79): 42–59.
———. "La ironía, la función del hablante y la experiencia del lector en la poesía de Angel González." *Hispania* 64 (1981): 570–81.
———. "Las voces de Angel González." In *En homenaje a Angel González: Ensayos, entrevista y poemas*, edited by Andrew P. Debicki and Sharon Keefe Ugalde, 7–23. Boulder, Colo.: Society of Spanish and Spanish-American Studies, 1991.
———. "Linguistic Parody and Reader Response in the Worlds of Angel González." *Anales de la Literatura Española Contemporánea* 7, no. 1 (1982): 11–30.
Bleiberg, Germán, and Julián Marías, eds. *Diccionario de literatura española*, 4th ed. Madrid: Revista de Occidente, 1972.
Bousoño, Carlos. "La poesía de Guillermo Carnero." Introduction to *Ensayo de una teoría de la visión: Poesía 1966–1977*, by Guillermo Carnero. Madrid: Hiperión, 1979.
———. *Teoría de la expresión poética*. 4th ed. Madrid: Gredos, 1966.

Brower, Gary. "Breves acotaciones para una bio-bibliografía de la vidobra de Angel González." *Mester* 5, no. 1 (1974): 10–12.

Cadalso, José. *Cartas marruecas.* 1789.

Calinescu, Matei. *Five Faces of Modernity: Modernism, Avant-Garde, Decadence, Kitsch, Postmodernism.* Durham, N.C.: Duke University Press, 1987. Revised edition of *Faces of Modernity.* Bloomington: Indiana University Press, 1977.

Carnero, Guillermo. "El último libro de Angel González: Alumbramiento de muchos caminos." *Informaciones de las Artes y las Letras,* 16 December 1976, 5.

———. "Precedentes de la poesía social de la posguerra española en la anteguerra y guerra civil." *Boletín de la Fundación Juan March,* 1973, 3–20.

Castellanos, Rosario. *Poesía no eres tú: Obra poética, 1948–1971.* Mexico: Fondo de Cultura Económica, 1972.

Castellet, José María. *Nueve novísimos poetas españoles.* Barcelona: Barral, 1970.

———. *Veinte años de poesía española.* Barcelona: Seix Barral, 1960.

Ciplijauskaité, Biruté. *El poeta y la poesía.* Madrid: Insula, 1966.

———. "Purificación y esencialidad en la más joven poesía." In *After the War: Essays on Recent Spanish Poetry,* edited by Salvador Jiménez Fajardo and John C. Wilcox, 109–28. Boulder, Colo.: Society of Spanish and Spanish-American Studies, 1988.

Cirlot, J. E. *A Dictionary of Symbols.* 2d ed. Translated by Jack Sage. New York: Philosophical Library, 1971.

Culler, Jonathan. *Ferdinand de Saussure.* England, 1976; reprint, New York: Penguin, 1977.

———. *The Pursuit of Signs: Semiotics, Literature, Deconstruction.* Ithaca: Cornell University Press, Cornell Paperbacks, 1983.

Díaz, Elías. *Pensamiento español en la era de Franco (1939–1975).* Madrid: Tecnos, 1983.

Díaz Castañón, Carmen. "«Avanzaba de espaldas aquel río.»" *Angel González: Verso a verso.* Oviedo, Spain: Caja de Ahorros de Asturias, 1987.

Debicki, Andrew P. *Angel González.* Madrid: Júcar, 1989.

———. "Angel González: Transformation and Perspective." In *Poetry of Discovery: The Spanish Generation of 1956–1971,* 59–80. Lexington: University Press of Kentucky, 1982.

———. "Poesía española de la postmodernidad." *Anales de la Literatura Española* 6 (1988): 169–75.

Delgado, Bernardo. "Las tres voces de Angel González." *Jugar con fuego: poesía y crítica* (Avilés, Asturias) 3–4 (1977): 77–86.

Drew, Elizabeth. *Poetry: A Modern Guide to Its Understanding and Enjoyment.* New York: Dell, 1969.

Eagleton, Terry. *Literary Theory: An Introduction.* Minneapolis: University of Minnesota Press, 1983.

Fisher, Diane R. "The Voices of Logocentrism and Decentering in Two Poems by Angel González." *Revista Canadiense de Estudios Hispánicos* 16, no. 1 (Fall 1991): 45–59.

Works Cited

Freud, Sigmund. *A General Introduction to Psychoanalysis*. 1924. Translated by Joan Riviere. New York: Permabooks, 1953.

Frye, Northrop. *Anatomy of Criticism: Four Essays*. 1957. Princeton: Princeton University Press, 1971.

Fuertes, Gloria. *Historia de Gloria: Amor, humor y desamor*. Edited by Pablo González Rodas. Madrid: Cátedra, 1981.

———. *Obras incompletas: Edición de la autora*. Madrid: Cátedra, 1981.

Gaggi, Silvio. *Modern/Postmodern: A Study in Twentieth-Century Arts and Ideas*. Philadelphia: University of Pennsylvania Press, 1989.

García Hortelano, Juan, ed. *El grupo poético de los años 50 (Una antología)*. Madrid: Taurus, 1978.

García Lorca, Federico. "Llanto por Ignacio Sánchez Mejías." In *Obras completas*, 535–45. Madrid: Aguilar, 1972

García Martín, José Luis. "La poesía última de Angel González." In *Guía para un encuentro con Angel González*. Luna de Abajo Cuaderno de Poesía no. 3. La Felguera, Langreo, Spain: Luna de Abajo, 1985.

———. Review of *Prosemas o menos*. *El Ciervo: Revista Mensual de Pensamiento y Cultura* 34, nos. 415–16 (September-October 1985): 23–29.

Gil de Biedma, Jaime. "Angel." In *Guía para un encuentro con Angel González*. Luna de Abajo Cuaderno de Poesía no. 3. La Felguera, Langreo, Spain: Luna de Abajo, 1985.

Gómez Segade, M. A., J. M. González Herrán, Y. Novo Villaverde, and M. Santos Zas. "Rumbos de la poesía española en los ochenta." *Anales de la Literatura Española Contemporánea* 9, nos. l–3 (1984): 175–200.

González, Angel. "Angel fieramente humano." Interview by Gracia Rodríguez. *Quimera* 35 (January 1984): 23–29.

———. "Angel González: el asturiano disimula con la ironía su sentimentalismo." Interview by Ignacio Gracia Noriega. *La Nueva España*, 5 October 1985.

———. "Angel González, poeta: Con esperanza, sin convencimiento." Interview by Victor Claudín and Alfonso González-Calero. *Ozono* 4, no. 36 (September 1978): 50–53.

———. "Angel González o la desesperanza." Interview by Federico Campbell. In *Infame turba*. Barcelona: Lumen, 1971.

———. *Antología poética*. Madrid: Alianza Editorial, 1982.

———. "Antología temática." *Guía para un encuentro con Angel González*. Luna de Abajo Cuaderno de Poesía no. 3. La Felguera, Langreo, Spain: Luna de Abajo, 1985.

———. *Antonio Machado*. Madrid: Júcar, 1986. Expanded edition of *Aproximaciones a Antonio Machado*. Mexico: Universidad Nacional Autónoma de México, 1982.

———. *Aspero mundo*. Madrid: Rialp, 1956.

———. *Astonishing World: The Selected Poems of Angel González, 1956–1986*. Translated by Steven Ford Brown and Gutierrez Revuelta. Edited by Steven Ford Brown. Minneapolis, Minn.: Milkweed Editions, 1993.

———. *Breves acotaciones para una biografía*. Las Palmas, Spain: Inventarios Provisionales, 1971.

———. "Breves acotaciones para una biografía: Angel González verso a verso." Interview by Miguel Somovilla. In *Angel González: Verso a verso*. Oviedo, Spain: Caja de Ahorros de Asturias, 1987.

———. "Conversación con Angel González." Interview by Faustino F. Alvarez. In *Una antología*, by Angel González. 2d ed. Oviedo, Spain: Automóviles Luarca, S. A., 1985.

———. "Cuestionario." In *Antología de la nueva poesía española*, edited by José Batlló, 342–44. Madrid: El Bardo, 1968.

———. "Entrevista a Angel González." Interview by Sharon Keefe Ugalde. In *En homenaje a Angel González: Ensayos, entrevista y poemas*, edited by Andrew P. Debicki and Sharon Keefe Ugalde, 111–25. Boulder, Colo.: Society of Spanish and Spanish-American Studies, 1991.

———. *Grado elemental*. Paris: Ruedo Ibérico, 1962.

———. "*Harsh World" and Other Poems*. Translated by Donald D. Walsh. Princeton: Princeton University Press, 1977.

———. *Muestra, corregida y aumentada, de algunos procedimientos narrativos y de las actitudes sentimentales que habitualmente comportan*. Madrid: Turner, 1977.

———. *Muestra de algunos procedimientos narrativos y de las actitudes sentimentales que habitualmente comportan*. Madrid: Turner, 1976.

———. *Palabra sobre palabra*. Madrid: Poesía Para Todos, 1965.

———. *Palabra sobre palabra*. Barcelona: Seix Barral, 1968; 2d ed. Barral, 1972; 3d ed. 1977; 4th ed. Seix Barral, 1986; 5th ed. 1992; 6th ed. 1994. (Successive versions of complete works.)

———. "Palabras pronunciadas en el acto de entrega de los premios Príncipe de Asturias 1985." In *Angel González: Verso a verso*. Oviedo, Spain: Caja de Ahorros de Asturias, 1987.

———. *Poemas: Edición del autor*. Madrid: Cátedra, 1980.

———. "Poesía española contemporánea." In *Angel González: Verso a verso*. Oviedo: Caja de Ahorros de Asturias, 1987.

———. "Poesía y compromiso." In *Poesía última*, edited by Franciso Ribes, 57–59. Madrid: Taurus, 1963.

———. "Poética: Defensa de la poesía social." In *Antología de la nueva poesía española*, 2d ed., edited by Leopoldo de Luis, 291–92. Madrid: Alfaguara, 1969.

———. *Procedimientos narrativos*. Santander: La Isla de los Ratones, 1972.

———. *Prosemas o menos*. Edited by Pablo Beltrán de Heredia. Santander, 1984. Privately printed. 2d ed. Madrid: Hiperión, 1985. 3d ed. Madrid: Hiperión, October 1985.

———. "Ramón Pérez de Ayala: verbalización del paisaje y credo estético." In *Angel González: Verso a verso*. Oviedo: Caja de Ahorros de Asturias, 1987. Reprinted from *Simposio Internacional Ramón Pérez de Ayala (1880–1980)*. Gijón: Imprenta Flores, 1981.

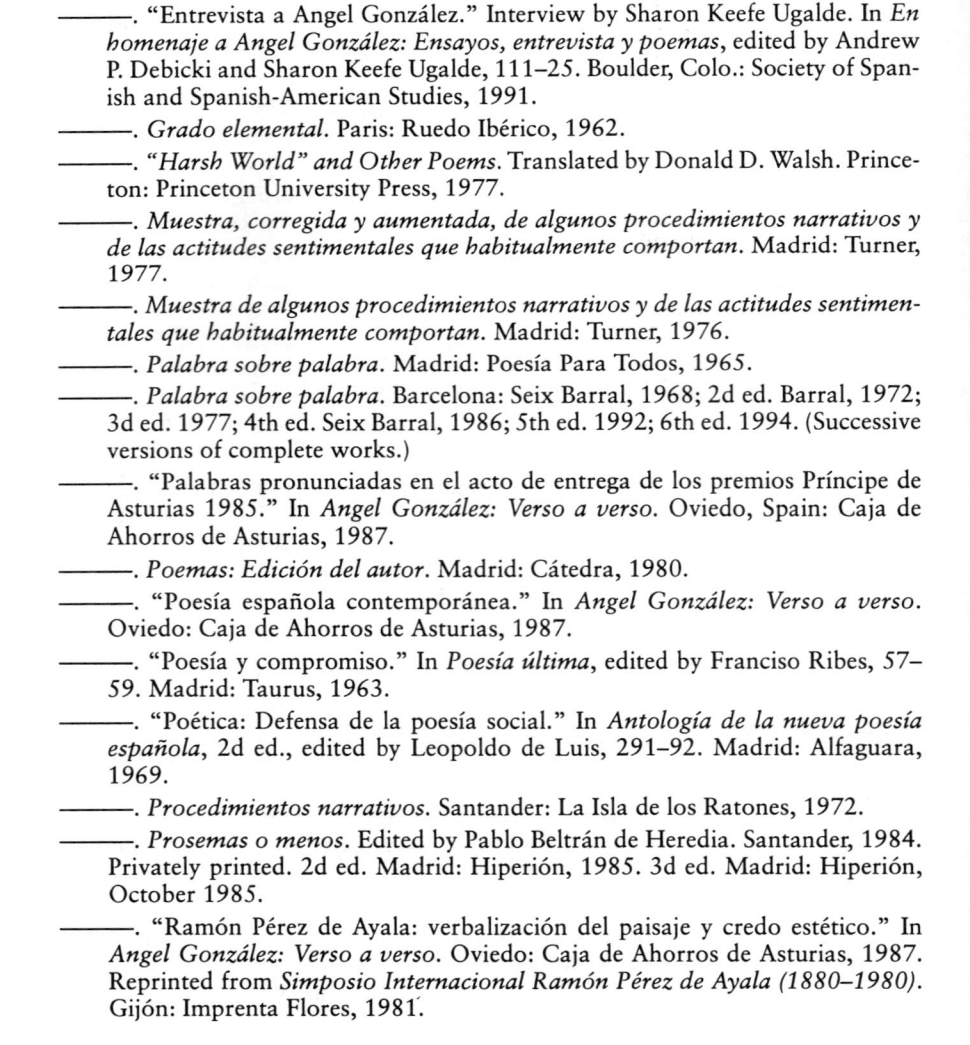

———. *Sin esperanza, con convencimiento*. Barcelona: Colliure, 1961.
———. "Sobre poesía y poetas." *Peña Labra: Pliegos de Poesía* 82 (1984): 4.
González Muela, Joaquín. "La poesía de Angel González en su primer período." In *Homenaje a Casalduero: crítica y poesía*, edited by R. Pincus Sigele and Gonzalo Sobejano, 189–99. Madrid: Gredos, 1972.
Goytisolo, Juan. *En los reinos de taifa*. Barcelona: Seix Barral, 1986.
———. *La isla*. Barcelona: Seix Barral, 1961.
———. *Marks of Identity*. Translated by Gregory Rabassa. New York: Grove, 1969.
———. *Señas de identidad*. Mexico: Joaquín Mortiz, 1966.
Guillén, Jorge. *Aire nuestro: Cántico, Clamor, Homenaje*. Milan: All'Insegna del Pesce d'Oro, 1968.
———. *Lenguaje y poesía: Algunos casos españoles*. Madrid: Alianza Editorial, 1972. First published in English under the title *Language and Poetry*. Cambridge: Harvard University Press, 1961. First published in Spanish in Madrid by Revista de Occidente, 1972.
Hassan, Ihab. *Paracriticisms: Seven Speculations of the Times*. Urbana: University of Illinois Press, 1975.
———. *The Postmodern Turn: Essays in Postmodern Theory and Culture*. Columbus: Ohio State University Press, 1987.
Hernández, Antonio, ed. *Una promoción desheredada: La poética del 50*. Madrid: Zero, 1978.
Herzberger, David K. "Narrating the Past: History and the Novel of Memory in Postwar Spain." *PMLA* 106, no. 1 (January 1991): 34–45.
Ilie, Paul. *Literature and Inner Exile: Authoritarian Spain, 1939–1975*. Baltimore: Johns Hopkins University Press, 1980.
Izquierdo, Luis. Introduction to *Angel González: Antología poética*. Madrid: Alianza, 1982.
Jameson, Fredric. *The Political Unconscious: Narrative as a Socially Symbolic Act*. Ithaca: Cornell University Press, 1981.
———. *The Prison-House of Language: A Critical Account of Structuralism and Russian Formalism*. 1972. Princeton: Princeton University Press, 1974.
Jiménez, José Olivio. *Diez años de poesía española: 1960–1970*. Madrid: Insula, 1972.
Jiménez, Juan Ramón. *Primeros libros de poesía*, 3d ed. Madrid: Aguilar, 1967.
Johnston, John. "Ideology, Representation, Schizophrenia: Toward a Theory of the Postmodern Subject." In *After the Future: Postmodern Times and Places*, edited by Gary Shapiro, 67–95. Albany: State University of New York Press, 1990.
LeCertúa, Patrick Josef. "Angel González: Poetry as Craft and the 'Word Upon Word' Experience." Diss., University of Kentucky, 1982.
Lyotard, Jean-François. *The Postmodern Condition: A Report on Knowledge*. Translated by Geoff Bennington and Brian Massumi. Minneapolis: University of Minnesota Press, 1984. Originally published as *La Condition postmoderne: rapport sur le savoir*. France: Les Editions de Minuit, 1979.

Makris, Mary. "Intertextualidad, discurso y ekfrasis en 'El Cristo de Velázquez' de Angel González." In *En homenaje a Angel González: Ensayos, entrevista y poemas*, edited by Andrew P. Debicki and Sharon Keefe Ugalde, 73–83. Boulder, Colo.: Society of Spanish and Spanish-American Studies, 1991.

———. *Under the Influence: Intertextual Strategies in the Poetry of Angel González.* Ann Arbor, Mich.: University Microfilms International, 1990. Microfiche, 9123297.

Mandlove, Nancy. "Used Poetry: The Trans-parent Language of Gloria Fuertes and Angel González." *Revista Canadiense de Estudios Hispánicos* 7, no. 2 (Winter 1983): 301–6.

Mangini, Shirley. *Rojos y rebeldes: La cultura de la disidencia durante el franquismo.* Madrid: Anthropos, 1987.

Martin, Sara A[nn]. "La experiencia desfamiliarizada de *Sin esperanza, con convencimiento*." In *En homenaje a Angel González: Ensayos, entrevista y poemas*, edited by Andrew P. Debicki and Sharon Keefe Ugalde, 59–72. Boulder, Colo.: Society of Spanish and Spanish-American Studies, 1991.

———. *The Poetry of Angel González: Standing with the Reader.* Ann Arbor, Mich.: University Microfilms International, 1987. Microfiche, 8727628.

Martínez Ruiz, Florencio. *La nueva poesía española: Antología crítica.* Madrid: Biblioteca Nueva, 1971.

Martino, Florentino. "La poesía de Angel González." *Papeles de Son Armadans* 57 (1970): 229–31.

Méndez, José. "La poesía en la ciudad." *Prólogo* 6 (January-February 1990): 22.

Miller, Martha LaFollette. "Inestabilidad temporal y textual en Angel González." In *En homenaje a Angel Gonález: Ensayos, entrevista y poemas*, edited by Andrew P. Debicki and Sharon Keefe Ugalde, 25–36. Boulder, Colo.: Society of Spanish and Spanish-American Studies, 1991.

———. "Literary Tradition Versus Speaker Experience in the Poetry of Angel González." *Anales de la Literatura Española Contemporánea* 7, no. 1 (1982): 79–95.

———. "The Ludic Poetry of Angel González." In *After the War: Essays on Recent Spanish Poetry*, edited by Salvador Jiménez-Fajardo and John C. Wilcox, 75–82. Boulder, Colo.: Society of Spanish and Spanish-American Studies, 1988.

———. "Political Intent Versus Verbal Play in 'La paloma' by Angel González." *Perspectives on Contemporary Literature* 11 (1985): 93–99.

———. "Society, History, and the Fate of the Poetic Word in *La realidad y el deseo*." In *The Word and the Mirror: Critical Essays on the Poetry of Luis Cernuda*, edited by Salvador Jiménez-Fajardo, 166–80. Madison, N.J.: Fairleigh Dickinson University Press, 1989.

———. "The Uses of Play and Humor in Angel González' Second Period." In *Simposio-homenaje a Angel González*, edited by Susana Rivera and Tomás Ruiz Fábrega, 113–26. Madrid: José Esteban, 1987.

Mitchell, W. J. T. *Iconology: Image, Text, Ideology.* Chicago: University of Chicago Press, 1986.

Moix, Ana María. "Veinticuatro horas de la vida de . . . Angel González." *TeleeXprés,* 4 November 1972, 25.

Montesquieu, Charles de Secondat, Baron de la Brède et de. *Considérations sur les causes de la grandeur des Romains et de leur décadence.* 1734.

———. *Lettres persanes.* 1721.

Ortega y Gasset, José. *El tema de nuestro tiempo.* Madrid: Espasa-Calpe, 1968.

Otero, Blas de. *Esto no es un libro (This Is Not a Book).* Río Piedras, Puerto Rico: University of Puerto Rico, 1963.

———. "Muy lejos." In *Poesía social: Antología, 1939–1968,* 2d ed. revised and enlarged, edited by Leopoldo de Luis. Madrid: Alfaguara, 1969.

Palley, Julian. "Angel González and the Anxiety of Influence." *Anales de la Literatura Española Contemporánea* 9, nos. 1–3 (1984): 81–96.

Parker, Stacey L. "Desfamiliarización en la poesía de Angel González." *Inti* 21 (Spring 1985): 75–82.

Pérez Firmat, Gustavo. *Literature and Liminality: Festive Readings in the Hispanic Tradition.* Durham, N.C.: Duke University Press, 1986.

Perloff, Marjorie. *Poetic License: Essays on Modernist and Postmodernist Lyric.* Evanston, Ill.: Northwestern University Press, 1990.

———. *The Poetics of Indeterminacy: Rimbaud to Cage.* Princeton: Princeton University Press, 1981.

Persin, Margaret H. "Presence versus Absence in the Early Poetry of Angel González." In *Recent Spanish Poetry and the Role of the Reader.* Lewisburg, Pa.: Bucknell University Press, 1987.

Persin, Margaret H., Andrew P. Debicki, Nancy Mandlove, and Robert Spires. "Metaliterature and Recent Spanish Literature." *Revista Canadiense de Estudios Hispánicos* 7, no. 2 (Winter 1983): 297–309.

Preminger, Alex, ed. *Princeton Encyclopedia of Poetry and Poetics.* Enlarged edition. Princeton: Princeton University Press, 1974.

Provencio, Pedro. "Angel González." In *Poéticas españolas contemporáneas: La generación del 50.* Madrid: Hiperión, 1988.

Redfern, Walter. *Clichés and Coinages.* Oxford and Cambridge, Mass.: Basil Blackwell, 1989.

Ribes, Francisco. "Nota preliminar." In *Poesía última.* Madrid: Taurus, 1963.

Riffaterre, Michael. *Semiotics of Poetry.* Bloomington: Indiana University Press, 1978.

Rivers, Elias L., ed. *Renaissance and Baroque Poetry of Spain.* New York: Dell, 1966.

Rodríguez Padrón, Jorge. "Angel González: 'Tratado de urbanismo.'" *Cuadernos Hispanoamericanos* 216 (1967): 674–80.

Rogers, Douglass. "Posturas del poeta ante su palabra en la España de posguerra." In *After the War: Essays on Recent Spanish Poetry.* Edited by Salvador Jiménez-Fajardo and John C. Wilcox, 55–65. Boulder, Colo.: Society of Spanish and Spanish-American Studies, 1988.

Rovira, Pere. "Los *prosemas* de Angel González." *Insula,* no. 469 (December 1985): 1, 10.
Rubio, Fanny, and José Luis Falcó. "Estudio preliminar." In *Poesía española contemporánea: Historia y antología, 1939–1980,* 2d ed. Madrid: Alhambra, 1982.
Sartre, Jean-Paul. "Commitment." In *Existentialism and Humanism,* translated by Philip Mairet. London: Philosophical Library, 1947. Reprinted in *The Modern Tradition: Backgrounds of Modern Literature,* edited by Richard Ellmann and Charles Fiedelson, Jr., 853–55. New York: Oxford University Press, 1965.
Schumm, Sandra. "El aspecto alusivo de la poesía de Angel González." *Hispanic Journal* 12, no. 1 (Spring 1991): 133–45.
Silver, Philip W. "What Are Poets For?: Reference, Unamuno, Social Poetry, Angel González." In *Simposio-Homenaje a Angel González,* edited by Susana Rivera and Tomás Ruiz Fábrega, 83–93. Madrid: José Esteban, 1987.
Singleterry, Gary Auburn. *The Poetic Cosmovision of Angel González.* Ann Arbor, Mich.: University Microfilms International, 1973. Microfiche, 73–8380.
Sobejano, Gonzalo. "Salvación de la prosa, belleza de la necesidad en la poesía de Angel González." In *Simposio-Homenaje a Angel González,* edited by Susana Rivera and Tomás Ruiz Fábrega, 23–54. Madrid: José Esteban, 1987.
Solomon, J. Fisher. *Discourse and Reference in the Nuclear Age.* Norman: University of Oklahoma Press, 1988.
Sontag, Susan. *Against Interpretation and Other Essays.* New York: Dell, 1978. Articles and reviews first published 1962–65.
———. Preface to *Writing Degree Zero,* by Roland Barthes. New York: Hill and Wang, 1968.
Sotelo, José Antonio, and Andrés Barba. *Literatura española contemporánea.* Madrid: Dossat, 1986.
Soufas, C. Christopher. *Conflict of Light and Wind: The Spanish Generation of 1927 and the Ideology of Poetic Form.* Middletown, Conn.: Wesleyan University Press, 1989.
Spanos, William V. *Repetitions: The Postmodern Occasion in Literature and Culture.* Baton Rouge: Louisiana State University Press, 1987.
Steiner, George. "Silence and the Poet." In *Language and Silence: Essays on Language, Literature, and the Inhuman.* New York: Atheneum, 1967.
Stewart, Susan. *Nonsense: Aspects of Intertextuality in Folklore and Literature.* Baltimore: Johns Hopkins University Press, 1978/1979.
Stycos, Maria Nowakowska. "Intertextuality in Selected Spanish Poets Since 1939: Intertext/Poetics/Reader." In *After the War: Essays on Recent Spanish Poetry,* edited by Salvador Jiménez-Fajardo and John C. Wilcox, 47–54. Boulder, Colo.: Society of Spanish and Spanish-American Studies, 1988.
Sueiro, Daniel. "Angel más poeta." In *Guía para un encuentro con Angel González.* Luna de Abajo Cuaderno de Poesía no. 3. La Felguera, Langreo, Spain: Luna de Abajo, 1985.
Tigges, Wim. *An Anatomy of Literary Nonsense.* Amsterdam: Rodopi, 1988.

Trotsky, Leon. "The Limitations of Formalism." In *Literature and Revolution*, translated by Rose Strunsky. New York: International Publishers, 1925. Reprinted in *The Modern Tradition: Backgrounds of Modern Literature*, edited by Richard Ellmann and Charles Fiedelson, Jr., 340–49. New York: Oxford University Press, 1965.

Vázquez Montalbán, Manuel. *Crónica sentimental de España*. Prologue by Guillermo Heras. Madrid: Espasa Calpe, 1986.

Villanueva, Tino. "*Aspero mundo*, de Angel González: De la contemplación lírica a la realidad histórica." *Journal of Spanish Studies: Twentieth Century* 8, nos. 1–2 (Spring-Fall 1980): 161–80.

———. "Censura y creación: Dos poemas subversivos de Angel González." *Hispanic Journal* 5, no. 1 (Fall, 1983): 49–72.

———. *Tres poetas de posguerra: Celaya, González, y Caballero Bonald (Estudio y Entrevistas)*. London: Tamesis, 1988.

Whitman, Walt. *Complete Poetry and Selected Prose*. Edited by James E. Miller, Jr. Boston: Houghton Mifflin, 1959.

Wilson, Christopher P. *Jokes: Form, Content, Use and Function*. London: Academic Press, 1979.

Index

"Acaso" (González), 104–7, 108
"Acoma, New Mexico, diciembre, 5:15 P.M." (González), 113
Adams, Hazard, 39
Addison, Joseph, 163
"¡Adiós, «Cordera!»" (Leopoldo Alas [Clarín]), 128
"A la poesía" (González), 130, 178–79, 181, 183, 188
Alarcos Llorach, Emilio, 19, 19–20, 31, 34–36; and substantive view of poetic language, 35, 49, 71
Aleixandre, Vicente, 30
Allende, Salvador, 68, 81, 83
Alloway, Lawrence, 131
"Alocución a las veintitrés" (González), 32, 63
Antología de la nueva poesía española (Battló), 39
"Aquí, Madrid, mil novecientos" (González), 96, 137
"A Roma sepultada en sus ruinas" (Quevedo), 91–92
"Así parece" (González), 182–83
Aspero mundo, 15, 30, 31, 31–32, 52, 95, 113, 137, 141
Aub, Max, 198n. 43
"Avanzaba de espaldas aquel río . . ." (González), 155–59, 188
"A veces" (González), 142–43, 175–76, 178
Ayala, Francisco, 62
"Ayer" (González), 96, 99–104, 105–6, 188

Bakhtin, Mikhail, 188–89

Ballestero, Manuel, 210n. 13
Barral, Carlos, 30–31, 70
Barth, John, 154; as a humanistic postmodern, 46, 124, 154–55
Barthes, Roland, 172
Batlló, José, 18, 39
"Beato sillón" (Guillén), 168
Bécquer, Gustavo Adolfo, 49
Benet, Juan, 38, 200–201n. 16
Benson, Douglas K., 21, 110, 186; on "El campo de batalla," 53–55, 61; on parody and irony in González, 44, 203n. 4
"Biografía e historia" (González), 182
"Birds in the Night" (Cernuda), 178
Bousoño, Carlos, 19, 30, 145; and crisis of reason, 22, 51, 70–71
Breves acotaciones para una biografía, 197n. 18, 199n. 15; as ludic work, 16, 19

Cadalso, José, 92
"Calambur" (González), 204n. 15
Calinescu, Matei, 188; and postmodernist self-referentiality, 83, 184; and postmodernist uncertainty toward reality, 95; and strong versus weak thought, 93; and the universalist conceptions of modernism, 83–84
Campbell, Federico, 40
"Campo de batalla, El" (González), 53–55, 59, 61
"Camposanto en Colliure" (González), 63, 66, 174
Cántico (Guillén), 144
"Capital de provincia" (González), 137

Carnero, Guillermo, 44, 48–49, 187; poetics and poetry of, in 1970s, 18–19, 19; on political art, 51; on pure and impure poetry, 49
Carnivalesque, 200n. 12
Cartas marruecas (Cadalso), 92
Castellanos, Rosario, 206–7n. 11
Castellet, José María, 30, 31, 39
Cela, Camilo José, 70
Celaya, Gabriel, 32; and instrumental view of poetry, 39, 49, 69
Censorship under Franco, 62, 70
Cernuda, Luis, 178
"Chatarra" (González), 141, 142
"Chiloé, setiembre, 1972" (González), 83
Ciplijauskaité, Biruté, 20
"Ciudad cero" (González), 34
"Civilización de la opulencia" (González), 34
Communist Party: and dissident writers of González's generation, 69
"Confesiones de un joven problemático" (González), 124–26, 128, 129
Considérations sur les causes de la grandeur des Romains et de leur décadence (Montesquieu), 92
"Contra-Orden. (Poética por la que me pronuncio ciertos días.)" (González), 172–74, 183
Coplas por la muerte de su padre don Rodrigo (Manrique), 151
"Crepúsculo, Albuquerque, estío" (González), 48, 110, 113
"Crepúsculo, Albuquerque, otoño" (González), 48, 110, 113
"Cristo de Velázquez, El" (González), 130–32, 177–78, 207n. 12
"Cuando el hombre se extinga" (González), 85–86
Culler, Jonathan, 160, 203n. 2; on the use of apostrophe in poetry, 57–59
"Cumpleaños de amor" (González), 96–97, 97, 98–99, 104
"Cumpleaños" (González), 36, 96–98, 99, 104

"Dato biográfico" (González), 119, 119–24, 129, 181–82

"De otro modo" (González), 183
Debicki, Andrew P., 142, 187, 198n. 15, 199n. 18, 200n. 10, 204nn. 9 and 10, 205n. 21; and clichés and parody in González, 16, 44, 101, 203n. 4; on "Camposanto en Colliure," 66; on González's cultivation of several tendencies at once, 50; and "poetry of discovery," 20; and role of reader in completing González's texts, 192n. 25, 208n. 28; and rupture of rules of reality in González, 96, 101
Deixis en fantasma (González), 46
"Del campo o de la mar" (González), 115–19, 123
"Día se ha ido, El" (González), 111, 112–13
"Diatriba contra los muertos" (González), 107–8
Díaz, Elías, 210n. 13
"Discurso a los jóvenes" (González), 32, 53, 58, 61, 63, 85
Dissident writers under Franco, 69
"Divagación onírica" (González), 81–82
"Dos versiones del Apocalipsis" (González), 132

Eagleton, Terry, 163, 205n. 36; on art as a fetish, 164
"Egloga" (González), 143, 144, 146–50, 160
"Elegía pura" (González), 143, 144, 146, 150–55, 160
"Empleo de la nostalgia" (González), 199n. 18
"Entreacto" (González), 32, 53, 59–61, 63, 64–65, 199n. 25
"Episodio último" (González), 113
"Eruditos en campus" (González), 126–28, 201n. 18
España cachonda, La, 103
"Estío en Bidonville" (González), 32, 63–65, 104
Esto no es un libro (Otero), 174
"Evocación segunda" (González), 34
Experimentalism in literature, in early 1960s, 70

INDEX

Falcó, José Luis, 18, 19, 38–39
"Ficha ingreso hospital general" (Fuertes), 122
Fisher, Diane R., 210n. 15
Fokkema, D. W.: and reality as a fiction, 95
Fowles, John: as humanistic postmodern, 46, 124
Franco regime, 37, 58–59, 63, 72, 83, 103, 183
French Lieutenant's Woman, The (Fowles), 123
Freud, Sigmund, 61; and challenge to reason, 114; and theories of humor, 41, 202n. 21
Frye, Northrop, 39, 149, 160
Fuertes, Gloria, 122, 174; testimonial poetics of, 164

Gaggi, Silvio: on Barth and Fowles as humanistic postmoderns, 19, 46, 124, 154; on classificatory systems in Fowles, 123; on postmodern aesthetics, 119, 131; on postmodern disillusionment with modernism, 45; on science and postmodernism, 113–14
García Hortelano, Juan, 25
García Lorca, Federico, 92, 93, 151
García Martín, José Luis, 38, 184–85
Generation of 1927, 30, 164
Gil de Biedma, Jaime, 30, 45, 60–61, 201n. 1; testimonial poetics of, 164
Gimferrer, Pedro, 19, 39
Gimferrer, Pere. *See* Gimferrer, Pedro
"Glosas a Heráclito" (González), 84–85
"Glosas en homenaje a J. G." (González), 207n. 13
González Cano, Pedro, 25–26, 27; ideological leanings of, 26, 27
González, Angel: and *antipoesía*, 17, 141, 172, 207n. 15; and the Apollonian/Dionysian duality, 31, 36, 42, 123–124; and Celaya's view of poetry, 39; and censorship, 33, 36, 50, 67; childhood and early adulthood of, 24–30 (*see also* González, Civil War and family of); as civil servant, 31, 40; Civil War and family of, 27–29; and the Communist Party, 30; crisis period of the early 1970s, 39–41; critical reception of, 44–45, 186, 187; and critical theory, 18, 39, 50, 209n. 4; and Cuban revolution, 63, 65, 79, 174; Dionysian aspect of personality of (*see* González, Angel, and the Apollonian/Dionysian duality); ethical bent of, 46, 49, 63, 67; and experience and schemes, 137, 144, 146, 150, 154, 160 (*see also* González, Angel, and mimesis and semiosis); first poetic stage of, 34; and history's relationship to poetry, 24; as a humanistic postmodern, 46, 124; ideological milieu of, 49–50, 51; ideology in early and later works of, 51; and images, distrust of, 162, 163, 164, 177, 178, 183; influence of Sartre on, 32; and inner priest, 29, 46 (*see also* González, Angel, and the Apollonian/Dionysian duality); and the instrumental view of poetic language, 50; as a literary critic, 43–44, 196n. 6; and literary theory (*see* González, Angel, and critical theory); and loss of faith in words, 16–19, 36–37, 39, 51, 54, 68, 71–74, 76–77, 83, 86, 129, 137, 175; love relationships of, 45; and ludic response to disillusionment with modernism, 45; and ludic, turn to, 25, 113, 137–38, 159, 174, 179; and Madrid, life in, 40–41; and "mala conciencia," 93, 199n. 18; and marginalization, sense of, 15; and Marxism, 49, 81, 84, 184, 189, 210n. 13; as member of second postwar generation, 31; and mimesis, 178–79, 189; and mimesis and semiosis, 143–44, 150 (*see also* González, Angel, and experience and schemes); and modernism, reaction against, 163; and

González, Angel *(continued)*:
modernismo, 169; and morality in art, 93; and mother's death, 41; in New Mexico, 41–44; *noctambulismo* of, 31, 106 (*see also* González, Angel, and the Apollonian/Dionysian duality); and the *novísimos*, 39, 49, 169; poetic self-portraits by, 179–83, 188, 189–90; poetics of, 32–33, 188; and postmodern aesthetics, 20, 21, 22, 23, 44, 45, 113, 129, 154, 159, 162, 183–84, 187–88; and Príncipe de Asturias Prize, 20, 34, 44; and reader as collaborator, 20–21, 24, 115, 187; reticent nature of, 128, 141, 145; and second poetic stage, 37, 86, 137, 179, 197n. 18; and second poetic stage, transition to, 36, 47, 66, 68, 71, 80–81; as social poet, 32–33, 165; and social realism, 31; and the substantive view of language, 35, 71–72

González Muela, Joaquín, 193n. 21

Goytisolo, Juan, 30, 69, 199n. 19, 201nn. 1 and 3; on exile and inner exile, effects of, 62–63; and *Señas de identidad*, 38

Grado elemental (González), 15, 33, 63, 66, 141; as social poetry, 32, 198n. 41

Guillén, Jorge, 92, 93, 106, 110, 144, 173, 202n. 15; and view of "la Obra," 20; and "well-made world," 168

Hassan, Ihab, 162, 188, 190, 209n. 34; on indeterminacy, 188; on negative capability, 189; on postmodern entropy of meaning, 113, 124; on postmodernism as disorder, 136; on postmodern pornography, 125; on self-subversion in postmodern literature, 75

Heisenberg, Werner: and physics and commonsense notions of time, space, and causality, 113–14

Herzberger, David K.: on novels of memory, 103–4

Hierro, José, 30, 32

Hypericons, 165

"If It's Tuesday, This Must Be Belgium," 106

"Igual que si nunca" (González), 111–12

Ilie, Paul: on inner exile, 55, 62–63

Institución Libre de Enseñanza, 26

"Intermedio de canciones, sonetos y otras músicas" (González), 76

Intertextuality and the ludic, 138

"Inventario de lugares propicios al amor" (González), 34, 104

"Invitación de Cristo" (González), 132–33

Isla, La (Goytisolo), 201n. 3

"J. R. J." (González), 176–77

Jameson, Fredric, 48, 160, 203n. 2

Jencks, Charles, 124

Jiménez, Juan Ramón, 21, 30, 144, 156–57, 158, 159, 164, 177, 178; influence of, on González, 95; as "pure" poet, 48; as stereotype of aesthete, 138; as topic of González book, 43

Language: relationship to politics and play, in literature, 48; referentiality of, 137

Latin American Boom novelists, 70

Leach, Edmund, 124

"Lecciones de buen amor" (González), 34, 36, 67

LeCertúa, Patrick Josef, 19, 36, 197–98n. 41, 204nn. 10 and 12

León, Fray Luis de, 129

Lessing, Gotthold Ephraim, 163, 173

Lettres persanes (Montesquieu), 92

"Liliputienses, Los" (González), 127. See also "Máximas mínimas"

Liminality, 200n. 12

Linguistics, 111

"Llanto por Ignacio Sánchez Mejías" (Lorca), 92, 151

"Lluvia, La" (González), 137
"Los sábados, las prostitutas madrugan mucho para estar dispuestas," 34, 142, 174
Lost in the Funhouse (Barth), 154
"Luz llamada día trece" (González), 109
Lyotard, Jean-François, 184, 188; delegitimation of grand narratives, 189
Lyric poetry, 145

Machado, Antonio, 34, 129, 130, 144, 174; as a cultural icon, 66; as inspiration to González, 46, 48–49, 63, 66; and symbolist aesthetic, 159; as topic of González book, 43
Makris, Mary, 176, 187, 207n. 15, 208nn. 20 and 28
Mallarmé, Stephane, 178
Mandlove, Nancy, 44, 204n. 15
Mangini, Shirley, 51, 68, 93, 199nn. 18 and 19, 200n. 4
Manrique, Jorge, 151
Marsé, Juan, 199n. 19
Martino, Florentino, 186
Martin, Sara, 201n. 24, 208n. 21
Marx, Karl, 177, 178; and dialectical materialism, 163; and iconoclasm, 163
Marxism: and iconoclasm, 163, 164
"Máximas mínimas" (González), 127, 133, 135
"Me falta una palabra" (González), 52, 138–39, 142, 156, 167, 169, 170
Méndez, José, 209n. 34
"Mensaje a las estatuas" (González), 56–60, 63, 65, 90, 91, 183, 199n. 25
"Meriendo algunas tardes," 205n. 21
Metafiction, 138
"Metapoesía" (González), 137, 138, 188
Metapoetry, 19
"Mi vocación profunda" (González), 111, 113, 188
Mitchell, W. J. T., 162; on iconoclasm and iconophilia, 163–64, 165, 173–74; on ideological content of images, 168
Modernism versus *modernismo*, 206n. 2
Moix, Ana María: 1972 González interview, 41, 42
Mondrian, Piet, 131
"Monólogo interior" (González), 208n. 31
Montesquieu, Charles, 92
"Muerte de máquina" (González), 142
"Muerte en el olvido" (González), 183
Muestra de algunos procedimientos narrativos y de las actitudes sentimentales que habitualmente comportan and *Muestra, corregida y aumentada, de algunos procedimientos narrativos y de las actitudes sentimentales que habitualmente comportan*, 44, 81, 115, 119, 129, 138, 144–46, 187; as ludic poetry, 16
Muñiz, María, 25, 26–27, 41
Muñoz Suay, Ricardo, 69
"Muy lejos" (Otero), 173

Neruda, Pablo, 30, 68
Ninfeas (Jiménez), 144
Niños de la guerra, 68
"No tuvo ayer su día" (González), 108–10, 113
Nonsense: and intertextuality, 138. See also Stewart, Susan
Nora, Eugenio de, 32, 62
"Notas de un viajero" (González), 86–93
Nouveau roman, 70
Novísimos, 19, 20, 91; the crisis of reason in the poetry of, 70; and loss of faith in the poetic word, 39; metapoetry in the poetry of, as critique of reason and language, 71
Nueve novísimos poetas españoles (Castellet), 39

"Oda a la noche o letra para tango" (González), 129–30, 182

"Oda a los nuevos bardos" (González), 81, 168–70, 173, 177
"Orden. (Poética a la que otros se aplican.)" (González), 170–72, 176, 182, 202–3n. 22
Ortega y Gasset, José, 166, 167
Otero, Blas de, 30, 173, 174; as social poet, 48
"Otra vez" (González), 81

Padorno, Eugenio, 19
"Palabra muerta, realidad perdida" (González), 71–72, 73
Palabra sobre palabra (collected works of Angel González), 31, 45; the absurd in, 95–96, 98–99, 104–6, 111, 113, 119; accidents and chance as generating devices in, 179–80, 189; the aleatory in, 189; anthropocentrism exposed in, 111; anti-aestheticism in, 23, 35, 49, 52, 81; the Apocalypse in, 85, 110, 132; apostrophe in, 57–59; appropriation of religious texts in, 135; art and life, the relationship between, in, 46, 83, 140, 162, 163, 164, 177, 178; the bourgeoisie, critique of, in, 168; bracketing of ideological or lyric expression in, 129, 135–36, 182, 189; carnival in, 189; clichés and conventions from literature and social discourse in, 119, 121–22, 150, 159; coded communication in, 52–53, 86; collage and fragmentation in, 21, 37, 77, 80, 111, 188; collective postwar illusions, critique of, in, 103; conceptual play in, 22; cultural order, critique of, in, 86; and deconstruction, 189; decontextualization in, 99, 113; defamiliarization in, 21, 67, 87, 91, 111, 118, 119, 177, 179, 189; the divine, the secularization of in, 131; double coding in, 124, 129; the elegiac in, 15, 22, 96, 103, 141–42, 143, 150–55, 157, 159, 189; *engagement*, social and political, in, 15, 25, 32–34, 35, 37–38, 50–53, 67, 80, 174 (*see also* González, Angel, as social poet; González, Angel, and social realism; González, Angel, and social satire); existence, interpersonal view of, in, 183; existentialism in, 30, 31, 45, 49, 55, 63, 67, 95, 98, 110, 118, 200n. 4; form/content duality in, 104 (*see also* González, Angel, substantive view of language); the Franco regime in, 58, 61; historical discourse, critique of, in, 81–84, 90; human solidarity in, 141; humanism, critique of, in, 81; humor in, 41, 51; iconoclasm in, 173–74 (*see also* González, Angel, and images, distrust of); indeterminacy and undecidability in, 17–18, 21, 75, 80, 110, 113, 114, 125, 135, 155; indirection in, 67; ineffability in, 141; inner exile in, 22, 55, 61–63; intertextuality in, 144; irony in, 15, 33, 36, 41, 50–51, 52, 145, 189; jokes in, 37, 129–30, 135, 182; juxtaposition of different classificatory and meaning systems in, 96, 118–19, 123; juxtaposition of material and spiritual realms in, 130–33, 142; language and reason, critique of, in, 51, 75, 81; leftist icons in, 174; life and death, inversion of, in, 182–83; ludic expression in, 20, 42, 114, 159–60, 165, 175, 176; ludic, shift from *engagement* to, in, 47, 50, 71, 94–95, 184, 186; lyricism, traditional, in, 50; materialist viewpoint in, 170, 173; mechanization in, 113; the memento mori in, 141; metanarratives of modernity, rejection of, in, 131; metapoetry in, 138–39, 142–43, 150, 159–60, 203n. 25; misdirection in, 106, 113, 118, 122; nature in, 110; nonsense in, 19, 37, 84–85, 119, 124–25, 159; nonsense, creation of through decontextualization, in, 99;

Palabra sobre palabra (continued): objective correlative in, 52–53, 58–60; overdetermination in, 153; paradox in, 141; parody in, 61, 157, 188; the pastoral tradition in, 22, 143, 149–50; play with categories and levels of discourse in, 106, 135; play with causality and arbitrariness in, 102, 106, 111; play with genres in, 137, 143, 144–45; play with literal and figurative language in, 101–2, 104, 107–8, 133, 157–59; play with literary traditions in, 22, 91–92, 119, 121, 137, 139, 141–44, 149–53, 159, 160; play with logic and common sense in, 22, 67, 94, 95–97, 111, 113; play with scale in, 103, 113; play with spheres of discourse in, 22, 115, 118–19, 121–23, 126, 128, 132, 135–36; poetic escapism, critique of, in, 162, 164–65, 167–73, 176–77 (*see also* González, Angel, anti-aestheticism in); poetry and poets in, 22–23, 162, 165; poetry as naming in, 106, 110–11; poetry as witnessing in, 72, 95, 96, 162, 175, 179, 182; political underpinnings of the poetry of, 22–23, 46, 52–54, 63, 77; postmodern shift from strong to weak thought in, 93; presence versus absence, dialectic of, in, 55, 62, 63, 197n. 28; puns as generating devices and evidence of linguistic instability in, 124–25, 140, 143; realism in, 122, 124; representation, critique of, in, 83; romantic elements and their undermining in, 125–26, 158, 181–82, 183; self-referentiality in, 81, 137, 184, 188; sexual imagery in, 168–72, 175–76; social satire in, 81; the speaker as a fiction in, 37; street language in, 173–74, 208n. 20; the sublime and the antisublime in, 165–67, 171, 177, 180, 181, 189; theme of love in, 46; theme of time in, 33, 46, 103, 108; time and space, unconventional and illogical treatment of in, 96–97, 104–6, 108–13, 118; titles in, 137, 144–46, 150–51; understatement in, 145; ungrammaticalities in, 144–47, 154; "universalist conceptions," rejection of, in, 83, 184; verbal play in, 16, 19, 37, 51; Vietnam war in, 79; violations of commonsense categories and hierarchies of relevance in, 98–99, 101–3, 106, 113, 159; violations of logic and common sense in, 101–2, 104, 109, 111
Palabra sobre palabra (love poetry), 33, 34, 73, 139, 141
"Palabra, La" (González), 139–40
"Palabras casi olvidadas" (González), 140
"Palabras del Anticristo" (González), 133–35
"Palabras inútiles, Las" (González), 73, 140–41, 198–99n. 15
Palley, Julian, 61
"Paloma, La" (González), 77–81, 142
"Para que yo me llame Angel González" (González), 95, 165–67, 174, 183
Parker, Stacey L., 201n. 24
"Parque con zoológico" (González), 34
Parra, Nicanor, 207n. 15
"Penúltima nostalgia" (González), 72–73, 103
Pérez Firmat, Gustavo, 200n. 12
"Perla de las Antillas" (González), 32, 63, 65–66, 85, 93, 174
Perloff, Marjorie, 104; on indeterminacy, 17–18, 113, 142, 155; on unmediated presentation, 142
Persin, Margaret H., 44, 62, 187, 192n. 25, 197n. 28, 208n. 28; on complexity of González's early poems, 53–54; on "Si serenases / tu pensamiento," 55; on the reading process, 61–62
"Piedra rota" (González), 58
"Poema, El" (Jiménez), 177
"Poemas elegíacos" (González), 137

"Poesía eres tú" (González), 179
Poesía última, 31, 33–34
"Poesías sin sentido" (González), 119, 181
"Poesía y compromiso" (González), 24
Poeta en Nueva York (Lorca), 92
Poetry of discovery, 31, 34
"Por aquí pasa un río" (González), 157
Postmodern aesthetics, 17, 23, 136; and the experimentalism of the 1960s, 38; form stressed at the expense of content in, 154; and the notion of authorship, 20; and the notion of representation, 18
"Preámbulo a un silencio" (González), 68, 74–76, 174–75, 181
Presagios (Salinas), 144
"Primavera delgada" (Guillén), 92
"Primera evocación" (González), 34
Procedimientos narrativos, 16, 44, 115, 137
Prosemas o menos, 45, 81, 108, 115, 129, 130, 182; as ludic work, 16
"Prueba" (González), 63
Puns, 124–25, 140

Quevedo, Francisco de, 91–92

Ramos, Mel, 131
Razón vital, 166, 167
"Realismo mágico" (González), 179–80
Redfern, Walter: on collage, 77
Reni, Guido, 177
Ribes, Francisco, 33–34
Ricoeur, Paul, 94
Riffaterre, Michael: on language, literary versus nonliterary, 47; on mimesis and semiosis, 143–46, 153, 161; on overdetermination, 153; on ungrammaticalities, 143–45
Rivera, Susana, 45, 46
Rovira, Pere, 200n. 6
Rubio, Fanny, 18, 19, 38–39

Salinas, Pedro, 144
Saussure, Ferdinand de, 111, 160–61, 203n. 2

Second postwar generation, 20; and loss of faith in the poetic word, 38; crisis of reason in the poetry of, 70
Segal, George: appropriation of Mondrian by, 131
Semiotics: and Spanish poetry, 19
Semiotics of Poetry (Riffaterre), 144
Semprún, Jorge, 69
Silver, Philip W., 197n. 28
Sin esperanza, con convencimiento, 52, 55, 59, 95; as social poetry, 32, 197n. 41; time in, 33
"S. M. nos contempla desde un daguerreotipo" (González), 178
"Sobre poesía y poetas" (González), 183
Social realism, 68, 103–4
Soledades (Machado), 144
Solomon, J. Fisher, 179
Somovilla, Miguel, 27, 29, 34
"Soneto a algunos poetas" (González), 52, 167–68, 169, 170
Sontag, Susan, 165; on morality in art, 63, 93
Soufas, Christopher C., 113, 207n. 18
Steiner, George: on twentieth-century disillusionment with language, 17
Stewart, Susan, 51, 84, 85, 159, 190, 202n. 10; on the link between art and play, 48; on commonsense notions of time, space, and causality in the creation of nonsense, 94, 106; on creating nonsense through juxtaposing spheres of discourse, 95; on culture as classification, 123; on the ludic genres, 138; on metafiction, 138; on misdirection, 106; on nonsense, 22, 99, 114, 125, 136; and postmodernism, 95; on the proliferation of details, 103; and provinces of meaning, 94–95, 115; on realism, 122; on the trickster, 180
Structuralism, 95
Stycos, Maria Nowakowska, 206n. 8

Tema de nuestro tiempo, El (Ortega y Gasset), 166–67

Index

"Teoelegía y moral" (González), 130–32, 135
"Te tuve . . ." (González), 113
Tigges, Wim, 113, 124
Time, in different cultures, 205n. 36
"Title" (Barth), 154–55
"Todos ustedes parecen felices . . ." (González), 168
Toilet of Venus (Velázquez), 131–32
Tratado de urbanismo, 33, 34, 67, 76, 137–38, 141, 142; as transitional volume, 16, 22, 36–39, 68, 71
Trotsky, Leon: and relationship of art and life, 177
Twain, Mark, 177–78

Ullán, José Miguel, 39
Unamuno, Miguel de, 48

Vallejo, César, 30, 142–43, 176, 178
Vázquez Montalbán, Manuel, 39; on the "vampirización del recuerdo," by the Franco regime, 72

Velázquez, Diego de, 130–32, 177, 178
Villanueva, Tino, 58, 197n. 41; on "El campo de batalla," 54–55; and objective correlative in González, 53; and the substantive view of language, 53
"Vino primero pura" (Jiménez), 178

Walsh, Donald D., 44
White, Hayden, 179
Whitman, Walt, 174
Wilcox, John C., 21
Wilde, Oscar, 130, 199n. 25; nature as imitation of art, 160
World War I: and postmodern skepticism, 114

"Yarg Nairod" (González), 83
"Yo mismo" (González), 183

"Zona residencial" (González), 34, 168, 183